Thank you Jeff and team for the bold challenge of your book *Ministry in the New Marriage Culture*. The downward trajectory of the sexual revolution, which is accelerating at an unprecedented pace, is challenging ministers, church leaders, and members in ways we have never experienced before. This book is timely and helps coach us through this difficult time in American history.

—Dr. Ronnie Floyd, president, Southern Baptist Convention and author of *Forward: 7 Distinguishing Marks For Future Leaders*

Timely. Practical. Insightful. Biblically-faithful. Gospel-centered. Convictional. Helpful. These are just some of the words to describe this incredibly important volume of thoughtful essays. Highly recommended!

—David S. Dockery, president, Trinity International University

Who would've ever thought we would be in a culture in which marriage needed to be defined and defended? It is very simple at its core but without God simplicity becomes complexity. *Ministry in the New Marriage Culture* will give you great insights of how to answer the questions our culture poses. What a blessing in the midst of society's confusion that God still has clear answers.

—Gregg Matte, pastor of Houston's First Baptist Church and author of *Unstoppable Gospel*

Jeff Iorg and his faculty have been living and working for years where the rest of us must now live, and that is in a circumstance of a fair level of cultural hostility. In the coming months the churches are going to be presented with every conceivable kind of difficulty related to the matter of ministry. *Ministry in the New Marriage Culture* acquaints a pastor, a student, or a layman with what that culture will look like and what it will ~~mean for churches in the~~ decisions to be made. I, for one, am treme̶ ̶ ̶ ̶ ̶ ̶ ̶ ̶ ̶ ̶ ̶ ̶ ̶ ̶ ̶ ̶ ̶ ̶ ̶ution that Golden Gate Seminary an̶ ̶ ̶ ̶ ̶ ̶ ̶ ̶ ̶ ̶ ̶ ̶ ̶ ̶ ̶ ̶ ̶ ̶ ̶ ̶ ̶ ̶ ̶e to make in reaching our world for

—̶ ̶ ̶ ̶ ̶ ̶ ̶ ̶ ̶thwestern Baptist Theological Seminary

D1510785

Jeff Iorg has been at the epicenter of the marriage revolution in America. As a strong Christian leader in the San Francisco bay area, he is a wise voice for Christians all over the country who find themselves suddenly in new terrain. In this book, an assembly of top notch evangelical scholars and thinkers engage questions of how to minister in a new marriage culture. Every church and church leader can benefit from this solid, winsome map of the way forward.

—Russell Moore, president, Ethics and Religious
Liberties Commission

# MINISTRY
## IN THE

# NEW
# MARRIAGE
# CULTURE

# MINISTRY
## IN THE
# NEW
# MARRIAGE
# CULTURE

### EDITED BY
## JEFF IORG

PUBLISHING GROUP
NASHVILLE, TENNESSEE

# CONTENTS

## Introduction

## Biblical Foundations for Ministry in the New Marriage Culture

## Theological Foundations for Ministry in the New Marriage Culture

## Models and Methods for Ministry in the New Marriage Culture

# INTRODUCTION

# CHAPTER 1

# MINISTRY IN THE NEW MARRIAGE CULTURE

*Jeff Iorg*

*What if this happened at your church?*
Your church sponsors its annual Vacation Bible School. A ten-year-old boy comes with a friend and hears the gospel for the first time. He commits himself to Jesus as his Lord and Savior and tells you about his decision. You are elated. He promises to bring his parents on family night at the end of the Bible school so they can also hear the good news about Jesus. On family night your new young friend brings his parents, two men married to each other. How will you respond? Will they be welcome in your church? How will this boy's perception of the gospel and the church change based on how his parents are treated? What will be your plan for continuing your church's relationship to this family in days to come?

One of the men in this same-sex marriage hears the gospel at the family night service. He's intrigued. His religious upbringing was a smattering of New Age confusion and overbearing Christian legalism. The gospel sounds like really good news to him! He returns with his son the following Sunday for both a Bible study class and worship service. Is he invited to your couples' class or sent to some other group for men? How do the church kids respond to the new boy with the two dads? Do church members invite these visitors to sit with them in the worship service? How about out for lunch after church?

This same man continues to attend church regularly. After a few weeks he indicates he has committed himself to Jesus. He presents himself for baptism and church membership. Will your church baptize him? Will he be welcomed as a member while still in a legally recognized same-sex marriage? Since he is now a Christian, will you encourage him to get divorced, thus ending his same-sex union? If he does this and risks losing custody of the boy who first started this chain of events by coming to Vacation Bible School, will you advise him to do it anyway, no matter what the courts decide about the child? Must a divorce precede the baptism? Are the two events connected at all?

*Welcome to ministry in the new marriage culture. Now what if . . .*

Your teenage son has his first girlfriend. You aren't surprised or displeased. It's a normal developmental phase of life; hormones are raging and romance is in the air. You meet the young lady, and you're impressed. She is smart, funny, articulate, and open about her Christian faith. You discover her mother—check that, both mothers—are actually pastors in a church in your community. Your son gets angry when you question the validity of their marriage and the legitimacy of their Christian faith. By extension he feels you are also attacking his girlfriend. He accuses you of being judgmental, legalistic, and unloving. He knows what you believe about marriage—and what you say the Bible teaches—but kindhearted Christian pastors are modeling a different message for him. How do you respond to your son's accusations? How do you relate to his girlfriend . . . her parents . . . their expressions of Christianity?

*Welcome to ministry in the new marriage culture. And, then this happens . . .*

Your good friend at church owns a photography studio. She decides her Christian convictions about marriage prohibit her from shooting same-sex weddings. This sets off an angry firestorm in your community and spills over into your church. She is accused of violating the civil rights of the people she refuses to serve. Some in your church side with the critics, claiming this situation is no different than restaurant owners in a previous generation refusing service to African-Americans. It's a civil rights issue, they claim, and Christians are on the wrong side again. What do you say to your friend? Should she treat all customers the same? Do her religious convictions allow her to discriminate in whom she serves? Would you counsel the Christian caterers, florists, and limousine drivers in your community to do the same thing? What will you tell them to do when their income dissipates because of their moral stand? Will you help them financially, stand with them legally, or allow them to handle the losses as the consequences of their own choices? How do you respond to fellow church members who see same-sex marriage as a civil rights issue?

In a similar vein you have a church leader who owns a company that has many employees. He does not want to grant family leave, medical benefits, or other privileges of married employees to same-sex couples. Can he discriminate in this way? Should he provide these benefits to all his employees, no matter their moral choices? Is this a demonstration of Christian love or a compromise of his Christian convictions?

On the other hand, what if you, as an employee, are impacted personally? Suppose your company terminates benefits for all employees rather than provide benefits to same-sex couples. You might lose your benefits not because of anything you have done but because your employer would rather not face the legal implications of granting benefits to some legally married couples but not to others. How will you respond? Will you lash out in anger at the employees who cost you your benefits? Will you initiate legal action against your employer for taking your benefits? Will you look for another job, perhaps even relocating, to find a company that provides the benefits you need for long-term security? How will you manage uprooting your family, changing churches, finding a new home, and building new friendships? If the fallout of the same-sex marriage movement impacts you negatively in this way, how will you respond when you interact with same-sex couples you know personally?

*Welcome to ministry in the new marriage culture. And then you get this phone call . . .*

A boy grew up in your church as Steven. Now, ten years after his high school graduation, he has returned to your community as Stephanie. Hormonal therapy and gender-reassignment surgery have given him/her feminine features and he self-identifies as a woman. Stephanie has a boyfriend. They call you, as a pastor, to ask if you will do their wedding and help them establish a Christian home. How do you respond? Do you meet with them? Counsel them? Do their wedding as an evangelistic outreach or simply refuse to get involved?

*Welcome to ministry in the new marriage culture.*

## Now What?

This book rests on the conviction that same-sex marriage is wrong—on every level, in every way—but also acknowledges it is a growing cultural reality demanding a ministry response from Christian leaders and churches. Orthodox Christian leaders have clearly articulated our moral position and engaged in political activism opposing this movement, but the culture changed anyway. We are now, like it or not, in a new marriage culture. The question this book attempts to answer is simple: Now what? The answers, unfortunately, are not as simple.

Same-sex marriage is here, and there's ample evidence it's here to stay. Every writer who contributed to this book agrees same-sex marriage is wrong. Every writer agrees the biblical model for marriage is one man joined with one woman for life. Nothing in this book contradicts or softens those convictions. Up until now communicating those standards and advocating for traditional marriage has been the church's primary message. We are not minimizing or denying the importance of those efforts. We are not advocating political activism or legal action to preserve traditional marriage be stopped. We are, however, insisting the church accept the reality of our present situation and address ministry issues emerging from this cultural change.

If same-sex marriage is really as bad for our culture as we claim—and it is—then the negative fallout will soon show up on our ministry doorsteps. Broken families, disillusioned parents, confused children, and disheartened believers who do not know how to relate to their child, parent, friend, or colleague will turn to us for help. This book provides resources for answering the "now what" questions people are asking or soon will be asking ministry leaders.

All the writers in this book are veteran ministry leaders. We care about people—all people—and want them to know the fullness of life in Jesus Christ and the life-shaping fellowship of a local church. We are not content with simply telling people what not to do and then allowing them to wallow in the consequences when they ignore us. We are compassionate leaders who willingly wade into the cesspool of human brokenness and help people find their way to healing and wholeness. We recognize though, despite our best intentions and efforts, some people will stubbornly refuse the gospel we offer and its implications and standards for holy living. Yet we still have compassion for them! Judging them does not effect real change. Loving them enough to pursue them might make a difference. We cling to that hope as we minister and as we write.

## What's Not in This Book and What Is

This book does not have a section on the reasons same-sex marriage is wrong, nor does it have an extended section on the validity of biblical or traditional marriage. Those are important issues, but other good books have already covered that ground. Excluding this information does not—we repeat—*does not* mean this information is unimportant. We simply assume those facts as background for this book and put our focus elsewhere—on solving ministry problems brought on by our failure as a culture to uphold the ideals of traditional marriage.

This book is about *ministry* in the new marriage culture. It's not about political activism to oppose same-sex marriage, moral foundations for biblical marriage, or philosophical reasons for traditional marriage. We agree those subjects are important and demand clear articulation in every appropriate venue, but just not here. We are moving on to the next big issue—responding to the ministry needs the redefinition of marriage is thrusting upon us. This book focuses on how to *minister* in the new marriage culture while upholding biblical convictions about gender, marriage, and sexuality. We will consider some of the biblical and theological support for ministering in this kind of cultural milieu, and rich resources are available. But even in those chapters, the focus will be on ministering in the new marriage culture, not defining or opposing same-sex marriage from Scripture.

Similarly, when we describe various ministerial approaches for specific age groups or issues, the focus remains the same. We recognize, for example, how unwise it is for children to be adopted or otherwise grow up in same-sex marriage households, but they are there and powerless to change their situation. We do not debate whether this is a healthy family arrangement. (We know it is not.) Instead, our focus is on ministering to people who are impacted by these arrangements—children, their friends, their parents, their grandparents, etc. Same-sex marriage impacts not only the couple in the union but also their extended family and community members who must adjust to and respond to their marital choice. The focus throughout this book—whether in biblical, theological, or applied sections—is on answering the question, "Now what?" and addressing the ministry needs created by this dramatic cultural shift in defining marriage.

We end the book with two special resources: a sermon manuscript you can adapt to preach on these issues in your church and an encouraging story of one pastor's attempt to engage the LGBT (lesbian, gay, bisexual, transgender) community in a constructive manner. We hope both of these resources will encourage and embolden you as you tackle this emotionally explosive issue in public ministry.

## Thanks for Being a Ministry Leader!

You may be soberly reading this book because you dread what's coming—additional ministry challenges piled on your already too-full plate! We empathize with you. We wish we had better news, but the truth is, same-sex marriage is unloosing a tsunami of negative results drowning our culture. No one—no matter how strongly they feel about avoiding same-sex marriage—will be untouched by this issue. As a ministry leader you will deal with the private fallout as people come to you for counseling and advice. You will also be forced to manage the public decision-making processes that determine how your church or organization will respond to never-before-imagined dilemmas. For example, what will you do when a same-sex engaged couple, who registered online, shows up for your church's premarital counseling classes? How will you console longtime church members who feel disgraced when their daughter marries another woman and invites them to the wedding? Situations like this, and manifold others, will present an ever-changing menu of new ministry challenges.

We believe this book will help you meet the demands of ministry in the new marriage culture. It will not answer all your questions, but it will provide a framework to move you toward positive solutions. Some parts of this book may make you angry. That's not our intention. You may disagree with us on some key points. We accept that and admit you may be right. We are on the leading edge with this book, and it may be the "bleeding edge" on some points. We are breaking new ground and have no illusion it will be an easy, clean, neat, or entirely accurate process. We have tried to be true to Scripture, while taking on the most explosive and destructive cultural change of our generation. We believe what we have written will help you be a more effective leader. For the mistakes we apologize. Point them out to us, and we will do better next time!

Thank you for bearing the burden of ministry leadership. It was already a difficult task, and it's only going to get harder in the next generation. But you do not have to go it alone. Jesus said, "Take my yoke upon you" (Matt. 11:29 NIV). Remember, it's a two-oxen yoke, and He's right beside you. Pressing the analogy, we are also yoked up with you in a multi-oxen team effort. Together, we can make a difference as we plow through the previously untouched ground of ministry in the new marriage culture.

Let's get started.

# Biblical Foundations for Ministry in the New Marriage Culture

CHAPTER 2

# MINISTRY FOUNDATIONS IN THE OLD TESTAMENT

*Paul Wegner*

Fifty years ago in America most people expected to marry. Most children grew up in fairly stable, traditional homes. But shifts in marriage and family have taken place over the past fifty years. On the website of the Archdiocese of Washington, Monsignor Charles Pope reflects with both nostalgia and concern about these changes:

> There was a time in this land when divorce was rare. When it occurred, people were shocked and whispered about it. Really it was not so long ago. . . . It is not as though every marriage was happy before 1965. Indeed, there were many "unhappy marriages." But people had a different outlook which empha- sized the importance of staying true to commitments that had been made and to sticking to them "for the sake of the kids." These attitudes were enshrined in law which made divorce difficult. Marriage was for the children and children had needs for stability and for parents who stuck to their commitments. Today, the attitude is that marriage is for the adults and the needs of the children are somewhat secondary.[1]

## Marriage Has Changed Rapidly in Our Society

In looking at today's social and demographic trends, a recent Bloomberg report for *Business Week* found (as of August 2014) more adults are now single than married.[2] Another survey from the National Survey of Family Growth (NSFG) found "more than one-in-four fathers with children 18 or younger now live apart from their children—with 11% living apart from some of their children and 16% living apart from all of their children."[3] Most analysts agree a drastic change began to occur in the cultural understanding of marriage in the 1960s and 1970s and has accelerated in the first part of this century.

At least one significant change that has impacted today's views on marriage was the introduction of no-fault divorce. W. Bradford Wilcox describes its inception: "In 1969, Governor Ronald Reagan of California made what he later admitted was one of the biggest mistakes of his political life. Seeking to eliminate the strife and deception often associated with the legal regime of fault-based divorce, Reagan signed the nation's first no-fault divorce bill."[4] Within fifteen years no-fault divorce was nationwide with state after state following California's lead. Between 1960 and 1980 the divorce rate in the United States more than doubled.[5] The snowball effects of divorce are highlighted in a study by Nicholas Wolfinger of the University of Utah, who found that adult children of divorced families are 89 percent more likely to divorce as compared to adults who were raised in intact, married families.[6]

Divorce is certainly not the only contributing factor in marriage trends today. Socioeconomic factors are also at play, according to another Pew nationwide study:

A new "marriage gap" in the United States is increasingly aligned with a growing income gap. Marriage, while declining among all groups, remains the norm for adults with a college education and good income but is now markedly less prevalent among those on the lower rungs of the socio-economic ladder. The survey finds that those in this less-advantaged group are as likely as others to want to marry, but they place a high premium on economic security as a condition for marriage. This is a bar that many may not meet.[7]

Andrew Cherlin, in an opinion column in the *New York Times*, wrote that marriage today is less about love and more about portraying a sense of having arrived in life:

> Today, marriage is more discretionary than ever, and also more distinctive. It is something that young adults do after they and their live-in partners have good jobs and a nice apartment. It has become the capstone experience of personal life—the last brick to be put in place after everything else is set. People marry to show their family and friends how well their lives are going, even if deep down they are unsure whether their partnership will last a lifetime.[8]

Children who arrive on the scene today find themselves in a variety of family units and households. A trend on the rise is women giving birth either before marriage or with no plan to marry: "Somewhere around 2000, the country underwent a profound shift: women, driven largely by 'middle-American' women, began putting the baby carriage before marriage. In fact, for women on the whole, the age of first birth is now 25.7 while the age at first marriage is 26.5. . . . And here's another startling fact: one in two mothers in America is now having a baby first and marrying later, if at all."[9]

Raising children in a single-parent home is difficult, as is growing up in one. (I know all too well since I was raised by a divorced mother.) Raising a family alone requires one parent to perform the roles of both father and mother and to take on the many jobs parenting entails.

Many different factors affect how we view marriage in American culture today—from divorce, to sexual orientation, to economic pressures. These and other factors are causing society to redefine marriage and family. As Christians, our desire is to connect people to God and His truth. But are we, as Christians, still sure of God's foundational truth about marriage? Let's look at four Old Testament passages that lay the groundwork for ministry in the new marriage culture.

## God's Principles for Marriage Have Not Changed

### Principle 1: Genesis 2—God's Foundation for Marriage

Two of the most popular sermon passages for Christian weddings are Ephesians 5:22–33 and Genesis 2:18–24. And well they should be since both passages go back to God's original plan for marriage. In Genesis 2 God declared it was "not good for the man to be alone" (v. 18); yet after creating every other being, none were found to be a suitable "helper" for man. The Hebrew language literally means: "there was not a help corresponding to him." God therefore created "woman." His intent was not simply to duplicate man but to make something that would "correspond to man." The idea is creating a person in a mirror image. It is like having a right hand and a left hand that fit together so as to hold hands. When God made "Eve," she was different from man in significant ways, but those ways were intended to complement "man." Whereas one person might be stronger in certain areas, the other person would be stronger in others—so together they would complement each other as a single unit with combined strengths. The two people together would be stronger than each one alone. This was a brilliant way to ensure the basic family unit—a man and woman as husband and wife—would have what is needed to meet the challenges that come at them through life.

Unfortunately, what was designed to complement can become instead a source of irritation in a marriage relationship. God intended the interaction between genders in marriage to help a couple become more complete and well-rounded as individuals, "sanding off the rough edges" so to speak. But the process can be uncomfortable. Over time spouses can view each other as a source of irritation, dragging each other down, blocking happiness. It is easy to interpret these conflicts as meaning a marriage is not healthy. Couples think of breaking up the marriage rather than learning from each other and helping each other grow. This is especially true when society tells couples that marriage is about meeting individual needs—not intended to change people. The conflicts in marriage are designed to help people learn to be more loving, more caring, or to teach self-denial. So the first thing in laying a foundation for healthy marriage is teaching God's true purpose for marriage. God intended a man and woman to join together, to complement each other, and to remake each other into more well-rounded people demonstrating godly character, not just to make each other happy.

***Woman Was Made from Part of Man:*** Eve was formed from the side of Adam, and he recognized right away she was different from all the other created things—"This one, at last, is bone of my bone and flesh of my flesh; this one will be called 'woman,' for she was taken from man" (Gen. 2:23). It is unclear in the text how much of Adam's body was taken to make Eve, but Adam's response suggests it included both flesh and bones. The connection between Adam and Eve is highlighted in the English translation of the words "man" and "woman," but the Hebrew is even clearer. The Hebrew word for "man" in this passage is *'ish* (שִׁיא), and the word for "woman" is *'ishshah* (הָשִׁא). Technically speaking, a feminine ending is added to the Hebrew word for "man." The Hebrew language could not show a much stronger connection between Adam and Eve. She was made from the essence of Adam. No other part of creation was formed this way. Eve was clearly created for man to become a partner unique to him.

***A New Family Unit Is Created:*** Genesis 2:24 makes clear a new family unit was being created. In the strongly patriarchal society to which Moses wrote, the bridegroom needed to leave his family and be joined to the bride. If he remained within the household of his father, he would continue to be under his father's authority. Creating a new family unit thus demanded he leave his family. The strong family relationship between a father, a mother, and a son was to be replaced by the even stronger relationship between the husband and wife. This relationship between a husband and wife is described by two phrases in the latter part of verse 24. They clearly indicate a husband is to be "united" with his wife and the two of them shall "become one flesh" (NIV).

The Hebrew word describing this uniting means "to stick together," "to cling to," or "hold together" and is explained even more clearly in the next phrase—"they will become one flesh" (ISV). These words clearly teach the concept of two people actually forming a "one flesh" unit. In a real sense they are no longer two people but one unit. It is somewhat similar to the mysterious concept of the Trinity where three persons of the Godhead are one and yet have distinct personalities. This one-flesh concept God envisions must not be taken lightly. In Matthew 19:6, Jesus underscored the significance of this union when He said, "What God has joined together, let no one separate" (NIV). Just as God intended a husband and wife to bring different gifts and strengths to their marriage to complement each other, He also envisions a strong marital bond. A couple trusts, honors, and commits to one another forever, vowing never to give up that connection and living out their vows. Divorce undercuts God's intention and disregards His plan for marriage.

In addition, when couples exchange vows before God, they are actually making a covenant before God and with God by asking Him to oversee the keeping of those vows. God takes covenants seriously and holds people responsible to keep their vows. To understand better how God views covenants, study Jeremiah 34:13–22, which describes how God punishes the people of Israel for breaking a covenant they had made. Pastors must help couples understand when God is invoked through prayer in a wedding ceremony, He serves as a witness to the promises the couple makes to each other. God does not force anyone to get married. But when a couple chooses to do so and calls on God to oversee their marriage, He holds them accountable to keep their covenant with each other and with Him.

***Applying These Principles in the New Marriage Culture:*** First and foremost, we must use Scripture to train Christians how God designed marriage and His purposes for marriage. From the beginning, as revealed in the Old Testament, God's plan for marriage has been clear. We must teach that a man and woman unite, complement each other in their relationship, purpose to form a unit stronger than two individuals alone, and keep marriage vows exchanged before God as a covenant that cannot be broken.

Second, premarital counseling is crucial to confirm these truths among newlyweds. Through premarital counseling a couple can be guided to learn principles that lead to a healthy relationship and how to handle issues that often bring conflict in marriage. Wise pastors do not assume young couples know the biblical framework and purpose for marriage and use premarital counseling as a teaching moment. These sessions can also be a witnessing opportunity to nonbelievers who want a "church wedding" and are open to learning about "Christian marriage" instead. Pastors have a responsibility to perform "Christian weddings," and premarital counseling can lead any couple to prepare for that distinctive event.

Third, churches must provide ongoing support for marriage relationships. A church should strive to be a resource to people who need help in their marriages—through teaching, mentoring, training, and counseling. It is great when a church can gain the reputation in a city of being a resource to people who need help in their marriages. Many conferences are available to enrich healthy marriages and to help those who are struggling. If the church needs to subsidize a conference for those who cannot afford one, that is a good investment. There are also excellent video presentations for small-group use on improving marriage relationships. These also provide a good opportunity to invite friends and neighbors, as many non-Christians have struggling marriages. Another helpful resource churches can provide is training couples with healthy marriages to serve as marriage mentors for those needing help.

Churches must take the long view—for good or for ill—that marriages serve as examples to the generations that follow. While divorce can lead to divorce in the next generation, strong marriages can also be a great witness to future generations of the power and fulfillment that come from healthy marriages.

## Principle 2: Genesis 19—God's View of Homosexuality

Ministry in the new marriage culture today is complicated by the strength of the LGBT (lesbian, gay, bisexual, transgender) agenda and confusion about how the church should respond. The LGBT community is influential out of proportion to its prevalence in society. According to The Williams Institute of the School of Law of the University of California, about 4 percent of adults in America consider themselves in one or more of the groups recognized as LGBT.[10] Yet despite being a small percentage of the American population, the views of the LGBT community have been given prominence in the media and government, prompting attempts to redefine marriage and various civil rights.

This is not a new problem for the church. Similar issues in Roman society presented the early church with challenges it had to face head-on. The early church had scriptural resources from the Old Testament to guide them as they formulated their response, some of which came to be canonized in the New Testament.

***Scripture's Guidance:*** Scripture, both Old and New Testaments, provides timeless guidelines both to understand and to respond to LGBT behaviors. Scripture is clear that gay, lesbian, bisexual, and transgender behaviors are condemned by God and are listed with other sins (Gen. 18–19 [Ezek. 16:48–49]; Lev. 18:22–24; 20:13–16; Judg. 19:22–24; Rom. 1:26–27; 1 Cor. 6:7–11; 1 Tim. 1:9–10). While these sexual sins are not new, what is new in American culture is the vehemence with which the LGBT community and sympathizers attack those who do not hold their views. The LGBT community has lobbied the nation to redefine who can marry, to legitimize homosexual behavior, and to normalize other biblically prohibited sexual behavior while demonizing those who oppose their efforts.

As part of their strategy, some religious leaders supporting the LGBT agenda argue that Genesis 18–19 (and Judges 19) refers to inhospitality, not homosexuality. Since Lot was responsible for the safety of those visiting his home, what was supposedly condemned was the violence intended, not the sexual orientation of that violence.

Let's look at the incident in Genesis (a similar incident is recorded in Judges 19) to see if this is really a feasible interpretation.

Genesis 19:4–5 indicates the men of Sodom came to Lot's house, asking to see his visitors so they could "know" them (ESV). Confusion has arisen because the Hebrew word "to know" (עָדַ yāda‘) has a broad range of meanings from "mere acquaintance" (just getting to know someone, Gen. 29:5) to the intimacy of a husband and wife who "know each other" through sexual intercourse (Gen. 4:1). The context clarifies the author's intent. In Genesis 19:7, Lot calls their request an "evil" (HCSB) or "wicked thing" (NIV). There is nothing evil or wicked about wanting to get better acquainted with someone. That kind of "knowing" is an honest demonstration of hospitality in the Old Testament. Some LGBT apologists argue Lot is condemning gang rape (not homosexuality). Why then does Lot offer his virgin daughters, since it would be just as bad to gang rape his daughters as the male visitors? When Lot attempts to redirect the expression of their desire toward his daughters, not only are the men uninterested in the daughters, but it inflames them to threaten worse harm to Lot than what they planned for Lot's visitors. The intensity of their lust is revealed when the men press against Lot in an attempt to break into his home.

Confusion about the Sodom and Gomorrah story can also influence how one interprets Ezekiel 16:48–50. Some argue Ezekiel 16 states Sodom's wickedness was her failure to help the poor and needy (even though they had means), and their wickedness is not identified as sexual sin. But failure to help the poor is just one item in a list of Sodom's sins: they did not help the poor/needy, they were haughty, and they committed an abomination before Yahweh. Because the abomination is listed as another sin, it most likely refers to the attempted rape of Lot's visitors by the men of the city (what Lot called a "wicked thing," NIV).

The term "abomination" (הָבְעוֹת tō‘ēbâ) is not used elsewhere in the Old Testament when describing failure to feed the poor. Instead it is used to describe behaviors like sacrificing children to other gods (Deut. 12:31), eating unclean meat (Deut. 14:3), offering imperfect animals as a sacrifice to Yahweh (Deut. 17:1), wearing clothing of the opposite sex (Deut. 22:5), giving the earnings from prostitution to the temple (Deut. 23:18), remarrying a woman after having divorced her (Deut. 24:4), dishonest measures (Deut. 25:16), and keeping secret images of deities (Deut. 27: 15). Of particular relevance to this discussion, the word *abomination* is also used in Leviticus 18:22 (ESV) and 20:13 (ESV) to describe the act of same-sex sexual relations between men.

These passages from the Old Testament are foundational to passages in the New Testament that also list homosexuality with other sins (Rom. 1:26–27; 1 Cor. 6:9–11; 1 Tim. 1:9–10; Rev. 21:8). The Romans passage is the clearest, saying women gave up their natural desires for unnatural ones and men burned with desire for one another. Again some LGBT proponents have suggested these New Testament passages do not apply to homosexuals who are in monogamous, committed relationships. This is hard to argue in light of the command against same-sex relations as described in Leviticus 18:22–24 and 20:13–16, as well as the clear prohibition of homosexual activity described in Romans 1:26–27 The Romans passage laments that men had abandoned the natural relations "with women" (v. 26 NIV) and "burned with lust for each other" (v. 27 NLT). This same verse describes this activity of "males with males" (DARBY) as a "shameful" (NIV) or disgraceful activity that is unacceptable to God.

***Demonstrating Love:*** Jesus is our best model for relating to people. He never ran from or shunned sinners. He told His followers the "sick" are the ones in need of a "physician" (both physically and metaphorically; Matt. 9:12; Mark 2:17; Luke 5:31). Jesus realized the gospel message was the only hope that could heal sinners. We must realize, no matter how offensive they may seem, homosexual relations are just one type of sexual sin. So is lust. So is addiction to pornography. So is adultery. Every sin, including all of these, is an affront to God. Any sin, from gossip to homosexuality, can become an ingrained pattern of behavior or an addiction. How then should a church respond since Scripture is clear that homosexual relations are sinful?

First, we must not hold prejudices about sin, thinking one sin is better or worse than another. Any sin can be and needs to be forgiven by God through Jesus Christ. One difficulty is the resistance people have to any behavior, particularly their behavior, being labeled as a "sin." Those who teach that homosexual relations are a sin will likely risk being labeled homophobic, intolerant, or bigoted. Unfortunately, many in the gay community think that conservative Christians hate them. Our best response is to live out our convictions through a loving, caring Christian community which effectively communicates both love for individuals and God's truth about sin.

Second, it is not likely people will come into our churches unless we have ways to meet them where they are. Jesus confronted sinners in their sin, met their needs, called them to repent, and then helped them overcome the consequences of their past actions. Churches follow Jesus' example when they care for people with AIDS, befriend people who are living alternative lifestyles, develop ministry to same-sex couples and their children, and otherwise extend themselves to connect with sinners.

Third, we must train our children about what God says about LGBT issues. These will be difficult discussions, but it will become more and more common for children to have a friend with either two mothers or two fathers. Our children must understand, in age-appropriate terms, God's plans for marriage, family, and sexuality. Children must be taught to navigate the many cultural changes in the family (divorce, death, single mothers who never married, same-sex parents, etc.), learning at an early age how to uphold God's standards while relating in a healthy way to their peers.

## Principle 3: Genesis 16; 29–30—God's Concession to Polygamy

A major problem some have when considering the Old Testament is how God can appear to condone polygamy, especially in light of Old Testament teaching on marriage in Genesis 2. In Mark 10:8, Jesus stated, "The two [notice it does not say "two or more"] shall become *one flesh*. So they are no longer two but *one flesh*" (ESV, italics added). Clearly, Jesus interpreted God's standard for marriage as one man and one woman for life.

While polygamy is included in the Old Testament narrative, it is not affirmed. Examples of polygamy in the Old Testament bristle with marital and family relationship problems. Sarah became so angry with Hagar she forced Abraham to send her out of the house (Gen. 21:10). Jacob's two wives fought over his affection (Gen. 30), and Solomon's many wives led his heart away from God (1 Kings 11:1–6). So why did God allow polygamy?

God's ideal for marriage is clear: one man and one woman become "one flesh" (Gen. 2:24). Rarely has humankind lived up to God's ideal; consequently, people always suffer for their failures. Yet God allows those choices, which often reflect cultural realities. There were, for example, sociological reasons polygamy occurred in the Old Testament. The ancient Near East was largely a patriarchal society. It was unusual for women to be able to own land or provide for themselves (an exception was the daughters of Zelophehad about whom God made a special pronouncement, Num. 27; 36). It was also customary for a father to take care of a daughter until she was old enough to marry, at which point her husband would then take care of her. In this way women were provided for in the Old Testament period. There were also times in Israel's history when there were not enough eligible males due to war, plagues, or famines. Yet women still needed to be protected and provided for (see Isa. 4:1) so polygamy was permitted. While polygamy was a pragmatic cultural adaptation, the practice remained less than ideal and sinful.

Beyond this permitted provision, many kings and wealthy men took multiple wives for different reasons: to demonstrate their wealth, to show their power, or to create alliances. Israelites often took foreign wives, which usually led them into apostasy. A number of Old Testament passages that are purported to support polygamy (e.g., Exod. 21:10; Deut. 21:15) are actually case laws that describe what to do when that particular situation arises. Case laws do not legitimize polygamy. They simply indicate what to do when it occurs.

In the New Testament Jesus refers back to the ideal in Genesis 2 (Matt. 19:1–6; Mark 10:4–8) when He spoke about divorce. He boldly said that anyone who divorces his wife and marries another commits adultery (Matt. 5:31–32; 19:8–9). Paul likewise goes back to God's original plan (Gen. 2) when he wrote about marriage (Eph. 5:31). He further required church leaders to be examples and only have one wife (1 Tim. 3:2; Titus 1:6).

Confronting polygamy may not seem like a frequent problem yet in the new marriage culture, but it soon may be the next step. This is actually a problem missionaries have already confronted for years. Our primary response on the issue of polygamy is teaching God's truth about marriage. This is a delicate issue since it takes a thorough understanding of Scripture to interpret correctly what it teaches. Clearly understanding God's view of polygamy has ramifications in the areas of divorce, cohabitation, ministry in international mission-ary settings, and perhaps soon in the United States as well.

## Principle 4: Song of Solomon—God's Affirmation of Love in Marriage

Song of Solomon is an unusual book included in God's revelation. Difficult questions revolve around its interpretation and its purpose. We can be assured, however, that there is a purpose for including this book in the Old Testament canon and that it contains pertinent infor-mation God wants us to know. One interpretational question basic to understanding this book is: How many characters are featured in the book? Some commentators designate two characters—Solomon and his Shulammite bride. Others indicate three characters—Solomon, his Shulammite bride, and the shepherd lover.

Whether there are two characters or three does not greatly affect the purpose of the book—describing godly love between a husband and wife. The number of characters, however, greatly affects how the book is to be understood. Old Testament culture often emphasized one of the purposes for marriage as being the means to have and provide for children. Encouragingly, the Song of Solomon elevates another purpose—romantic love between a husband and wife. A few other Old Testament passages mention this type of love between a husband and wife (Isaac's love for Rebekah, Gen. 24:67; Jacob's love for Rachel, Gen. 29:18, 20, 30; Elkanah's love for Hannah, 1 Sam. 1:5; Michal's love for David, 1 Sam. 18:20, 28; Rehoboam's love for Maacah, 2 Chron. 11:21; Ahasuerus's love for Esther, Esther 2:17; see also Prov. 5:18–20).

Ancient Near Eastern cultures likely did not often highlight romantic love between a husband and wife because they considered true love to be better demonstrated through actions of commitment and provision (i.e., the husband's care for his wife and children). Still, a book like the Song of Solomon emphasizes how romantic love could and should be demonstrated between a couple.

The book's message is also inspiring in how it showcases the depth of commitment of married love. If two characters are assumed in the story, then it portrays how Solomon pursues the Shulammite woman to win her heart and explore the joys of married love with her.

It seems more likely, however, that the book contains three characters with an interesting twist that emphasizes genuine love even more. At the beginning of the book, the Shulammite woman is brought into Solomon's palace (1:4b, "the king has brought me into his chambers," esv). She was likely a new arrival into Solomon's harem, whose beauty was recognized by all. As she entered a period of preparation for marriage, the Shulammite truly realizes the honor that has been bestowed upon her by coming into the king's harem. She fully expects to have a growing love for Solomon.

Then, in the middle of chapter 2, the bride's beloved shepherd comes bounding over the hills (v. 8) and peers in the windows to find his beloved (v. 9). Solomon was never a shepherd and, as king, would not have needed to stand behind a wall peering through the windows to see his beloved. In the rest of that chapter, the shepherd lover tries to convince the Shulammite woman to come away with him. She is torn between the prospect of marriage to a king or returning to her former shepherd lover. Chapter 3 begins with a dream (possibly a repeated dream, v. 1) wherein the Shulammite longs for the shepherd lover. Later (possibly still part of the dream), she envisions her wedding to Solomon (vv. 6–11), probably with increasing angst.

In chapter 4, Solomon woos the Shulammite, but then again in chapter 5 she is asleep, apparently dreaming about her shepherd lover. Chapters 6 and 7 may be a continuation of the dream or simply a conversation between the Shulammite and the shepherd lover (or less likely Solomon). The most important verses for understanding the Song of Solomon are found in chapter 8: "Mighty waters cannot extinguish love; rivers cannot sweep it away. If a man were to give all his wealth for love, it would be utterly scorned" (v. 7).

Taking this verse within the story's broader context, it suggests Solomon, even with all his great wealth, could not buy the Shulammite woman's love. This meaning is further elaborated a few verses later: "Solomon owned a vineyard in Baal-hamon. He leased the vineyard to tenants. Each was to bring for his fruit 1,000 pieces of silver. I have my own vineyard. The 1,000 are for you, Solomon, but 200 for those who guard its fruits" (Song 8:11–12).

This section appears to contrast Solomon, who has a vineyard with valuable fruit, with the Shulammite who has only her own vineyard. If the author used the word *vineyard* figuratively to refer to Solomon's harem of hundreds of beautiful wives, this is in stark contrast to the Shulammite who only has herself in her vineyard. The term *vineyard* was also used earlier in the book when referring to the Shulammite's body. She states in Song of Solomon 1:6 she was put in charge of the family vineyard, but she did not take care of her own "vineyard" (suggesting her hard work tending the family vineyard did not allow her to protect her own body from the sun). If this is how the song is interpreted, then Solomon had many wives, but the Shulammite had only herself that she could give. She could choose to whom she would give herself and apparently it was not to Solomon but to the shepherd lover.

With this interpretation the book's message is clear: love cannot be bought; it must be given. This message would not only stand in strong contrast to the message that pervaded the ancient Near East; it is also timeless and just as relevant today. In a generation that seeks satisfaction instead of genuine commitment, this message is a breath of fresh air. The Shulammite woman could give her "vineyard" to whomever she chose, but she chose to keep it for the one person she truly loved. It would have been easy to allow her "vineyard" to be purchased for money or fame, but she chose to keep herself only for her shepherd lover. Our generation needs to hear this message over and over again.

## Conclusion

These four passages provide a strong foundation for marriages and families our generation needs to hear. Many influences are at work today, eroding the church's understanding of marriage and family. Divorce, cohabitation, foregoing marriage, same-sex marriage, and polygamy are a few of the primary challenges to marriage in the new marriage culture. While society's values sway to and fro without an anchor, God's foundation for marriage and family has remained firm. Starting in the Old Testament and continuing through the New Testament, God has advocated marriage as one man united with one woman for life.

The culture is now affecting and often controlling how Christians view marriage and the family. Without being grounded in a biblical portrait and significance of marriage, we will lose our ability to be salt and light to this generation. But it is never too late to believe and promote God's standards! God is using thousands of churches all over the world to continue to teach the truth of Scripture. We must continue to welcome people into our churches with "baggage," who have not yet found forgiveness from sin—any sin, including sins against marriage—and new life in Jesus Christ. We also need to ensure our marriages and families are models of God's standards. When we fail to do this, we must allow God to pinpoint our sin and forgive us. We must then redouble our efforts to build homes that honor God. Jesus said, "Let your light shine before men, so that they may see your good works and to give glory to your Father in heaven" (Matt. 5:16). What a glorious opportunity we have in this generation to live our lives in such a way that our Father in heaven is glorified!

# CHAPTER 3

# Ministry Foundations in the New Testament

*Richard R. Melick Jr.*

Many Christians believe cultural changes like the advent of a new marriage culture including same-sex marriage are a modern problem originating in cities like San Francisco. That's simply not true. Confusion about sexuality and dysfunction about marriage are old problems, first found in an ancient city familiar to Bible students.

Famous for many of its attributes, infamous for many others, the city of Corinth held a strategic place in the Roman world. The glory days of Greece had passed. Rome defeated the Greeks in 146 BC, and with that defeat Corinth was changed forever. In approximately 44 BC, Julius Caesar rebuilt the city over its ancient ruins. In a few years, as the city took a new form, Christianity arrived and thrived. The resurrection was preached, a church was started, and the gospel's implications expressed themselves in shaping new behavior among previously secular people. Their story is illustrative and helpful for addressing foundational biblical issues for ministry in the new marriage culture today.

## The City of Corinth

Paul traveled to Corinth on his second missionary journey and entered one of the most complex cities of the ancient world. Corinth was rebuilt as a haven for Roman freedmen and retiring soldiers. Because of its flourishing economy, entrepreneurs relocated from around the empire hoping to capitalize on this unique opportunity for economic success. Tradesmen flocked to the city, taking advantage of a positive economic climate. Workers came too, moving their families in hopes of a better life. The rich got richer; the middle class did well for a while; and the lower class was growing with its slums and struggles.

Vestiges of its Greek ancestry abounded, such as the forerunners of the Olympic Games. Paul's visit coincided with one of the three-year cycles of the games (AD 51). Like today the games brought tourists, athletes, businessmen, and spectators.

Both the Greeks and the Romans practiced various religions at Corinth; evidence of at least sixteen different religions has been enumerated by historians. Corinth also offered ethnic religions from around the world, along with occult magic. Above all, the emperor cult flourished in Corinth as it did in all Roman cities. For all its ancient history, at the time of Paul's visit, Corinth was geographically in Greece but culturally in Rome.[1]

Corinth was also corrupt. The world recognized the city's reputation for free-living, freewheeling, and freethinking lifestyles. Prostitution flourished, including both male and female prostitutes. Perhaps more than a thousand priestess prostitutes descended nightly from Aphrodite's Temple on the Acrocorinth. While many scholars dispute that number, it certainly fits the overall characterization of the city given by early Roman historians.

Because of cultural distance between then and now, the relevance of the Corinthian church for today can be questioned. Yet biblical scholars see many similarities between Corinth and contemporary culture. British scholar Anthony Thiselton notes the similarities of Corinth to today's "postmodern" mood and writes, "First Corinthians stands in a *distinctive position of relevance to our own times.*"[2]

In summary Corinth was centrally located, politically and economically cosmopolitan, multicultural and multiethnic, with a legacy of both Roman and Greek influence. It was also morally corrupt, which produced a church reflecting those qualities and problems. Corinth, then, seems to offer a relevant model for developing ministry in the new marriage culture.

## The Church at Corinth

The Church at Corinth received more care and energy from Paul than any other church. Paul made at least three trips to Corinth— one as part of its founding, plus two others. The Bible contains two epistles to the church which, combined, are the longest letters to any church of the first century.

In addition to the canonical epistles, most scholars (including this author) believe Paul wrote at least two other epistles to Corinth. One was written before 1 Corinthians and one between 1 and 2 Corinthians. Together Paul probably communicated at least seven times with the church: three visits and four letters. Paul also sent both Timothy and Titus there in his stead.

The content of the epistles reveals why Paul invested so much in the Corinthian church. It was a problem-riddled group of new Christians, caught between the pull of their newfound Christianity and their acculturation to the practices of the city. They struggled to live in light of the kingdom of God while living with the ever-present pressures of this world. Yet Paul planted seed and nourished it in hopes of harvesting a bastion of Christian truth in the midst of cosmopolitan confusion.

## Sexual Activity Outside of Marriage: The Roman Worldview

A common theme unites Paul's concerns about the Corinthians. A man in the congregation had an ongoing sexual affair with his stepmother. Paul had addressed this problem in previous communication and had been misunderstood (1 Cor. 5:1–2). The letter called 1 Corinthians is, in part, a correction to that misunderstanding. Within this context Paul wrote 1 Corinthians 5–7, an extended passage on sexual purity demanded of the church. In 1 Corinthians 6:9, he listed vices that concerned him. Notably, two of these ten sins include homosexual acts. His discussion parallels the other two places in the New Testament that identify homosexual conduct specifically: Romans 1:26 and 1 Timothy 1:10.

## Homosexuality in First-Century Roman Culture

Before considering these texts, it will be helpful to survey how homosexuality was perceived in the Roman Empire. In general Romans followed the Greeks in their sexual practices. Many leaders, such as Alexander the Great and several Roman emperors, reportedly had sexual relationships with men. Judging from ancient writings and drawings on urns and murals, homosexuality was a commonly accepted practice among men of status. Again, generally speaking, the records often portray dominance, physically demonstrating who was superior in the relationship. Those who took the subordinate role were ridiculed and disrespected, while the dominant role had prominence. Ancient writers reveal masters could have sex with slaves of either gender without fear of retaliation. Prostitution, again with either gender, was accepted culturally and was even part of worship in many religious temples.

Some scholars dismiss Greco-Roman homosexual acts as simply an acculturated way of establishing social and class hierarchy. They claim Paul abhors the misuse of persons and clamor for social position rather than the homosexual acts themselves. Paul did express deep concern about the abuse of people. While sex may have been one way of demonstrating dominance, it was still sex. For whatever reason one might suggest the practices were culturally acceptable, they were still clearly forbidden in the church.

Though homosexual practices commonly occurred, there is no evidence the Roman worldview endorsed same-sex marriage. Virtually all of those known to engage in homosexual activity also had heterosexual marriages. There were, however, some famous cases of same-sex union ceremonies. Paul wrote 1 Corinthians (AD 53–55) and, later, Romans (AD 55–57)[3], during Emperor Nero's reign. Nero's sexual deviations are well documented. His passions drove him to extremes unacceptable even in Roman culture. Among them he publically married two different men. While his wife Poppea Sabina was alive, he asked Pythagorus, a freedman, to formalize their relationship with a marriage ceremony (AD 64). In it Nero took the role of the woman! Later, when his wife became pregnant, in a fit of rage Nero kicked her in the stomach until she died. He married another woman, Statilia Massilina (AD 66), then publicly married a teenage boy, Sporus, who took the role of the woman in the relationship.[4] These ceremonies took place eight to ten years later than the writing of 1 Corinthians and Romans, but the political atmosphere and social attitudes leading to them were clear.

### Homosexuality in Romans and 1 Corinthian Texts

Romans 1:27 and 1 Corinthians 6:9 are the most prominent New Testament texts related to homosexuality. Let's first consider the Romans text:

> The males in the same way also left natural relations with females and were inflamed in their lust for one another. Males committed shameless acts with males and received in their own persons the appropriate penalty of their error. (Rom. 1:27)

This is Paul's most well-known passage on homosexuality and the locus of much debate. It continues the progression of Romans 1:18: "For the wrath of God is revealed from the heaven against all ungodliness and unrighteousness and men, who by their unrighteousness suppress the truth." The implications are clear. First, regarding idolatry, people go their own way, drifting into a situation where they finally "worshiped and served the creature rather than the Creator" (Rom. 1:25 ESV). Second, regarding morality, three times Paul states, "God gave them over."[5] The first time is to heterosexual promiscuity.

The second is to lesbian and homosexual activity. The third is to total egocentricity. The three stages may be progressive, and all are evidences of those who fail to worship the true God.[6]

The text seems clear, but at least two major objections have been raised to interpreting it as condemning all homosexual activity. First, many have assumed the text speaks of pederasty, a common practice in Greco-Roman culture. Pederasty is the practice of older men seducing young boys for sexual purposes.[7] Since this was a prevalent cultural practice, some interpreters limit Paul's condemnation to that practice only rather than all homosexual activity.

At least three points mitigate this interpretation. First, a Greek word for *pederasty* was available when Paul wrote Romans, and he did not use it. Surely Paul would have used that word if that issue were his concern. Second, the previous verse describes lesbian activity, a conduct seldom discussed and not as prevalent in the Roman world. Third, Paul uses the terms "female" and "male," rather than "woman" and "man." In this, he follows the biblical account of creation where God "created them male and female" (Gen. 1:27). This highlights the specific gender function of the sexes.

The second major objection states that Paul is concerned with "contrary to nature" issues. It suggests Paul decries "going against one's nature." Properly each should follow his nature, whether heterosexual or homosexual. Almost all biblical scholars debunk this, noting that for Paul "nature" generally means the natural order or the natural way things are. Paul speaks of homosexual activity itself as contrary to nature. The plain reading of the text reveals that Paul speaks against homosexual activity.

A second important text for this discussion is 1 Corinthians 6:9. While it does not contain as extended a discussion as Romans 1, it does have a precise description and condemnation of homosexual activity:

> Don't you know that the unrighteous will not inherit God's kingdom? Do not be deceived: No sexually immoral people, idolaters, adulterers, or anyone practicing homosexuality, no

thieves, greedy people, drunkards, verbally abusive people, or swindlers will inherit God's kingdom. (1 Cor. 6:9)

Two explanations are essential for understanding this verse. First, the phrase "sexually immoral people" translates the Greek word *pornoi*. The general use of the word describes a broad sexual deviation. Some try to confine it to heterosexual intercourse outside of marriage, but various contexts reveal it has the meaning of any sexual activity outside of marriage. It is a general term. Second, two different words are used in this passage for those practicing homosexual activity. The Greek word *malakoi* means "soft" and is generally understood as the passive partner. The other word, *arsenokoitai*, combines two words, "men" and "sexual intercourse" to indicate the active partner. Together the words paint a vivid picture.

Paul uses ten words in the vice list in 1 Corinthians 6:9. Four clearly describe sexual activity outside of marriage. Homosexuality is included, but it is only part of the list. *Porneia*, the general term, covers all forms of sexual immorality. When the term occurs by itself without contextual modifiers, it covers a broad range of extramarital sexual involvements, whether specific sex acts or not. Further, Paul makes no distinction between homosexuality and extramarital heterosexual activity in how the church understands and relates to those involved in them.

Both Romans and 1 Corinthians texts clearly describe homosexual activity. Two overall conclusions may be drawn. First, Scripture opposes homosexual acts. Second, homosexual acts are often included in the lists of vices generally called *porneia*.

## Corinth: A Case Study of Theological Response

An excellent case study for ministry in the new marriage culture is the church at Corinth. Paul wrote extensively to them regarding sex and marriage, and the instructions are applicable for today. Two foundational principles guide what follows. They are pragmatic, relating to how we ought to live. Each, however, rests solidly on theological platforms.

First, the Christian worldview best meets the needs and ambitions of any society, providing a proper environment for all. This does not mean every Christian holds a Christian worldview. Numerous examples of wrongful action can be attributed to people who "thought they were doing God's will." The distinction is delicate. Nevertheless, a truly Christian approach to life allows those who differ to do so (unless the conduct is immoral or unethical) but affirms what is best for all.

Second, a properly functioning church provides the best environment for satisfying the longings of the heart. One may have difficulty finding a "properly functioning church"! Nevertheless, the church ideal described in Scripture best meets human needs.

First Corinthians 5–7 is the most extended Pauline passage on sexual misbehavior. From this section of the Bible, five theological emphases can be summarized that guide the church in these matters. These principles outline what the church must do to protect itself and to offer a redemptive, alternative sexual ethic in our world. Theological responses are theological. That is, they center on God (Theos) and His revealed will. Too often, the church (like society) builds its program on a pragmatic and/or relational theology. That is, we live in light of those around us, whether we do so attempting to reach them or out of fear of them. We must be called back to a God-centered approach to deciding issues related to sexual behavior. Here are five principles to facilitate this response.

## 1. Express God's Love through His Grace

Christians are supposed to love everyone. Unfortunately, it is often more an ideal than a description of reality. Similarly, Christians are supposed to extend grace to everyone. Unfortunately, grace is often perceived as permission and love as tolerance. Both concepts need clarification.

Paul introduced his discussion in Corinthians with a correction. They had been debating his previous letters on these matters.

Paul had recommended a strong stance against a church member who willfully and continually violated God's expectations of sexual purity. He advised the man having an affair with his stepmother be dismissed from the congregation for his own good. First Corinthians 5:9–13 contains instructions about the Christian offender and provides insight as to our attitude:

> I wrote to you in a letter not to associate with sexually immoral people. I did not mean the immoral people of this world or the greedy and swindlers or idolaters; otherwise you would have to leave this world. . . . For what business is it of mine to judge outsiders? Don't you judge those who are inside? (1 Cor. 5:9–10, 12–13)

"Sexually immoral" translates *pornois*, the general term for those who practice wrongful sexual activities.[8] It occurs in a list of vices that include idolatry, sexual practices, and wrongful social relationships. Furthermore, if the church judges those outside the church, it can become preoccupied with what is God's business, not theirs.[9]

Paul corrects their misunderstanding of his previous letter that he meant some kind of Christian monasticism. He wrote: "In that case you would have to leave this world" (1 Cor. 5:10 NIV). If the church leaves the world, it fails in its most important mission: to reach the world for Christ. Rather than leaving the world, the statement assumes Christians will know the people of the world and have a relationship with them. The church belongs in the world. We cannot love those whom we do not know!

Love has many dimensions. First Corinthians 13 beautifully describes the persistence and power of love. It does not, however, address what love actually is. Love can be defined as "enriching the lives of others." Love cannot be reduced to allowing people to do whatever they want. Ultimately, no one accepts that definition. We all realize some things are harmful for individuals and society. Love is always expressed through the lens of truth. Love always intends to bring people closer to Jesus.

This principle of the transforming power of love leads to one of Paul's most powerful statements. After describing the vices of those who will *not* inherit the kingdom of God, Paul stated: "And that is what some of you were. But you were washed, you were sanctified, you were justified in the name of the Lord Jesus Christ and by the Spirit of our God" (1 Cor. 6:11 NIV).

Amazingly, "the unrighteous" can become the righteous, the "right doers." The church is living proof salvation works! God changes people through Jesus Christ and by the power of the Holy Spirit. This is not human work; but transformed humans, now called saints, joyously exemplify this truth.

This first theological principle gives us perspective. Christians must not express anger, vindictiveness, or judgmentalism toward those who disagree with them. God desires their salvation and expects us to deliver that message. Looking at lost people, we see what some of us were! By loving others and offering grace to change, we celebrate our transformation as well.

## 2. Affirm a Biblical Worldview

Worldviews encompass everything. A biblical worldview[10] begins where the Bible begins and ends where the Bible ends. What is not included in the Bible must be consistent with, and not contrary to, the Bible. The Bible begins with "in the beginning God" (Gen. 1:1) and then reveals God to us. Modern society, to its detriment, spends little time thinking about God.

Among the many dimensions of a proper theology, Scripture locates sexual purity in God Himself. For example, at the conclusion of an explicit warning about sex outside of marriage, Paul wrote:

> The Lord will punish all those who commit such sins, as we told you and warned you before. For God did not call us to be impure, but to live a holy life. Therefore, anyone who rejects this instruction does not reject a human being but God, the very God who gives you his Holy Spirit. (1 Thess. 4:6–8 NIV)

It seems insufficient, and perhaps vague, to say simply "God" will judge. Instead, Paul explicitly identifies sexual purity with each person of the tri-unity of God: God (the Father) calls; the Lord (Jesus) as judge; the Holy Spirit within the believer. Paul identifies each person of the Trinity for emphasis. Perhaps, even further, each is called as a witness to sexual purity because, in marriage, the two sexes mirror the relationships of the Trinity. The highest form of human intimacy, sealed through the sexual union, reflects the satisfying intimacy found within the Godhead.

This Trinitarian viewpoint may provide the rationale for Paul's discussion in Romans 1. Describing the downward plight of humanity, Paul links it to the tragic consequences of not honoring God. He wrote:

> For although they knew God, they neither glorified him as God nor gave thanks to him, but their thinking became futile and their foolish hearts were darkened. . . . They exchanged the truth about God for a lie, and worshiped and served created things rather than the Creator . . . just as they did not think it worthwhile to retain the knowledge of God, so God gave them over. (Rom. 1:21, 25, 28 NIV)

Three specific consequences are enumerated. First, heterosexual promiscuity outside of marriage dishonors God. Second, homosexual activity is forbidden. Third, idolatry through egocentricity is condemned.

Homosexual activity is described vividly as "men also abandoned natural relations with women and were inflamed with lust for one another. Men committed indecent acts with other men" (Rom 1:27 NIV). The Greek text is more explicit. Literally, rather than "men" and "women," Paul wrote "males" and "females." Going back to the most basic physical gender distinctions, Paul's words exactly replicate the Greek of the creation accounts.[11] Humans created in the image of God are "male and female" (Gen. 1:27).

In Romans 1, the "natural" partner of a woman is a man, and the "natural" partner of a man is a woman. While Paul reflects on the biblical creation account, his language points even to the created order outside of Scripture.[12] Paul expects perfect synergy between what is found in the natural world and explanations provided by Scripture. His argument, then, even finds support in nature. Natural law provides a "natural theology." The laws and theology of nature require explication, which is provided in part in Scripture. But apart from Scripture, Paul argues natural law affirms heterosexual relationships as the norm. Male and female complement each other.

Even with the symmetry of both natural and scriptural evidence, there are several other insights about why improper sexual relationships imperfectly reveal God. First, God is perfectly complete in and of Himself without anything outside Himself. Second, God is a social being able to communicate and enjoy intimacy at the highest level, untainted by imperfection. Third, God created humans in His image reflecting the social capacities and satisfaction intimacy brings. Finally, God created male and female because together they uniquely approximate the intimacy of God Himself.

When we consider all this, we affirm a biblical worldview that begins with God and creation as the foundation for understanding human sexuality.

## 3. Exalt a Biblical View of Marriage

Many themes in 1 Corinthians suggest first-century believers often had a low view of marriage. In Greco-Roman society a simple axiom prevailed: marriage is for procreation, sexual pleasure is found outside marriage.[13] This perspective seems to have found its way into the Corinthian church. In this sexually pluralistic environment, Paul made two important points related to marriage: Christians must not seek extramarital sexual pleasure, and God's purpose for married sexual expression includes pleasure.

In rejecting extramarital sexual pleasure, Paul based his argument on the second creation account, "This is why a man leaves his father and mother and bonds with his wife, and they become one flesh" (Gen. 2:24). God created Eve to meet Adam's need for companionship. The deepest levels of intimacy are sealed by "becoming one flesh," after a man and wife commit to each other. Throughout Scripture this verse serves as the foundation for marriage.

For example, Paul wrote about the high and holy place the institution of marriage has in God's economy (Eph. 5:22–31). Healthy marital relationships include a wife who submits to her husband and a husband who loves his wife. Marriage pictures the relationships God has with His people, particularly modeled by Jesus Christ and the church. No other institution enjoys as lofty a comparison.

In Roman culture there was an ongoing discussion about the purpose of marriage. Was it for *procreation* only? Or could it be for *pleasure*? Roman culture generally did not frown on prostitution or homosexuality as a means of personal satisfaction. Paul enters the debate with a biblical solution.

In 1 Corinthians 7:1–6, Paul advocates one of the purposes of marriage is providing companionship and pleasure. The issue he addressed was *porneia*, the plural of fornication, "fornications." He was not likely speaking of repeated individual acts with a prostitute but all the vices he had already listed. He underscores that neither husbands nor wives own their own bodies. Rather, they should consider their bodies as belonging to their spouses. There is no mention of procreation.[14] The entire context is that of mutual companionship and sexual satisfaction. Only prayers, agreed upon mutually, should interfere with normal sexual relations (1 Cor. 7:5). Clearly he sees a normal, happy, and healthy marriage as a strong deterrent to sexual wanderings outside the relationship.

In ministering to a new marriage culture, the church must exalt a biblical view of marriage. Marriages are in trouble. Divorce is rampant. Cohabitation is common. Celibacy is chosen by many, not as a spiritual practice but because young adults fear emotional and physical hurt in marriage relationships. Marriage is often denigrated, rather than praised, for several reasons. First, some think an undue focus on marriage may reveal their own marriage is in jeopardy. Second, some fear talking about marriage problems will discourage the unmarried from marriage. Finally, some leaders lack confidence in their own marriages, therefore undermining what they might teach on the subject.

In sexually pluralistic Corinth, Paul both warned about extramarital relationships and commended positive Christian relationships. He lifted up marriage and expanded on those ideas in his other writings. Rather than shy away from these standards, churches must enthusiastically affirm God's way of being married satisfies deep needs for companionship and intimacy.

## 4. Teach Respect for the Body

People are intimately and concretely connected to their bodies. Bodies often shape personalities, vocations, and activities. The body is the vehicle through which a person feels and communicates. Perhaps more than any other entity or possession, people instinctively believe their bodies are their own. Whatever they wish to do with their bodies, they believe they have the right to do. This modern philosophy is not so new. It raised its head in ancient Corinth and was a major concern when Paul wrote about confronting and combating sexual impropriety.

Some in the Corinthian church apparently claimed this mantra for their inappropriate actions: "I have the right to do anything," you say—but not everything is beneficial. 'I have the right to do anything'—but I will not be mastered by anything. You say, 'Food for the stomach and the stomach for food, and God will destroy them both'" (1 Cor. 6:12–13 NIV).

Ostensibly the argument is about personal freedoms. Some church members joined the chorus, claiming they owned their bodies and could do whatever they wanted. For additional support they added a theological twist related to the stomach and food: "God will destroy them both." The theology reflected a conviction that the resurrection was spiritual, involving the nonmaterial parts of the person, but the body was suited to this earth and would remain in dust after death.

This argument is sometimes echoed today in the church when people say, "If it is natural, it is right," or, "If it feels good, do it," or,

"You only live once." These popular sayings support the perspective that following desires and inclinations is right, no matter the resulting behavior.

The argument about food belied the real issue. Paul answers, "The body, however, is not meant for sexual immorality but for the Lord, and the Lord for the body" (1 Cor. 6:13 NIV). This verse is followed with an extensive discourse on the nature of the body, which countered the idea of sexual freedoms outside marriage in several ways.

First, "the body is meant for the Lord, and the Lord for the body." When God created physical bodies, He intended for them to be related primarily to Him. The body is for service of and fellowship with the Lord Jesus Christ, and He expects the sanctity of the body. Further, just as God raised Jesus in His body, God will raise us also. The argument the stomach is made for food fails. The stomach, like the rest of the body, is made for a higher purpose. It is also eternal, to be enjoyed in a glorified state by none other than our Lord Himself (1 Cor. 15). There is uniqueness to the physical body. Christians have a stewardship responsibility to use the body (the entire body) for its intended purpose, that of glorifying our Lord.

Second, our bodies are members of Christ himself (1 Cor. 6:15). In Jesus Christ's resurrection we find identity with Him as "members" of His body. We are spiritually joined with Him and cannot segment our bodies for use that disregards our union with him.

Third, sexual sin is sin against the body (1 Cor. 6:18). A believer's body belongs to the Lord and is destined to be united with Him in resurrection. Any sexual sin is contrary to that union and its ultimate destination. Paul further argues the body is a temple of the Holy Spirit (1 Cor. 6:19) and was purchased by Christ's death (1 Cor. 6:20). The word *body* occurs in this context seven times. Clearly sexual sin involves the body. The critical question, then, is, who owns a believer's body?

The answer in 1 Corinthians is extended. First, the proper use of the body involves only what is acceptable to the Lord, for whom it was created. Second, the body is a temple of the Holy Spirit and must not be defiled. Third, sexual desires of the body are only satisfied in a healthy marriage. Fourth, not all bodily desires will be satisfied on earth.

This last statement is foundational for an important section of 1 Corinthians 7. Some believers are counseled not to get married, even though it is a natural part of creation and satisfies deep needs for companionship. God's will is for people to discipline strong desires. Living according to God's will is better than trying to please self, including with sexual activities. Nearly all people have strong sex drives. They occur before, outside of, and during marriage. God does not intend that everyone will satisfy personal sexual drives. Many unmarried long for the satisfaction marriage can bring, but God has not willed it for them. They may be "eunuchs who have made them-selves that way because of the kingom" (Matt. 19:12). They choose sexual celibacy. They cannot violate God's will by engaging in pre-marital sex.

The consistent biblical teaching is people find their satisfaction first in God alone and then in human relationships that accompany living in God's will. The church must emphasize respect for the body. Glorifying God in our body means, among other things, avoiding premature or unnatural ways of satisfying the desires. Churches must emphasize total satisfaction of the entire person, not just the physical drives, through a vital relationship with Jesus Christ. Allowing Him to be Lord brings ultimate satisfaction.

## 5. Appreciate the Power of Church Community

For many Americans religion is a personal and individual matter. Some who become Christians keep their faith to themselves. They seek to handle life's difficulties on their own, often discouraged when their strength is insufficient to accomplish their holy ambitions.

The church is a corporate community, a body of believers. Entrance into the church is intensely personal. It requires confession of sin, faith in Jesus' death and resurrection, and obedience symbol-ized by baptism. Being in the church, however, is essentially com-munal. The Bible uses several metaphors for the people of God but none more powerful than the body of Christ (1 Cor. 12:12–31). Each believer has a unique place in the local church as a fully accepted member of the body of Christ.

In the Corinthian church the man who had an affair with his stepmother repented. He sought reconciliation and reinstatement into the church. It was exactly what mature believers hope will happen. In response Paul wrote specific commands as to how to embrace him: "The punishment inflicted on him by the majority is sufficient for him. Now instead, you ought to forgive and comfort him, so that he will not be overwhelmed by excessive sorrow. I urge you, therefore, to reaffirm your love for him" (2 Cor. 2:6–8 NIV).

The church was commanded to support this brother in three ways. First, forgive him. Christians often have difficulty forgiving those who have failed in sexual sins. His sin was egregious, but God's grace was sufficient. Second, comfort him. The word for "comfort" suggests coming alongside to support and help toward complete restoration and Christian maturity. Third, love him. Clearly communicate renewed love for the one who failed them all.

These are good instructions to apply today for anyone who repents of any sexual sin. The church must forgive as Christ forgives. The church must come alongside to lend support to avoid lapses and further failure. Finally, the church must make sure its love is felt and known. People with sexual sins in their pasts often need special care. Instead, the church often rejects them. Though initially happy with their conversion, Christians often avoid them as though contamination comes from personal contact. Paul wrote of these former sinners, "You were washed" (1 Cor. 6:11). The church must rally around those with special needs and issues as they attempt to grow in their newfound faith. The church is a place of grace and love. It is a hospital for the spiritually sick who are becoming well by God's grace.

## Conclusion

Christians must love all people, relating to them through the eyes of grace. Many people will have a different marital worldview. They may have little regard for the joys of marriage as God intended. They may be pleasure driven, thinking they can do what they want with their body. They may even go so far as redefining biblical marriage. The church must love such people just as they would any other sinner, for all have sinned. Once they are converted, the church must be a place of redemption and restoration to the wholeness God intended in creation. More than ever, in the new marriage culture, the church needs to be the church God intended.

# Theological Foundations for Ministry in the New Marriage Culture

CHAPTER 4

# GOSPEL CONFIDENCE IN THE NEW MARRIAGE CULTURE

*Christopher W. Morgan
and Gregory C. Cochran*

As a local and zealous mosque leader in Pakistan, Zahid marched from house to house ambushing Christians, often confiscating and burning their Bibles. One day Zahid decided not to burn all the Bibles but to keep one. His mission? To study the Bible well enough to refute those converting to Christianity. But instead of finding inconsistencies, Zahid found Jesus Christ through the gospel. Zahid now loves and ministers among those he once persecuted. And like the apostle Paul, Zahid has returned to witness to those of his former religion.[1]

The gospel was at work in Paul's diverse first-century contexts, and the gospel is at work in our multiple twenty-first-century contexts. Through the gospel God still turns antagonists into His children. And through the gospel God still forms gospel communities who display and communicate the realities of God's grace. Indeed, the gospel has been, is, and will always be powerful in every culture, including the new marriage culture.

But what is the gospel? How does it have power? How does the powerful gospel form a kingdom community? And how can we find confidence in God and His powerful gospel? These questions are massive in importance and breadth, but our space is limited so we will primarily focus on how Paul addresses them in his correspondence to the Corinthians.

## The Gospel

In Paul's first epistle to the Corinthians, he stresses the gospel fundamentally challenges human systems, is routinely rejected as foolishness, but comes from God and bears His power (1 Cor. 1:17–31). Paul also expresses his obligation to preach the gospel to all, his engagement with varied cultures for the sake of the gospel, and his hope to share in the gospel's blessings (1 Cor. 9:14–23; cf. 2 Cor. 11:7). Paul further crystallizes the gospel he received and proclaimed (1 Cor. 15:1–8).

In his second epistle to the Corinthians, Paul states, "But if our gospel is veiled, it is veiled to those who are perishing. In their case, the god of this age has blinded the minds of the unbelievers so they cannot see the light of the gospel of the glory of Christ, who is the image of God" (2 Cor. 4:3–4). In fact, Paul laments, "For if a person comes and preaches another Jesus, whom we did not preach, or you receive a different spirit, which you had not received, or a different gospel, which you had not accepted, you put up with it splendidly!" (2 Cor. 11:4; cf. Gal. 1:6–7). Yet there is no gospel other than the one preached by Paul.[2]

But of all these incredible passages, 1 Corinthians 15:1–8 most thoroughly defines the gospel:

Now brothers, I want to clarify for you the gospel I proclaimed to you; you received it and have taken your stand on it. You are also saved by it, if you hold to the message I proclaimed to you—unless you believed for no purpose. For I passed on to you as most important what I also received:

that Christ died for our sins
according to the Scriptures,
that He was buried,
that He was raised on the third day
according to the Scriptures,
and that He appeared to Cephas,
then to the Twelve.

Then He appeared to over 500 brothers at one time;
most of them are still alive,
but some have fallen asleep.
Then He appeared to James,
then to all the apostles.
Last of all, as to one abnormally born,
He also appeared to me.

Here Paul clarifies the gospel he received and proclaimed.

First, Paul shows that the gospel is the good news to a story that has been unfolding since creation. Not only has Christ died for our sins, and not only has Christ been raised for our sins, but He has also died and been raised "according to the Scriptures." This brief phrase indicates that Paul understands Jesus (and the gospel) to be tied to a far-reaching biblical story line. Anthony Thiselton notes that Paul views "the continuity of the cross of Christ with the history of the saving purposes of God as revealed in the Old Testament, which find their climax and fulfillment in the saving work of Christ."[3] Further, Paul considers the biblical story line as vital for "understanding the meaning of the saving role of the death of Christ by means of 'interpretation in OT categories—for example, of sacrifice . . . atonement . . . sufferings . . . the good time to come.'"[4] Thus, the gospel is the good news of Jesus in the context of the biblical story line.

Second, Paul clarifies that the gospel is the good news about Jesus, especially centered on His life and saving work. What Paul preached and deemed "most important" is that Jesus died for our sins, was buried, and was raised on the third day, all according to the Scriptures.

Both the historical realities and the theological significance of Christ and His saving work are underlined here. Note first the emphasis on historical fact: Christ died, was buried, was raised on the third day, and appeared on multiple occasions to an extensive exhibition of eyewitnesses: Cephas, the Twelve, more than five hundred brothers at one time, James, all the apostles, and Paul. Paul even records some of these eyewitness were alive at the time of his writing, letting the Corinthians and others know their testimony could be assessed and ultimately verified. Further, the historicity of the resurrection is central to Paul's argument throughout the remainder of 1 Corinthians 15.

But Paul makes clear the gospel is more than historical data about Jesus. Even if all accept every fact—that Jesus lived, died, was raised from the dead, and appeared to a wide range of valid eyewitnesses— that alone would not mean all believe *the gospel* in the fuller New Testament sense of that term. Thus, Paul's listing of the historical facts of Christ's death in 1 Corinthians 15:3–5 includes the small but significant phrase: "for our sins." The inclusion of "for our sins" draws attention to the inherently theological nature of the gospel. Jesus not only lived, died, was buried, was raised the third day, and appeared to many valid witnesses, but He also died for our sins. By "for our sins," Paul stresses Christ's death is central to His saving work, particularly declaring that Jesus' death is an atoning death (cf. Rom. 3:21–26).

Later in 1 Corinthians 15, Paul elaborates on the theological significance of the resurrection. Indeed, Jesus' resurrection is critical for the validity of our faith, preaching, forgiveness, hope of our future bodily resurrection, the hope of Christ's final victory over all powers and authorities, and the ultimate establishment of His kingdom (15:12–58). As Oliver O'Donovan shows, Christ's resurrection vindicates the created order in a "double sense: it redeems it and it transforms it."[5]

Third, the gospel is also depicted by Paul as the crystallized summary of all this. Graeme Goldsworthy captures the threefold sense of gospel:

The word *gospel*, then, is used in several ways. First, the NT uses it to describe the heart of the OT promises of salvation. Secondly, it is used of the saving event of Jesus of Nazareth as the grounds of salvation for all who believe. Thirdly, it designates the proclamation of that saving event as the means by which people are confronted with the truth about Christ.[6]

Matthew Emerson similarly concludes:

Thus when defining "gospel" through the lens of the canonical shape of the NT, we see that Christ's life and work, its proclamation by the church, and the call for an individual response are all part of that definition. The term "gospel" therefore ". . . embraces both the objective content that forms the substance of the Christian faith (Jesus' person and work as saving event), the present effectiveness of that substance as a living determinant of the human situation, and the proclamation of the content and its effect."[7]

## Gospel Power

Paul's gospel clarity in 1 Corinthians carries not only theological significance but also practical significance. Paul therefore urges the Corinthian church to live in light of the gospel's power. Indeed, from the beginning of 1 Corinthians, Paul stresses Christ's power:

For the message of the cross is foolishness to those who are perishing, but it is God's power to us who are being saved. . . . For the Jews ask for signs and the Greeks seek wisdom, but we preach Christ crucified, a stumbling block to the Jews and foolishness to the Gentiles. Yet to those who are called, both Jews and Greeks, Christ is God's power and God's wisdom, because God's foolishness is wiser than human wisdom, and God's weakness is stronger than human strength. . . .

When I came to you, brothers, announcing the testimony of God to you, I did not come with brilliance of speech or

wisdom. For I didn't think it was a good idea to know anything among you except Jesus Christ and Him crucified. I
came to you in weakness, in fear, and in much trembling. My
speech and my proclamation were not with persuasive words
of wisdom but with a powerful demonstration by the Spirit,
so that your faith might not be based on men's wisdom but on
God's power. (1:18, 22–25, 2:1–5)

Note how Paul contrasts the power of the gospel with human
wisdom. The gospel, here called "the message of the cross," is "God's
power to us who are being saved" (1:18). Christ is "God's power" and
"God's wisdom" and, as such, is more powerful and wiser than anything human. Further, God has chosen "not many" who are powerful
or wise but mostly those who are weak and insignificant. In doing
so, God undercuts all human boasting and spotlights His power and
wisdom. Because of this Paul thinks it would be foolish to base his
ministry practices on human power and wisdom. Instead, his ministry flows from confidence in God's powerful gospel. Clint Arnold
explains:

> Paul endeavored to root the faith of his converts in God and
> his power. The Corinthian Christians, however, were tempted
> to be more impressed with the form and style of delivery . . .
> rather than the content of the message. Paul thus calls them
> to focus on the content of the preaching—Jesus Christ and
> him crucified—and the demonstration of the Spirit's power
> in his preaching, evident in the transformed lives of the
> converts.[8]

What was the demonstration of the Spirit and of power which
Paul deems so compelling? Some have argued that the proof must
have referred to signs and wonders accomplished by the Holy Spirit
in Corinth. This is possible, but Gordon Fee offers a plausible interpretation. Fee suggests: "[Paul's] intent is clear from the context:
Even though he was weak and his preaching lacked 'rhetoric' and
'wisdom,' their very coming to faith demonstrated that it did not

lack power."⁹ Fee then shows the close relationship between Spirit and power in Paul's writings: "In Paul, the terms 'Spirit' and 'power' are at times nearly interchangeable (cf. 5:4). To speak of the Spirit is automatically to speak of power (cf. Rom 15:13, 19)."¹⁰ Fee then asks,

> To what powerful demonstration of the Spirit does this refer? It is possible, but not probable given the context of "weakness," that it reflects the "signs and wonders" of 2 Cor. 12:12. More likely it refers to their actual conversion. . . . Throughout this passage the power of God has the cross as its paradigm. The true alternative to wisdom humanly conceived is not "signs" but the gospel, which the Spirit brings to bear on our lives in powerful ways.¹¹

In sum, these believers were not naturally wise or powerful or noble people (1:26). They were, in fact, regarded as weak, foolish, and despised (1:27–28). Yet they were the chosen objects of God's effective grace. Therefore, the actual and plain proof of God's power "lies with the Corinthians themselves and their own experience of the Spirit as they responded to the message of the gospel."¹²

## The Gospel Community

Gospel power is demonstrated in the conversion of the Corinthians, and so it is likewise demonstrated in the church itself. Christ's saving work defines the nature of His new community. His life calls for a loving and holy community, His death redeems them unto His people, and His resurrection inaugurates a community presently (even if partially) living out the realities of God's kingdom. His messianic fulfillment of God's covenant promises forms the church as a new humanity, body, field, building, temple, and kingdom (1 Cor. 3:9, 16–17; 12—14). This gospel community, Paul asserts, is to be marked by unity (1:10–17), humility (1:18—2:5), wisdom (2:6–16), truth (3:10–15), holiness (3:16–17; 5:1–13; 6:9–20), and love (13:1–7).¹³ Living out the realities of God's inaugurated kingdom, this new community of Jesus both verbalizes and embodies the gospel and its power.

Note how distinct passages such as 1 Corinthians 6 and 13 shed light on the empowered gospel community. Like the epistle itself 1 Corinthians 6 is governed by Paul's concern for spiritual unity within the church and, as such, speaks to the nature of the church. The church is pictured in 1 Corinthians 6 as a united, organic whole. Each individual is a member of Christ (v. 15). Stephen Wellum explains, "By the agency of the Spirit (who not only regenerates us but now indwells us, individually as Christians and corporately as Christ's church), we now have become God's new temple (1 Cor. 3:16–17; 6:19; 2 Cor. 6:16; Eph. 2:21; Heb. 3:6; 1 Pet. 2:5)."[14] Uniting together as the intimate body of Christ (or as the temple of God) means, necessarily, being distinct from the world or culture at large. Paul makes this message clear by posing the questions of 1 Corinthians 6:15: "Don't you know that your bodies are a part of Christ's body? So should I take a part of Christ's body and make it part of a prostitute? Absolutely not!" The church is not a collection of individuals who occasionally congregate but a gospel-empowered entity called out of the world and into fellowship for gospel mission. Just as an individual part of a human body cannot visit a prostitute without the entire body being present, so also the individual member of the church body does not live unto himself. The body is an organic whole, a corporate entity.

Therefore, the body must be concerned for its own members. So when Paul sets forth the vice list in 1 Corinthians 6:9–11, he is not simply offering a moral checklist of recommended do's and don'ts. Rather he offers the church a distinguishing list, a list illuminating distinctions between those who have received the Spirit-powered gospel and those who have not. Not surprisingly, Paul chastened the Corinthians for their failure to make the proper distinctions based on the sexual immorality of 1 Corinthians 5. Paul reiterated the point again in 1 Corinthians 6, where some members were apparently taking others to court before unbelievers rather than making judgments themselves. Paul expects a congregation of gospel-empowered saints to be able to make decisions on matters of justice and morality (6:1–8).

One of the matters about which the gospel community would need to make clear judgments is the practice of homosexuality.[15]

Those characterized by fornication, idolatry, adultery, homosexuality, thievery, drunkenness, or swindling were failing to discern the basic salvific distinction between righteousness and unrighteousness. Righteousness characterizes those who have received Paul's God-powered gospel message, as is clear from verse 11: "And some of you used to be like this. But you were washed, you were sanctified, you were justified in the name of the Lord Jesus Christ and by the Spirit of our God." Thiselton comments, "The last of these verses brings welcome relief to this somber catalogue: And this [is what] some of you used to be."[16] The church is composed of people who have come in contact with Christ and have become washed clean from their sin and become set apart by God as holy ones.

The nature of the gospel community is also clarified by 1 Corinthians 13.[17] In this famous passage Paul points to the highest ambitions of these believers, or what these church members considered the pinnacle of spirituality. Some aspired to speak in the tongues of heaven, attain the deepest of knowledge, possess faith that led to miracles, sacrifice all their money to help the poor, or die a martyr's death for Christ. Paul strategically points to their highest spiritual aspirations and then turns the tables on them (13:1–3). Paul asserts that to reach our highest aspirations—in their case, to experience spiritual gifts beyond measure, to have faith that leads to miracles, to know truth as much as it can be known, to give all of our money to the poor, or to be willing to sacrifice our lives for the gospel—to reach all of these but to do them without having love is likened to being worthless: "I am nothing" (13:2); "I gain nothing" (13:3). Even radical spirituality/religion without love is worthless.

Then in 13:4–7, Paul points them to true spirituality, which at its core is true Christian love. He does not so much define love as describe and personify it, as a person who thinks and acts. Addressing the real-life problems of the Corinthian church, Paul warns them that their approach to religion is warped, portrays love as what is "central, characteristic, and irreplaceable in biblical Christianity,"[18] and selects particular facets of love they needed to hear. Some were impatient and unkind, filled with jealous ambition, egos, and were puffed up. They insisted on their own way, were feisty, and resentful. They even rejoiced in wrong rather than righteousness (1 Cor. 5). Some in the church promoted themselves rather than sought to promote the good of the overall body. Instead of humbly serving others, they humiliated others. Instead of rejecting the social class system, they highlighted it. Instead of following Jesus' example of service, love, and sacrifice for the good of others, they used the symbol of His sacrifice for self-promotion. Instead of viewing their spiritual gifts as a God-given means to strengthen the church, they boasted of their superior knowledge and spirituality.

Paul describes love by its response to others in the church. He offers several descriptions:

- Patient: endures suffering and difficult people (6:7).
- Kind: tenderness; Paul often links kindness with forgiveness (Eph. 4:32).
- Not jealous/envious: wants the best for others, not wishing that the successes of others were only ours (3:3).
- Not boast/vainglorious: unpretentious, not promoting ourselves so others would praise us (1:17; 2:1).
- Not proud/puffed up (4:6, 18, 19; 5:2; 8:1): humble, not arrogant.
- Not indecent/shameful/rude (5:1–2): pure, not immoral.
- Not insist on its own way (10:24, 33; cf. Phil 2:3–4): generous, not self-seeking.
- Not irritable: long-suffering, not given to fits of anger.
- Not resentful/keep records of offenses: having a forgiving spirit, not easily offended (6:7: "Why not rather suffer wrong?" ESV).
- Not rejoice over injustice; supports justice not wrongdoing.
- Rejoices in the truth; delights in and endorses truth.
- Bears all things: puts up with all things.
- Believes all things: generously trust, not suspicious or cynical (does not mean gullible).
- Hopes all things: hopes for the best, not pessimistic about others.
- Endures all things: perseveres.

Though the forms of love are as wide-ranging as the contexts, Paul demonstrates that love desires the good of others and gives of oneself for the sake of others.

Both 1 Corinthians 6 and 13 depict the church as the community of Jesus, in which unity, holiness, and love are prized. Even more, the unity of the gospel community requires such holiness, and it requires such love. In contemporary society unity is often sought at the expense of truth, and love is often defined as incompatible with holiness. But the church knows these virtues are unified, even interwoven, as Jonathan Edwards explains:

> The graces of Christianity are all connected together, and are mutually dependent on each other. . . .
> They so go together that where there is one, there are all. . . . Where there is faith, there are love, hope, and humility; and where there is love, there is trust; and where there is a holy trust in God, there is love for God. . . . Where there is love for God, there is a gracious love for man; and where there is a Christian love for man, there is love for God. . . .
> [T]he graces of Christianity depend on one another. . . . [T]here is also a mutual dependence between them, so that one cannot be without the other. . . . Faith promotes love. . . . Then again, love enlarges and promotes faith. . . . So love promotes humility. . . . Humility promotes love. . . . Love tends to repentance. . . . And repentance tends to humility. . . . A true love for God tends to love for men who bear the image of God.[19]

Note further that the gospel community is both characterized by such unity, love, and holiness, and it is to strive toward unity, love, and holiness. As the kingdom community the church necessarily bears the marks of both the already and not yet of the kingdom. As such, the church is both holy, and its members are gradually becoming more and more holy—which also means it has members who still sin. The church is a community of love, but as Paul's rebukes in 1 Corinthians 13 make clear, it is still composed of people who still have a long way to go in their love. Just as the individual believer is simultaneously justified and sinful, as Martin Luther reminds, so the church (and each individual member) is simultaneously holy and has a lot of growing to do—in holiness, love, unity, etc. However, while the church is never fully indicative of the kingdom, it remains a central means by which believers grow in unity, love, and holiness.

Thus, 1 Corinthians 6 reminds us that the gospel community, marked by unity, holiness, and love, distinguishes itself from the surrounding society and its norms. The gospel community follows a higher ethic, one rooted in God and His character. And the gospel community urges its members to live out this ethic, holding them accountable to it and helping them find ways to embody it.

First Corinthians 13 likewise reminds us that the gospel community is particularly distinguished from the surrounding society by love, its genuine desire for the good of others and practical, day-to-day prioritizing of the good of others, even at the expense of personal agendas and cultural values. The gospel community marked by such love is itself an apologetic for the gospel, as it demonstrates the goals of the gospel (reconciliation, new life, new humanity, etc.) as well as its life-giving power. As such, the church is "the gospel made visible," a new display of people in which God's reign has begun.[20] Francis Schaeffer referred to the church's love as the "final apologetic."

> We as Christians are called upon to love all men as neighbors, loving them as ourselves. . . . [W]e are to love all the Christian brothers in a way that the world may observe. This means showing love to our brothers in the midst of our differences—great or small—loving our brothers when it costs us something, loving them even under times of tremendous emotional tension, loving them in a way the world can see. In short, we are to practice and exhibit the holiness of God and the love of God. . . . Love—and the unity it attests to—is the mark Christ gave Christians to wear before the world. Only with this mark may the world know that Christians are indeed Christians and Jesus was sent by the Father.[21]

## Gospel Confidence in a New Marriage Culture

Through his Corinthian correspondence Paul explains the gospel is the good news for an already existing biblical story, centered on the person and saving work of Jesus, and often depicted as the crystalized message about Jesus. Paul elaborates that the gospel is powerful, through the work of Christ and the Spirit. This power is most clearly seen in the conversion of sinners and the establishment of the community of Jesus, the church. The church bears witness of God and His power through the faithful proclamation of the gospel as well as the community demonstration of unity, holiness, and love.

These gospel realities ground our gospel confidence in all situations. And these gospel realities ground our gospel confidence in the new marriage culture. How? While the rest of this volume will address the issues and applications in more detail, it seems appropriate here to suggest a few ways the gospel, gospel power, and the gospel community ground our gospel confidence in the new marriage culture.

First, the nature of the gospel enables us to view the "new marriage culture" through an appropriate lens. The biblical story includes dramatic tension, frequent sharp turns, and recurrent surprises. But Jesus has come, He has accomplished salvation, He has included all who have faith in Him into His community, and He will ultimately set the record straight. This current cultural shift is one of the millions of challenges God's people have had, do have, and will face. It is neither the largest nor the most important. We can and must engage it with careful reflection, with love, and with hope, as several essays in this volume articulate. But Christ has defeated the biggest challenge, sin and death (1 Cor. 15). Everything else pales in comparison.

Second, the gospel has power to transform lives. It changed the apostle Paul, it changed Zahid, it has changed many of us, and it will keep changing others. The strongest of human power structures and the finest of human theoretical systems are incomparable to the power and the wisdom of the cross of Christ (1 Cor. 1:18—2:5). We can and should reflect on how to wisely promote values in our manifold cultures, but central to our mission is the faithful proclamation and loving demonstration of the gospel.

Third, the goal of the gospel is not heterosexuality but holistic life in Christ. The confidence of our ministry in the new marriage culture is not merely that homosexual men and women can become heterosexual. Our confidence is that the gospel of Jesus Christ is divinely powered to redeem sinners and set them apart as holy unto the Lord in a Spirit-powered church. That gospel-powered transformation will lead, in time, to a life of holiness and love, which will ultimately relate to every aspect of life, including sexuality.

Fourth, God has established a gospel community to proclaim and display the gospel. The church's unity, holiness, and love are means by which God displays His own oneness, holiness, and love. A church marred by failure to live distinctly in a wide array of moral issues is a church that will be given a minimal platform to speak to these culturally unpopular issues. The more we are marked by unity, holiness, and love, the more our lives can ably paint the picture of how life ought to be, and the more our countercultural kingdom community can effect change in one another and in the broader society as salt and light (Matt. 5:3–16).

Fifth, while we should stress the power of the gospel and the community of Jesus to change lives, we should not give the impression change normally comes instantly, fully, or easily. Believers repent when they come to Christ, but the whole Christian life is marked by repentance. All believers struggle with temptation and sin. Real change can and does happen but rarely as easily or quickly as we would prefer. Those struggling with homosexuality who genuinely come to Christ will likely still face years of battles as they progressively walk in holiness. The church should lovingly and patiently stand with these brothers and sisters. As we noted, love marks the church, but Paul still has to encourage such love and its forms in his epistles. Unity marks the church, but Paul still has to rebuke pride and discord. Holiness marks the church, but Paul still has to urge the church and its members to repent of sin and live according to the kingdom. Everyone in the church struggles with something; everyone needs grace. Indeed, all of us need grace all the time. The church is no place for pseudotriumphalism but a gospel community characterized by unity, holiness, and love, which includes patience. As such, the church is used by God to transform us gradually but genuinely.

Finally, we can have great confidence the gospel we proclaim is the same gospel which changed Saul the persecutor into Paul the apostle, the same gospel which changed Zahid the imam into the resolute Pakistani evangelist he is today. The same gospel has also changed Rosaria Champagne Butterfield, who told her story in a recent edition of *Christianity Today*.[22]

Rosaria thought Christians were stupid, pointless, and menacing. By her own admission she was a radical, leftist, feminist professor with tenure. Her worldview was shaped by Hegel and Marx, not Paul or Jesus. Rosaria was comfortably living with her lesbian partner when, much like Zahid in Pakistan, she decided to read the one book that provided the fuel for her adversaries' fire: the Bible. Rosaria took up reading the Bible in order to refute it.

One day she wrote an article countering the Promise Keepers movement. She says she received significant pushback, much of it hateful. But one response came from a pastor who seemed truly concerned for Rosaria. He did not attack her. Instead, the pastor and his wife befriended her, shared Christ's love with her, explained the Bible to her, and prayed vulnerably with her, until one day Rosaria came to Christ. Once a champion of the gay and lesbian lifestyle, Rosaria walked away from it all, leaving people she honestly loved and, ultimately, exemplifying the power of the gospel of the Lord Jesus Christ.

The church at Corinth was made up of many believers like Zahid and Rosaria. And the church today is composed of many believers just like Zahid and Rosaria. Why? Because the same gospel is powerful to change lives. And through the gospel the community of Jesus still faithfully proclaims and lovingly displays the historic, divinely powered gospel.

## CHAPTER 5

# ROBUST ECCLESIOLOGY FOR THE NEW MARRIAGE CULTURE

## *Rodrick (Rick) K. Durst*

First and last, be encouraged. The gospel is still the power of God unto salvation. When the church is gospel driven, it has incredible resilience to flourish through any cultural transition. When Constantine and Licinius ended the Diocletian Persecution in 313, the culture changed for churches within the Roman Empire overnight. Churches quickly designed and tested practices for receiving lapsed Christians (who had worshipped the emperor or surrendered Scripture) back into their fellowship. These lapsed believers were intentionally received back after a time of testing and restitution.

After apartheid ended in 1994, South African churches needed to rethink fellowship and friendship across congregations. Conservative evangelical churches found themselves with little influence in the new culture because they had been less than vocal against the racial injustices of the apartheid government. Baptist churches, however, have regained their witness and prophetic influence in South Africa. They have opened nursing centers for those infected and dying of HIV-AIDS. Many congregations have erected makeshift nursing centers next to their worship buildings. These Baptists imagined a gospel way to live in grace without compromising the truth about lifestyles that offend God and damage lives, while also offering free nursing and lodging to the diseased and dying. These good works are renewing goodwill in the culture toward Baptists in South Africa.[1]

Be encouraged! The Lord has called His church to minister in His name and power in this rapidly changing new marriage culture. Historic and contemporary models like these motivate and instruct today's church on addressing this issue.

## Ecclesiological Disclaimer

This chapter offers, as its ultimate goal, an applied ecclesiology. Thoroughgoing ecclesiologies like *Sojourners and Strangers: The Doctrine of the Church* by Greg Allison or John Hammett's *Biblical Foundations for Baptist Churches* rightly put ecclesiological ontology before functionality—being before doing. This chapter focuses on what the church must do, resting on a thorough understanding of what the church must first be. This chapter is a first responder's emergency triage kit. The Trinitarian doctrine of the church and the many biblical images of the church, while not addressed here, provide needed direction when designing practical ecclesiology. Since this chapter is written to address a ministerial emergency requiring an immediate response, some foundational truths will be assumed as we focus on an applied ecclesiology.

## The Way Forward

A biblical ecclesiology is essential for effective ministry in the new marriage culture. In this brief chapter we can only focus on a few aspects of that doctrine. First, the terms of the discussion must be given theological definition. Second, a summary of basic ecclesiology will be constructed to explain the Protestant way of being Christian together. Third, three historic church practices will be described that churches have used to navigate disciple-making in new cultural contexts through the centuries. Finally, use of the church ordinances (baptism and the Lord's Supper) as a safety net for discipling and sustaining Christians emerging from the new marriage culture will be considered.

## Defining Terms

The "new marriage culture" means we are "not in Kansas anymore." There is a new "normal," and the rules have changed. While many of us came to faith in a time when Christianity held a privileged place in the public sector, this is no longer the case. If America has not fully moved to a culture of unbelief, it certainly has moved to a culture where evangelicals are suspect and open to often unexamined and uncivil prejudice. International missionaries have faced this kind of cultural distance and disrepute from the beginning. For centuries people in West Africa have come to faith and to the church with plural marriages. As African church leaders and international missionaries examined the Scriptures together in that polygamous marriage culture, at least in some instances, decisions were made to receive persons in plural marriages into the church upon their profession of faith and believer's baptism. There was also the understanding that until (through discipleship) the plural marriage had been scripturally and responsibly resolved, that member could not assume a leadership role in the church.[2]

American churches now face receiving men and women touched by the gospel who have lived with same-sex attraction, entered into marriage, adopted children, and/or have undergone gender reassignment surgery. If a eunuch could be considered a recipient of voluntary or involuntary gender-reassignment surgery, then the church has been facing similar issues about its membership since the first century with Philip and the Ethiopian official. Philip baptized this man in the spirit of Isaiah's prophecy that when the Messianic community arises then even faithful eunuchs will be welcomed by Yahweh into His temple (Acts 8:26–40; Isa. 56:4–7).

In the Roman *pater familias* culture, newborns unacceptable to the head of the household were routinely tossed into a nearby river. The early church responded by wading into rivers to rescue and raise these abandoned infants. Outspoken critics of Christianity grudgingly admired this display of concern and care.[3] How can we minister today in the new marriage culture so critics disputing the scriptural truths for which we stand might grudgingly acknowledge our gracious care for their outcasts? Churches need fair warning and adequate preparation to respond graciously when gospel power brings a new generation of broken people to the church out of the tragedies generated by this cultural quake.

In a nearby private school, which celebrates "diversity," the staff was alerted that the father of two students had announced he is now a woman. He wants to be addressed as "Miriam" and participates in school events dressed as a woman.[4] The homosexuality and transgender advocates in the school saw this event as the perfect opportunity to affirm diversity. Despite an early attempt to maintain the marriage, "Miriam" and his/her spouse are now involved in an acrimonious divorce proceeding, and their young son has fallen into significant emotional illness. This collateral damage goes unaddressed by school leaders lest it diminish the celebration of the husband/father's choice. Could your church be the healing place for that little boy, his sister, and their mother? For this to occur in many churches, the ministerial implications and applications of our ecclesiology need retooling.

*Ecclesiology* is the biblical doctrine of the church. Congregations are healthy in proportion to their being and doing what Scripture lays out for the church to be and do. This chapter is written from the viewpoint of believers' church congregationalism. This refers to a regenerate church whose membership is persons who have experienced and expressed repentance from sin, placed faith in Jesus as Lord and Savior, and have united with the congregation by profession of that commitment through believer's baptism.[5]

*Robust* ecclesiology refers to a congregation's capacity to retain and accelerate its unity, purity, faithfulness, and fruitfulness for gospel impact despite the changing marriage culture. A robust doctrine of the church mobilizes a congregation to contend for the faith, engage in community ministry, and offer the transforming message of the gospel. People come to church for four reasons: worship, because all week long they are downward-looking in their labor; fellowship, because they dwell in a hostile environment; forgiveness, because of missing the mark of holy choices and actions; and inspiration, because they need a word of breath-giving encouragement to go back to the daunting daily responsibilities. A robust ecclesiology delivers on these key points (Matt. 21:12–13; Mark 11:15–17; Luke 19:45–46).

*Membership* acknowledges the need to belong is universal and timeless. God declared it is not good for man to be alone, and it never will be (Gen. 2). People need the Lord, and people need one another to be wholly human. Church membership has multiple connotations: institutional, organic, and spiritual. Today the institutional sense of church membership is considered an unnecessary vestige of denominationalism in a postdenominational age. Postmodern evangelicals eschew the concept of membership as dividing attendees into insiders and outsiders because it is politically uncomfortable to be called an outsider.[6] For them, if membership is merely a matter of organizational affiliation and institutional satisfaction, then membership has lost its spiritual and organic meaning. Unless churches intend to operate without legal status and religious exemption as a nonprofit corporation, then these congregations must decide what constitutes a "voting member" in their articles of incorporation. Further, and more important for our purposes, lax membership standards can contribute to confused decision-making about responding to same-sex marriage issues. Membership, the capacity to identify who does and who does not have the privilege of identifying with a local congregation, does have a viable institutional meaning. That meaning, however, must be informed by the spiritual-organic meaning established by thoroughgoing discipleship.

The New Testament is not averse to the word *member* or the concept of church membership. Believers are members of the body of Christ (Rom. 12:5; 1 Cor. 12:12). Disciples are identified as branches grafted into the True Vine, Jesus (John 15:5). Meaningful membership involves accountability, intimacy, and engagement in ministry in the church community (Eph. 4:16). Believer's baptism is the public recognition of a person into membership (Matt. 28:19–20; 1 Pet. 3:21) because the person has been grafted into the body of Christ by the work of the Spirit (1 Cor. 6:19–20). The Lord's Supper is the regular spiritual checkup to see how faithful and fruitful that connection is (1 Cor. 11:28).

## Ecclesiology 101: Jesus Is the Church Builder

A brief but cogent ecclesiology of a believer's church can be hammered out from Matthew 16:15–23. (Eph. 4:1–32; 1 Cor. 11:17–34 and 12:1–31; and 1 Pet. 2:4–10 are other pillar passages for constructing a biblical doctrine of the church.)

With reference to *church membership*, we are *confessional conversionists.* Jesus required Peter and the disciples to confess personally who He was. Peter professes in Matthew 16:16, "You are the Messiah, the Son of the living God!" Jesus blessed Peter's confession (v. 17) and then critiqued Peter's subsequent pronouncement (v. 22), saying, "Get behind Me, Satan!" (v. 23). Peter earned this critique because he rebuked Jesus for teaching on the necessity of His sacrificial death on the cross. Confession of Christ without the cross is inadequate. "The Son of Man came to seek and to save what was lost" and "to give his life as a ransom for many" (Luke 19:10; Mark 10:45 NIV).

With reference to *theology proper*, we are *supernaturalists* and *revelationists.* In Matthew 16:17 NIV, Jesus declares, "Blessed are you, Simon son of Jonah, for this was not revealed to you by man, but by my Father in heaven." The church is constituted as it affirms there is one true triune God, who speaks and inspires human instruments to inscribe His will and ways into authoritative Scripture. E. Y. Mullins asserted that Jesus Christ has a right to be the boss in the church, and we know what the boss wants through His Word.[7]

With reference to *church polity* or *governance,* Jesus says in Matthew 16:18, "I will build My church." The church belongs to Jesus. The church is built by Jesus under His lordship and by the Spirit illumi-nating the Word of God. The church is built through the balance of gifted members ministering both to believers and unbelievers under the equipping leadership of pastors. Cleansing and commissioning always go together in Scripture. A robust ecclesiology, which insists, "For by grace you have been saved" (Eph. 2:8 NASB), is never separated from, "For we are . . . created in Christ Jesus for [not because of] good works" (Eph. 2:10 NASB). As members are recognized, equipped, and led into ministry (particularly directed toward unbelievers), mercy will be given to doubters, and those aflame with destructive habits and attitudes will be snatched to safety (Jude 22–23).

The *security of the church* is addressed in the famous passage about the forces of Hades not prevailing against the church (Matt. 16:18). This promise might look like an overpromise. From one perspective the world, the flesh, and the devil often infect churches with dis-ease and decline. From a broader viewpoint, however, we know the church has overcome countless attacks, trials, and persecutions over the centuries. The practice of securing believers, and thus the health of churches, is outlined in Matthew 18:15–20: "If your brother sins against you, go and rebuke him in private." To the measure church members discipline one another personally and corporately, to that extent nothing is able to separate them from the love of God in Christ. The gates of Hades cannot prevail as believers stand together.

*Ministry and mission* in the church are identified in Matthew 16:19, arguably the most terrific and terrifying verse in the Bible: "I will give you the keys of the kingdom of heaven, and whatever you bind on earth is already bound in heaven, and whatever you loose on earth is already loosed in heaven." This text is often avoided for two reasons. First, Roman Catholics use it to make Peter the first recipient of the keys of salvation, enabling him only to pass them to succeeding popes. Second, this verse offers more ministry authority than believers are used to exercising.

Yet two chapters later (Matt. 18:18), these keys are again men-tioned, but this time Jesus gives them to all twelve disciples. After His resurrection Jesus reiterates His entrusting of ministry authority to His disciples with these words, "If you forgive the sins of any, they are forgiven them; if you retain the sins of any, they are retained" (John 20:23). What, then, are these keys? The authority of God's Word vested in the canonical Scriptures and employed by Christ's disciples. In Luke 11:52 Jesus indicts the scribes and rabbis for their failure to be effective keepers of the keys of the kingdom through their knowledge and interpretation of the Scriptures. In Matthew 23 Jesus announced multiple woes against these key-carrying Pharisees and scribes. He discredits them for misuse of the keys and turns over that authority to His disciples.

Jesus often invited questions during His earthly ministry. The nature of those questions could be organized in two stacks. One stack would be about how to enter the kingdom of God, like when Nicodemus asked, "How can anyone be born when he is old?" (John 3:4). The second stack could be labeled "ethical questions related to living nobly within the kingdom of God." These questions were either evangelistic (about entering the kingdom) or ethical (about living rightly for the King). The mission of the church is, therefore, to exercise spiritual authority to share Scripture and gospel so men and women will know how to enter the kingdom of God and live holy lives as its citizens. This is the mission and ministry of the church, no matter cultural and contextual shifts. Churches have used those keys effectively over the centuries through three core congregational practices.

## Three Historic Church Practices

### 1. Make Confessions

Protestants in general and Baptists in particular were charged as nonconformists during the English Reformation. Henry VIII had no intention of being anything other than Catholic. He just wanted to be English Catholic and not Roman Catholic. Because of the prevailing church-state paradigm, Henry and the Anglican archbishop perceived the emerging expressions of Protestants, Quakers, and Separatists as lawless nonconformists subject to arrest, exile, or death. In response

Baptists sought to establish their orthodoxy within the context of Scripture.

In 1644, and then again in 1689, Baptists in London published confessions of faith addressed both to the king and to ecclesiastical authorities. These confessions were intended to show the continuity and discontinuity in Baptist beliefs with reference to the state-church creed and that those differences did not constitute disloyalty or danger to crown or country. Confessions of faith as statements of core beliefs became a key feature for both discipleship of those coming into the nonconforming churches and a key witness to the wider community.

Today doctrine is often perceived as dry and distant from Christian living. But Scripture asserts sound doctrine is essential to sound living. Theologically God makes and keeps covenant and calls us into the same. Confessional living is at the core of Scripture—from the Mosaic covenant to Christ in the new covenant. Historically confessions have provided the content to form the structure for Christian identity and character. A primary ministry strategy in the new marriage culture context must be inviting persons interested in the gospel and church membership into a discipleship discovery course that uses a church's confession of core beliefs as its curriculum. Sound doctrine is the beginning point for practical discussions about sound living. *The Baptist Faith and Message* 2000 speaks specifically into our new marriage culture:

> God has ordained the family as the foundational institution of human society. It is composed of persons related to one another by marriage, blood, or adoption. Marriage is the uniting of one man and one woman in covenant commitment for a lifetime. It is God's unique gift to reveal the union between Christ and His church and to provide for the man and the woman in marriage the framework for intimate companionship, the channel of sexual expression according to biblical standards, and the means for procreation of the human race.[8]

Missiologists and anthropologists advise the further a culture is from biblical standards, the more discipleship is necessary for persons to incarnate biblical truth. The new marriage culture shows America has taken serious steps away from biblical norms addressing marriage and family. A robust ecclesiology will refocus a church on its confession of faith and make it a required text for all members to revisit in constructive ways—through worship, preaching, and teaching.

## 2. Keep Covenants

If a confession of faith defines what a congregation believes, then a church covenant defines how the congregation intends to live together.[9] A church covenant outlines the core values and ethical framework of church fellowship. It formalizes our commitment to live a covenant of accountability together. When churches have defined their core values and practices in a church covenant and regularly revisit that covenant at the celebration of the Lord's Supper, then congregational angst gives way to esteem, and there is increased capacity for spiritual discipline.

Candidates for baptism deserve to know what the church expects of them as disciples and what they can expect from the church. These expectations are communicated in the church covenant. The covenant commits a congregation to live under the instruction of the Lord as agreed upon by the church and mandated in Scripture. Those regenerated by the Holy Spirit will give evidence of a desire to work out their salvation with fear and trembling (Phil. 2:12). If a church uses its covenant and confession as curriculum in a graciously taught orientation course, it will become clear to those in a same-sex marriage or other immoral life pattern that to obey Scripture, they will have to amend their lifestyle.

With reference to the issue of homosexuality, distinction between desire and behavior is critical. According to one study, same-sex attraction is possibly amendable so a believer is able to enter into a long-term heterosexual relationship in marriage only about 25 percent of the time.[10] About 10 percent of the time, homosexual believers seem unable to experience any change in same-sex attraction or even in behavior and can end up either denying the gospel or claiming that same-sex lifestyle is an acceptable Christian lifestyle. The majority of believers coming out of a same-sex lifestyle practice a commitment to be celibate, whether same-sex attraction remains or diminishes.

Exodus International was founded by four gay Christian men with a vision that homosexuals can change and "pray the gay away."[11] First Corinthians 6:9–11 was part of the biblical basis for this vision:

> No sexually immoral people, idolaters, adulterers, or anyone practicing homosexuality, no thieves, greedy people, drunkards . . . will inherit God's kingdom. And some of you used to be like this. But you were washed, you were sanctified, you were justified in the name of the Lord Jesus Christ and by the Spirit of our God.

Their interpretation of this passage assumed salvation meant not only forgiveness of past sins but cessation of continued immoral behavior *and* repair and change from same-sex attraction to heterosexual attraction. This overpromise and unrealistic expectation birthed "reparative therapy," which at times used psychological manipulation to force participants toward an artificial heterosexuality. The result was "shame, sexual misconduct and depression" as fragile new believers desperately thought their pledge to live with a good conscience meant not only cessation of homosexual actions but also attractions.[12] This situation substituted quick outward conformity for slow inward healing and transformation. These struggling believers saw only two choices: either conform to righteous action and feigned heterosexual attraction or retreat back into the same-sex lifestyle. Churches that have been most helpful, according to former lesbian and gay Christians, are those that welcomed them, shared the gospel with them, received their confession of faith by baptism as a "work in progress and not a finished work," patiently discipled them in the Word, and then let the Word do the work of transformation[13] (2 Cor. 4:1–2).

Ministry in the new marriage culture means churches must step up their discipleship practices to offer both entry-level and advanced support groups for those seeking to live the gospel in the context of a church community (Eph. 4:15). Within the first group (perhaps leading to church membership and service), participants must be challenged to affirm the church's confession of faith and endorse the church's covenant. In light of the changing marriage culture, churches may want to amend their present covenants to include an additional paragraph like the following:

> Believing we are created in the image of God and are persons for whom Christ died, and believing the gospel of Jesus Christ has grace and power to save any who repent and trust in Him, and believing it is the work of the Holy Spirit to grant us new life and to sanctify our lives as believers together for the glory of God; therefore, we pledge to live for Christ with a good conscience by trusting in the saving work of the cross, in the forgiveness of confessed sin, and in mutual accountability with one another by confession and confrontation to nurture our walk with Christ.

After careful analysis of the relationship between the Second Great Awakening and practices of church discipline among Baptist churches in the nineteenth-century American South, Gregory Wills contended that the Awakening's local impact was in proportion to the capacity of churches in that region to sustain discipline.[14] Congregational terms of endearment and engagement are found in the published church confessions and covenants of that era. When a church covenant clearly states what is expected of members and what they can expect of the church, it forms both an instructive and evaluative tool for congregational health. Engaging in meaningful conversation around a church's covenant and confession is the essence of the third practice of a robust ecclesiology, catechism.

## 3. Practice Catechism

The Greek word for instruction is *catechism,* a word some Baptists regard as a "high-church practice." The need for more intentional teaching, training, discipling—for catechism—is significant in modern churches facing the new marriage culture. Spiritual movements usually start with great preaching and vision-casting, but they are sustained by thorough catechism. Young and new believers need instruction to learn how to live out their faith.

Martin Luther authored his *Small Catechism* as a user-friendly guide for new converts to the Protestant movement. Benjamin Keach wrote a famous Baptist catechism to strengthen the growing but persecuted Baptist movement in seventeenth-century England.[15] Catechisms exist today but sometimes not by that name. Ralph Neighbor published the much-appreciated *Survival Kit for New Christians* in 1991, Henry Blackaby wrote *Experiencing God: Knowing and Doing the Will of God* in 1990, and Avery Willis produced the *MasterLife* discipleship series in the late 1980s. Established curriculums like these allow consistency and sustainability in congregational catechism for maturing new believers into effective church members.

Core Christian competencies—such as how to understand and interpret Scripture, how to praise and pray effectively, how to engage in a ministry that expresses joy and effectiveness, overcoming temptation, and how to share your faith and invite others into the kingdom—ought to be learned in the first year or two of coming to faith. Sometime early in their catechism, in the safety of a caring discipleship group, people emerging from same-sex lifestyles begin to experience the sanctifying work of the Spirit. This work renews their conscience and moves them toward ministry. While same-sex attraction may or may not diminish, the practice of homosexual action loses habituation and power.

## Baptism and the Lord's Supper

Scripture teaches the church has two ordinances, baptism and the Lord's Supper. Believer's baptism is the public expression of the inward reality of new life in Christ. Water baptism in the name of the Father, Son, and Holy Spirit does not regenerate. Rather, because one has already experienced the new life that forgiveness brings, baptism is the formal public uniting with a church in a pledge to maintain a clear conscience as one walks with Christ and other believers (Rom.

6:3–7; 1 Pet. 3:16, 21). The rite of baptism, practiced correctly, is the voluntary witness of a candidate to Christ and to the congregation of his/her commitment to follow Christ. Baptism is also the witness of the congregation that the candidate's testimony is affirmed and he/she is received into the community of those who are committed. Baptism publicly expresses a voluntary commitment to live the core beliefs and practices of the church, its confession and covenant.

Now comes the touchy part in relating to persons in same-sex marriages. Who is a proper candidate for baptism? Should we baptize only people who are "finished works," or should we baptize people who are "works in progress"? The baptismal pledge of a clear conscience suggests candidates be asked if, in obedience to Christ as Lord, they have made a break with known sin and are willing to avoid any future sin the Holy Spirit makes known to them through the Word of God. Can a person who self-identifies as having a same-sex orientation experience saving grace without having experienced a change in that orientation? Should a continued struggle with orienta-tion (temptation or desire) be equated with outward actions?

Baptismal commitment has never been a promise of perfection and never been an ordinance of a finished work. Willingness to refrain from future sex outside of heterosexual marriage has been a fair test for baptismal candidacy. When Christianity experienced a privileged place in the previous marriage culture, it was assumed that baptismal candidates would live a more moral life in line with the culture at the time of their baptism. Now that the culture is changing, baptism is the drama of seeing persons "snatched from the troubles and grip" of a fallen lifestyle into the "ark of salvation" by faith in Christ (see Jude 23; 1 Pet. 3:20–21). Even with this change, however, prebaptism perfection cannot be mandated. If we required perfection of sinners still tempted by alcohol, pornography, bitterness, and all forms of fornication, then who could be baptized? My experience has been that divorced persons and children of divorce (the collaterally damaged by the most common shortcoming of God's standard of marriage) are deeply appreciative of the affirmation and reception baptism represents as a full welcome into the household of God.

Persons impacted by same-sex relationships need that same sense of belonging to their new family.

The Lord's Supper is the regular opportunity of baptized disciples to examine their conscience in regard to the faith. A robust ecclesiology in the new marriage culture requires the church step up its discipleship practices. Churches must take seriously the baptizing of new believers by receiving them as new Christians in significant need of nurture and maturation. Churches that develop a sustained and vital program of discipleship (catechism) will be more than able to thrive in this challenging environment. We are in a rigorous spiritual battle for souls. There will be casualties. People will fail, quit, and repent, return, and reengage. The Lord's Supper can be the refueling table for this marathon.

John Wesley found that "penitent's classes" were needed for those who had fallen back into old habits of sin but wanted help to climb back out of the gutter.[16] Today's church must similarly commit to the work described in Jude 23, "save others by snatching them from the fire; have mercy on others but with fear, hating even the garment defiled by the flesh."

A good conscience is formed by instruction in Scripture. Believers are to be committed to growing in such instruction. When believers recognize truth, they must walk in it no matter the trouble that comes. All believers need companionship as they work out their salvation with fear and trembling. Godly affection means a congregation is committed to walking with, caring for, and rendering encouraging accountability to each and every member in his/her struggle to leave the old life behind and pursue the new life in Christ. Toward this end the Lord's Supper is a celebration of fellowship leading to healthy Christian living.

## May Grace Abound

Some of my friends who have left a same-sex lifestyle have been able to experience sexual attraction reorientation; however, most have not but have chosen instead to live a celibate life.[17] Accepting this reality is challenging for many churches, but it is the reality they must live with while rescuing people in the new marriage culture.

But what about people who have gone much farther than orientation and activity? What about receiving into church membership a person who has undergone gender reassignment surgery? This is a person who has undergone extensive surgical and hormonal procedures necessary to pursue life in a reassigned gender role. What does the Holy Spirit require if such a person comes to faith in Christ? What must the church require prior to welcoming him/her into fellowship?

In New Testament churches people were allowed to remain in the state in which they embraced Christ, namely allowing a single to stay single or the married to stay married (even if the spouse was an unbeliever, 1 Cor. 7:17). This principle should be applied to those who have had gender-reassignment surgery. If they acknowledge their choice as a sinful mistake, they can be received into membership in that state of existence. Whether they can reverse the procedure or not is a difficult decision requiring wise medical and spiritual counsel.

What about a person who becomes a believer but who had entered into a same-sex marriage prior to conversion? Paul wrote when one person in marriage becomes a believer and the other does not, the believer may allow the unbeliever to depart uncontested (1 Cor. 7:11–16). If the unbelieving spouse (even a same–sex spouse) wants to stay in the relationship, it seems the believer must be discipled toward church membership while the illicit relationship is reconfigured into a biblically affirmable relationship. A believer may need to redefine a same-sex marriage for purposes of property and parenting into a biblically acceptable platonic relationship. My pastoral hunch is while this approach is defensible biblically, practically such celibate relationships are not likely sustainable.

Ray Stedman, pastor of Peninsula Bible Church near Stanford University for forty years, wrote of a Sunday night worship experience in which he read 1 Corinthians 6:9–11 to the congregation:

No sexually immoral people, idolaters, adulterers, or anyone practicing homosexuality, no thieves, greedy people, drunkards . . . will inherit God's kingdom. And some of you used to be like this. But you were washed, you were sanctified, you were justified in the name of the Lord Jesus Christ and by the Spirit of our God.

He then asked people to stand if they personally identified with one of the people mentioned in the passage. No one stood up. After a while, the most saintly elderly woman in the congregation stood. This was followed by a newly baptized hippie. Soon everyone was standing. In that list of Corinthian church members who had been justified and sanctified, Paul listed homosexuals. This means persons who had come out of the Greco-Roman culture affirming homosexual activity and relationships and into the redeemed culture of Christ were recipients of both baptism and the Lord's Supper. Does it mean they were participants even though they continued to practice that lifestyle? Certainly not! Does it mean that the washing work of the Spirit and the Word changed their practice and what we call their orientation or attraction? A change in practice? Yes. A change in attraction? Maybe. Nevertheless, the redeemed from all sinful backgrounds were and can be sanctified by Jesus and included in His church.

Today a testimony of God's grace might sound something like this: "Hello folks, I was born Robin Smith, weight 6.8 pounds, 32 inches. When I was born again, my name was still Robin, but I was no longer legally or physically female. I had pursued and experienced gender reassignment surgery and for five years had been living as a man. I had even entered into marriage with a female with her full knowledge of my story. Now something has happened to me. I have discovered there is a true God to whom I am accountable as my Creator and now as my Redeemer. I found out that there is full forgiveness in the family of God. Look at me! I'm a born-again person, physically a male, chromosomally a female, married with two adopted children who call me 'Daddy.' I know I am a product of a sin-crazed world, but I am what I am now by the grace of God and want to find the way forward for God's glory with your love and help."

Let's get first things first, namely getting people gloriously saved! Then secondary issues can be resolved over time through discipleship aligning all else with the new life found in Jesus. If we put second things first, we will never get unbelievers to the first thing— salvation. A robust ecclesiology seeks first to bring people into the kingdom of God and then trusting the King to build His church by shaping, changing, and healing His followers in every way.

# CHAPTER 6

# A POSITIVE SEXUAL ETHIC FOR THE NEW MARRIAGE CULTURE

*Adam Groza*

All religions address two fundamental questions: What is wrong with the world, and what can be done to fix it? The first of these questions often arises empirically. It is evident to any rational person something is wrong with the world. For example, children go hungry, women are abused, and men murder. Evil abounds. Therefore, it is an incontrovertible, observable reality: we live in a broken world.

Brokenness is not merely a fact about the external world. Brokenness is both an external and internal problem. G. K. Chesterton was once asked to write an essay answering the question, "What is wrong with the world?" He replied:

Dear Sirs,

I am.

Yours truly,

G. K. Chesterton

Chesterton's admission stuns the proud ears of modern man. External brokenness stems from internal brokenness. It is easy to decry unjust wars among nations but difficult to admit our inner turmoil of guilt and shame.

## Brokenness Is Personal

The seventeenth-century Christian philosopher Blaise Pascal wrote about human brokenness in *Pensées*. Pascal observed man is both great and wretched. His greatness is evident in art, science, and other human advancements. His wretchedness, however, is also evident in war, injustice, and other ills. Pascal used this observation to contend Christianity alone can adequately explain both the greatness and wretchedness of man. Our greatness comes from being made in God's image, and our wretchedness from our fall into sinful rebellion against God. Pascal knew on a personal level both the glory of significant achievement and the shame of sin.

We live in a broken world, and we are broken. The Bible describes how this began when Adam and Eve's sin plunged humanity and all of creation into death (Gen. 3). Adam, Eve, the serpent, and the ground were all cursed. Sin turns humans into prideful cowards. Adam blamed Eve, and Eve blamed Satan. Sin brings immediate and lasting brokenness to all aspects of life and to all relationships.

In a scene part comedy and part tragedy, Adam and Eve hid from God, who is ever-present and all-knowing. Rather than run to God for a cure, they flee God as if He were the curse. Rather than faithfully bearing God's image, Adam and Eve joined a rebellion against God. Paul later wrote that every human has joined the rebellion (Rom. 3:23), and none can save themselves (Eph. 2:1). Everything and everyone is broken.

### Responding to Sexual Brokenness

Jesus had compassion on broken people, even as He proclaimed the kingdom (Matt. 9:35–38). Christian ethics must therefore be both biblical and compassionate. This can be challenging when sexual sins, such as homosexuality, are flaunted and celebrated in popular culture. Christians can be tempted to justify sinful anger or prideful condemnation instead of drawing on the experience of God's grace and the reality of God's power to have compassion.

Homosexuality, like all sin, is evidence of brokenness. We are all tempted to look down on others we perceive to be more sinful than ourselves. This is a form of self-idolatry and self-exaltation reminiscent of the Pharisee and tax collector (Luke 18:9). To single out a particular sin (such as homosexuality) for selective condemnation is to preach a false gospel. The true gospel declares that Jesus Christ alone is righteous. The false gospel, proclaimed when heterosexuals look down on homosexuals, declares residual faith in self, as if to say, "At least we're not like them." Jesus abhors and condemns this kind of self-righteousness. Christians cannot look down on homosexuals, nor can we look the other way and ignore or approve of homosexuality and same-sex marriage. All humans are broken and in need of a Savior, including each one of us.

## Evolution, Gender, and Sexuality

A positive sexual ethic offering hope for homosexuals starts with the biblical account of creation. When God made humans, He first made a man. From man God made a woman. God put man and woman together for their good and for His glory. Genesis 1:26–31 and 2:18–25 tell a unified story of God's creation of Adam and Eve and explain why God created them "male and female." Sexuality and gender are created by God for a purpose, and they are good.

A different story of sexuality and gender is increasingly dominant in Western society. The Darwinian evolutionary model affirms natural selection and random genetic mutation to explain the diversity, advancement, and complexity of nature. These mechanisms are also claimed to account for the development of gender and sexuality.

But when, where, and how do these developments occur? Evolutionary biology offers many theories but no verifiable evidence. In fact, the question of gender is puzzling for naturalists. Graham Bell concludes:

Sex is the queen of problems in evolutionary biology. Perhaps no other natural phenomenon has aroused so much interest; certainly none has sowed as much confusion. The insights of Darwin and Mendel, which have illuminated so many mysteries, have so far failed to shed more than a dim and wavering light on the central mystery of sexuality, emphasizing its obscurity by its very isolation.[1]

In 2001, Mark Ridley addressed the same subject. Ridley is a zoologist who studied at Cambridge and Oxford and completed his doctoral research under atheist Richard Dawkins. On the subject of sex, he writes: "Evolutionary biologists are much teased for their obsession with why sex exists. People like to ask, in an amused way, 'isn't it obvious?' Joking apart, it is far from obvious. . . . Sex is a puzzle that has not yet been solved; no one knows why it exists."[2]

Ridley is certainly correct: sexuality is a puzzle for those who accept evolutionary presuppositions. As he says, it is "far from obvious" why humans are engendered, sexual beings. This confusion over gender and sexuality is at the heart of the debate over homosexuality.

The theory of evolution assumes the emergence of complexity as the result of time, changes in the environment, reproduction, and mutations. Biological systems develop, some of which are more complex and others quite simple. There are distinct advantages to simple forms of life, especially those that can self-replicate. Amoebas, for instance, reproduce by a process called binary fission. In this process cell chromosomes replicate, and the cell elongates and breaks off to form a new, identical cell.

The amoeba does not search for a mate or compete for the right to reproduce. Clearly gender complicates the process of reproduction. What is not clear in the evolutionary model is why gender is good. It would seem the simpler path of self-reproduction would be enviable, especially if the driving concern of evolution is the development of reproductive success by which mutations are passed along.

If all life has evolved by natural selection and random genetic mutation, then maleness and femaleness are also random. In the evolutionary model gender and sexuality have instrumental value but not intrinsic value. Something is said to have instrumental value (or worth) based on its ability to produce something else of value. Something is said to have intrinsic value if it is good in itself, apart from what it can produce.

If Darwinism is true, then gender and sexuality have instrumental value but no intrinsic value. Gender and sexuality, then, are only means to an end. Their value, role, function, and purpose change or evaporate, detached from whatever purpose or good they serve in society at any given time. A society that believes itself to be over-populated will tend to devalue marital sex and with it marriage itself. If gender and sexuality are only about children, then once a society has enough children, it will conclude it no longer needs marriage.

The evolutionary perspective on gender and sexuality is nihil-istic in the sense gender and sexuality have no inherent meaning. The meaninglessness of gender and sexuality stems from the way in which they are presumed to have developed—without purpose, design, or intent. Any meaning a Darwinist may ascribe to gender and sexuality is arbitrary.

Those who value gender and sexuality are deeply troubled by the evolutionary explanation of them. Evolution, as a theory, renders the human experience of gender and sexuality an exercise in self-delusion. People are only fooling themselves when they think there is value to being engendered and sexual apart from the utilitarian act of reproduc-tion. Since homosexual sex cannot result in progeny, it would be con-sistent for Darwinists to be either indifferent or opposed to the value of homosexuality since it does nothing to propagate the species.

The evolutionary account of sexuality is not only nihilistic because it takes away any objective meaning to gender and sex, but it is also fatalistic. The fatalism of homosexuality is reflected in the lyrics of a popular song: "And I can't change, even if I tried, even if I wanted to."[3] In one sense this is true. It is not within the power of humans to change their core identity. But thankfully, in another sense, a person can be changed through faith in Jesus Christ who alone is able both to save and to sanctify.

## The Bible, Gender, and Sexuality

In contrast to the evolutionary theory of sexuality and gender is the story set forth in the Bible. In it gender and sexuality have intrinsic value. This means there is objective value in being a man or a woman. Gender is valuable because it is part of humanity's being made in the image of God. Men and women are equal, but different, image bearers. In this way humanity reflects the triune nature of God, being equal in essence but diverse in function.

Gender is also intrinsically valuable because it reminds us God is merciful and understands our weakness. When God looked on Adam alone in the garden, He had mercy on him and made Eve. The presence of gender diversity is more than a means to an end. The presence of gender diversity reminds us that God graciously designed and created gender as an expression of mutual dependence.

Gender reflects the mystery of God. Men and women are, in some ways, much alike. Yet there is still a profound mystery to the genders. A man and woman can commit themselves to an exclusive, intimate, lifelong, covenantal marriage relationship, spend their entire lifetimes getting to know each other, and never fully exhaust each other's intricacies. As the singer Bono puts it, there is a "mysterious distance between a man and a woman."[4] The mystery of gender reminds us a person can be known and unknown simultaneously and without contradiction. Humans are made in the image of God and made to know God; yet God is also mysterious and impossible to know fully.

As with gender, sexuality originated with God. Human anatomy makes obvious man is made for woman and woman for man. Reason alone suggests heterosexual sex is natural and homosexual sex is not. The brokenness of sin makes us blind to both reason and revelation.

In contrast to the nihilism of evolution, the Bible is clear that sexuality and gender have intrinsic value. Sexual desire itself points to the greater reality man is not made for himself or woman for herself, but rather humans are made for God and for each other. Deep longing for "Other" is a constant reminder we do not exist for ourselves and cannot truly satisfy ourselves. This sentiment echoes the words of Saint Augustine, who wrote in *Confessions,* "Thou hast made us for Thyself, and our hearts are restless till they rest in Thee."[5]

## Homosexuality Is Idolatry

Sin ruins everything and turns the human heart into an idol factory. Worshipping anything or anyone other than God through Jesus Christ is idolatry. It is idolatrous to divorce gender and sex from the ultimate purpose of worship. In the first chapter of Romans, Paul described idolatry as exchanging the glory of God for anything else in creation. Human sexuality is created by God and intended for His glory. Therefore, sexual sin (like homosexuality) is a form of idolatry (Rom. 1:24–27). The Bible warns about the results of idolatry in Psalm 135:15–18: "The idols of the nations are of silver and gold, made by human hands. They have mouths but cannot speak, eyes, but cannot see. They have ears but cannot hear; indeed, there is no breath in their mouths. Those who make them are just like them, as are all who trust in them."

Idolatry brings death. It creates spiritual zombies who are physically alive but spiritually dead (Eph. 2:1). Greg Beale concludes we become what we worship.[6] Gender and sexuality are meant to reflect God's image. Apart from that worshipful purpose, they are idolatrous and bring death. Idolatry renders a person unable to respond to the gospel. An idolater has eyes that cannot see, ears that cannot hear, and is therefore unable to repent. There is only an appearance of life.

# The Promise of Wholeness

Christianity offers both a diagnosis and a cure for human brokenness. Since all sin is evidence of brokenness stemming from the fall and since homosexual behavior is sin, then homosexuality is evidence of brokenness. It is wrong to make too little of the brokenness evident in homosexuality. It is also wrong to make too much of that same brokenness.

When we make too little of homosexuality, we disregard God and His Word. When we make too much of homosexuality, we make a different mistake. We focus too much on sin, which is never to be our ultimate focus, but rather a reality that draws our attention to Christ. When we give too much of our time, thoughts, and attention to sin, we disregard Paul's admonition to focus on what is true, honorable, just, pure, lovely, commendable, and morally excellent (Phil. 4:8). Christians should not ignore sin (or any particular sin), but neither should they fixate on it. To wage war against sin and pursue the good life, Christians must be focused on the resurrected Savior. His glory and salvation are the message of wholeness to our broken world.

## Resurrection Hope

Jesus offers hope to homosexuals because when He rose from the dead He defeated sin and death for anyone willing to repent and believe. The hope of Christian ethics is not self-improvement or man-centered therapy. It is a resurrected Savior who brings inside-out change. Jesus' victory over death means no sin is able to hold a Christian captive (Rom. 6:18). Conversely, apart from the resurrection, humanity is enslaved to sin (John 8:34). The imagery of baptism testifies to the idea saving faith is embracing the death of Christ and joining Him in resurrection life through the Spirit.

Resurrection freedom is essential to understanding Christian ethics and the hope the Bible offers homosexuals. Apart from the power of the resurrection at work in believers through the Spirit, there is no hope for wholeness. God's transforming work is comprehensive, affecting thoughts, emotions, desires, and behavior. This inside-out transformation begins with a new heart and initiates sanctification.

The newness of resurrection life has everyday implications for living. Peter wrote: "Dear friends, I urge you as strangers and temporary residents to abstain from fleshly desires that wage war against you" (1 Pet. 2:11). Peter wrote specifically about sinful desires. The life of faith is a constant war against sinful impulses and passions. It is a process of dying to self and living according to the unseen realities of the kingdom and the resurrected King.

The comprehensiveness of resurrection freedom offers hope for transformation in the inner life. Thoughts and desires can be sinful in and of themselves. Jesus taught that a man's sexual desire for a woman other than his wife is adultery (Matt. 5:28). The desire itself is sinful. Paul told Christians to take "every thought captive to the obedience of Christ" (2 Cor. 10:5 NASB).

As any Christian can attest, sinful desires and thoughts do not stop at the moment of conversion. A heterosexual man does not immediately lose adulterous sexual desires when he is saved. But, through the sanctifying work of the Spirit, he is no longer captive to those thoughts and desires or the sinful actions they produce.

A person who becomes a Christian out of a homosexual past enters a new lifestyle of waging war against their particular "fleshly desires." There is an important distinction between fighting or waging war against sin and being captive to sin. A fighter identifies sin as sin while a captive refuses to admit his sin and will never confess, repent, and be forgiven. Denial is a hallmark of captivity to sin. If nothing is broken, then nothing needs to be fixed.

A believer fighting against sin is concerned for the glory of God in all aspects of life (1 Cor. 10:31). Living for the glory of God means living according to the light of Scripture. Therefore, the fight of faith involves knowing and applying God's Word to every sphere of life, including sexuality.

Persons still captive to their sin do not agree with God about what is morally acceptable, do not care about obeying God's Word, and refuse to be corrected by Scripture (2 Tim. 3:16). Sin induces a form of "Stockholm Syndrome" whereby a person in captivity to sin comes to believe he or she is free and develops a bond, identity, and affection for the sin holding him or her captive. Like the unbelieving Israelites who longed to return to the chains of Egyptian slavery, a captive to sin has not experienced the inward transformation of resurrection freedom.

### Salvation and Sanctification

The good news of the gospel is wholeness from sexual sin and is found in Jesus. Wholeness refers to the act of living, body and soul, in accord with God's will and character. For this reason wholeness is not only possible through a saving relationship with Jesus; it is *only* possible through a saving relationship with Jesus. Anyone seeking respite from the brokenness and alienation of sin must first come in faith to Jesus as Savior and Lord.

The moment a person comes to faith in Jesus, he or she is accepted as a child of God. Paul wrote, "Therefore, since we have been declared righteous by faith, we have peace with God through our Lord Jesus Christ" (Rom. 5:1). The sin that once defined us, like homosexuality, no longer applies. Not because all broken desires cease but because the reality of God's saving work is greater than both sinful desires and resulting actions.

Salvation is instantaneous and immediately conveys a glorious new identity: child of God (John 1:12–13). A child of God is set apart unto Christ at the moment of conversion: "By this will of God, we have been sanctified through the offering of the body of Jesus Christ once and for all" (Heb. 10:10). The sacrifice of Jesus is sufficient to confer a new identity on anyone who comes to saving faith and to initiate a lifelong process of change marked by repentance.

*Sanctification* refers to both a believer's secure position in Christ and the process by which he or she is conformed to the holiness of Jesus. For instance, Paul says to believers, "This is God's will, your sanctification: that you abstain from sexual immorality" (1 Thess. 4:3). This passage notes several things about the sanctification process. First, sanctification is God's will for believers. Second, sanctification involves human effort. Third, sanctification is holistic and therefore includes sexuality.

Sanctification includes saying no to behaviors that come naturally to the fallen nature. Martin Luther famously noted that Christians are simultaneously righteous and sinner. This state has a significant implication for Christian ethics: that which is good does not come "naturally"; that which comes "naturally" is not always good. The resulting question in regard to morality is not, What comes naturally? but rather, What is good? In the Bible what is good is that which conforms to the character of God.

Sexual immorality is an especially heinous and resilient foe in the fight for sanctification. Sanctification requires abstaining from sexual immorality, which refers to a range of moral impurity (1 Thess. 4:3). The Greek word *porneia* is the root for the English word *pornography*. Paul also uses *porneia* in Romans 1:29 amid a list of sins that stem from idolatry.

Both heterosexuals and homosexuals have strong desires for sexual immorality. Basically any sexual behavior outside the marriage covenant between a man and woman is immoral and involves giving oneself away inappropriately. Paul wrote it is God's will for believers to deny themselves (abstain) from that which comes naturally to the fallen nature (sexual immorality) and to pursue by faith the new nature in Christ (1 Thess. 4:3). Because sexuality and gender are essential to being human, and to be human is to bear the image of God, sexual sin is an affront to both God and oneself.

Wholeness requires a person be awakened from the nightmare of captivity to sexual sin. Paul wrote, "Do not let sin reign in your mortal body, so that you obey its desires" (Rom. 6:12). Peter echoed this idea in his calls to grow in respect to salvation (1 Pet. 2:2–3) and godliness (1 Pet. 1:5–7). Positively sanctification means growing in holiness. Negatively it means increasingly capturing sinful sexual thoughts and refusing to act on them (2 Cor. 10:5). Both the positive and the negative aspects of sanctification describe the slow road to sanctification for all believers, including former homosexuals.

It is possible for a person to be saved and instantaneously delivered from addictions or other long-standing sinful patterns. But even Christians who experience instantaneous deliverance from one sin still struggle with other sins. Jesus is perfect, and one day when we get to heaven, we will be perfected with Him (1 John 3:2). Until then the Bible warns against anyone who claims to have already been made perfect (1 John 1:8). God knows we will continue to sin and graciously invites us to confess it and experience forgiveness (1 John 1:9).

## The Path to Wholeness

The journey out of a homosexual past and into sexual wholeness is one of daily repentance. Repentance is an act of faith whereby a person believes the promises of God and turns from sin to follow God. Repentance replaces what is sinful, broken, and harmful with what is holy, life-giving, and eternally good.

The word *holy* is most often associated with God: God is holy, has always been holy, and will always be holy. His holiness is part of who He is, and He does not need anything outside of Himself to aid His holiness. God commands believers to "be holy, because I am holy" in both the Old and New Testaments (Lev. 11:44–45; 19:2; and 20:7 as well as 1 Pet. 1:16).

No one is saved by repentance, but it is the necessary expression of faith as the sole means by which one comes to the Savior. So much so, Peter's core gospel message is, "Repent and return" (Acts 3:19 NASB). Peter preached repentance because Jesus taught repentance (Mark 1:15). The call to follow Jesus is a call to repentance.

Some people wrongly assume preaching repentance is unloving. Nothing could be further from the truth! No one has ever been more loving than Jesus, and He preached repentance. Inviting someone to turn from harmful and deadly behavior to abundant life is an act of love, particularly when it is done reasonably and respectfully (1 Pet. 3:15–16). It would actually be supremely *unloving* to silently watch another human being, made in God's image, wallow enslaved in the filth of sin and, by a lack of repentance, store up wrath for the day of judgment (Rom. 2:5). Warning these persons is an act of love.

When a person self-identifies as a homosexual, he commonly says, "I'm gay." This kind of statement is telling about the nature of sin. Sin is not just something we do; it defines us. The person who steals is a thief. The person who lies is a liar. The person who embraces same-sex attraction is a homosexual. Apart from Christ, sin is not just what we do; it is who we are. We are sinners and are defined by our sin.

Repentance is, therefore, not behavior modification. Any approach to homosexuality that simply attempts to change behavior apart from the grace of God and centrality of the gospel is idolatry. Sinful man is unable to change his ways without repentance and faith in God. Jeremiah asked, "Can the Cushite change his skin, or the leopard his spots? If so, you might be able to do what is good, you who are instructed in evil" (Jer. 13:23). Apart from God's saving work and subsequent sanctification, a person cannot truly change.

## Sanctification Takes Time

The process of repentance and sanctification takes time. It is, in fact, a lifelong endeavor. Despite this reality of the Christian life being marked by lifelong penitence, it is an enduring myth that repentance is only what a person does at the point of conversion. This myth perpetuates frustration among Christians who continue to struggle with sinful desires. They wrongly conclude if they were truly saved they would not be struggling with sin.

The life of repentance and faith entails a daily struggle with sin. We are counseled, "If we confess our sins, He is faithful and righteousness to forgive us our sins and to cleanse us from all unrighteousness" (1 John 1:9–10). This passage is vital for a positive sexual ethic for several reasons.

First, an ongoing struggle with sexual desires may be an expected part of the Christian life. The instruction to confess sin assumes Christians will have ongoing sins to confess. Christians have no biblical reason to expect perfectionism, or the total absence of sin, during their lifetime. God knows we will continue to struggle with sin. He offers believers the opportunity to confess, repent, and be forgiven. A person who claims to have no sin is calling God a liar and shows evidence of unbelief (1 John 1:5–10).

Second, genuine believers should confess their ongoing struggle against sexual sin. This confession is first to God (1 John 1:9), but mutual confession in appropriate settings is also warranted (James 5:16). A confessant Christian agrees with God that sinful actions, desires, and habits are contrary to God's Word and character. Confession exposes what Satan has been using to haunt believers— their old identities and entrenched life patterns.

Third, human effort is part of the repentance process. While we are saved by grace, we are saved unto good works (Eph. 2:8–10). The grace of God instructs us to deny ungodliness and be zealous for good works (Titus 2:11–14). Both the concepts of denying sin and being zealous for good works speak to the human effort expected of repenting Christians. A homosexual who contemplates coming to Christ should count on a daily struggle against sexual temptation, requiring confession and much effort to overcome.

The fruit of this daily struggle and the corresponding effort of faith is the increasing experience of new life. In Ephesians 4:22–24, Paul illustrates repentance by using the metaphor of "putting on" and "taking off." A Christian will experience the ongoing discipline of exchanging old and sinful habits with godly and holy habits as a result of faith. Repentance does not happen without conscious and willful effort on the part of the believer.

Some people pray a prayer of faith in Jesus but never make an effort to part with their former life. They are either unwilling to leave old ways behind or lack discipleship to do so effectively. Jesus warns that on judgment day many people will claim they are saved when in fact they are not (Matt. 7:21–23). Unrepentance and self-deception are symptoms of unbelief.

## Sanctification in Community

Christians should not sugarcoat the difficulty of consistent repentance when witnessing to homosexuals. The LGBT (lesbian, gay, bisexual, transgender) community sees the struggle involved in "coming out" and coming to terms with one's sexuality as a badge of honor. This struggle has a community-building effect because nothing worthwhile is easy, and supporters sustain the effort. The gospel is free but not easy. Former homosexuals who have embraced Jesus often talk candidly about the hardships in leaving the gay community, the loss of friends, and their daily struggle with sin. The church should become their new community to sustain their positive choices.

Many professing Christians have never been taught repentance takes effort. This is a discipleship failure among churches. Consequently new Christians may wrongly think holiness will come automatically, and sinful desires will simply disappear upon conversion. When sinful desires persist, professing believers become discouraged and assume their experiment with Christianity has been a failure.

A life of repentance is lived most effectively in the context of a healthy local church. In this context a healthy local church is a collection of Christians in covenant agreement with one another to follow God's Word in a community of repentance. In a community like this, believers receive the care, accountability, and counsel to experience victory in their daily struggle against temptations (including sexual desires). A community of repentance like this should be a welcoming place to anyone who is honest about his or her struggle with sin, willing to confess his or her sin and expend energy in developing new and godly habits. A healthy church will have appropriate discipleship opportunities for new believers to receive practical instruction and wisdom from older Christians (Titus 2).

Discipleship is essential to move all believers from theory to practice. To live a godly life, we need both instruction and examples. True discipleship includes observing a life well lived, which can be imitated in practical ways. When Jesus called His disciples, He invited them to follow Him (which includes learning from Him and emulating His behavior). The call to follow Jesus is still a call to be a disciple on mission for Jesus. The goal of discipleship is a deeper faith in Jesus resulting in holy habits. Prior to forming a relationship to Jesus, every person is an amalgam of sinful habits.

The process of replacing old (sinful) habits with new (holy) habits is the work of repentance in the context of discipleship. Wisdom (application of Scripture to complex life experiences) is required to put new habits into practice. Growing in wisdom involves two steps: learning behavioral principles from Scripture and observing mature believers who are modeling application of those principles. Those coming out of homosexuality need more than a good sermon or book. They need life-on-life relationships with maturing believers to teach them how to win the battle against their former fleshly habits on a daily basis.

Aristotle taught virtues are formed in man by his doing actions related to those virtues.[7] Or, as Will Durant famously put it: "We are what we repeatedly do. Excellence, then, is not an act but a habit."[8] Too many Christians come to faith and then expect sanctification to happen *ex nihilo*. Sanctification is achieved through repentance, and this process takes work. Some Christians attend a conference or read a new book in hopes their life will be rid of unholy desires. This is a ludicrous pipe dream. A virtuous life is achieved over time by faithfully seeking Jesus Christ and turning from sin in the context of the local church. Anything claiming to shortchange that process is false advertisement. Being honest is essential when counseling repentant homosexuals about the difficulty of life change. They have been told lies about their sexuality all their lives. Do not compound the problem with lies about the spiritual struggle they will face as they choose a new lifestyle.

### Real Change

Permanently changing behavior is a long, hard process, but the payoff is greater than many can imagine. Paul outlines the process and payoff in Ephesians 4:28: "The thief must no longer steal. Instead, he must do honest work with his own hands, so that he has something to share with anyone in need." This passage raises a fascinating question: When is a thief no longer a thief? According to evolutionary theory of behavior, anything genetically determined is unchangeable. So, if a person could be proven to have a genetically induced propensity for stealing, then that person would always be a thief. He could not change even if he wanted to change.

The Bible offers hope and freedom for those who embrace Jesus by faith and commit to the hard work of repentance. A thief is no longer a thief when he puts repentance into practice. First, he agrees with God stealing is wrong and stops. This, however, is not enough. Repentance is not simply behavior modification because the goal is not to stop stealing. The goal is wholeness. The thief ceases to be a thief when he stops (takes off) the old way of life (stealing) and starts working to give to others in need (puts on generosity). Charity is the new way of life that replaces thievery. This is a picture of total transformation and freedom in Christ!

So, when is a homosexual no longer a homosexual? Sin no longer defines a person set free from captivity to sin who embraces a life of repentance. Sinful desires and thoughts linger but no longer enslave. The greater reality of a resurrected Lord controls a child of God who lives by faith and not by feelings.

The hope and assurance of resurrection freedom and the good life of faith is made possible by the power of the Holy Spirit. Those who deny the possibility for change do not believe in God and the reality of the empty grave. God is omnipotent, meaning He can do anything He pleases (Ps. 115:3). Any approach to sexual ethics that denies His transformative power fails to take God seriously. A God who creates out of nothing and who raises dead people to life is surely powerful enough to aid His repentant children in finding victory over any enslaving behavior.

## It Gets Better . . . in Christ

Over the past few years, many celebrities have made videos promoting homosexuality in which they declare, "It gets better." The goal of these videos is to deter young people struggling with their sexual identity from committing suicide. Christians agree with the goal of these videos but not the message. The truth is embracing sexual sin does not lead to a better life. In reality, life only gets worse the longer it is lived apart from Jesus Christ.

The gospel is good news. In Jesus Christ life really does get better. Sins are forgiven. Identities are changed. Healing takes place. Everything is being made new. The gospel's message to homosexuals is not, "Stop being gay." It is not "stop" but "come." Come to Jesus in repentance and faith. He alone can re-create broken people and bring wholeness. Jesus can do this for every person, including those captured by distorted visions of sexuality, gender, and marriage.

# MODELS AND METHODS FOR MINISTRY IN THE NEW MARRIAGE CULTURE

# CHAPTER 7

# Preaching on Marriage Today

## Tony Merida

Preaching on marriage today reminds me of the film *Gran Torino*, starring Clint Eastwood as Walt Kowalski. Walt is a grumpy old widower, a blue-collar American living in Detroit (and owner of a sweet 1972 Gran Torino). He's bothered that his neighborhood is deteriorating and social norms are not what they used to be. His family says he's stuck in the 1950s. Walt especially struggles to understand his next-door neighbors, the Hmongs, who live totally within their ethnic community. Walt does not understand them and has no interest in getting to know them. The Hmongs feel the same way about Walt. Mutual incomprehension and animosity mark their relationship.

What the two groups need is a communicator, a person who understands both parties and can mediate between them. They need a *bridge builder*. In the movie this is what the teenage Hmong girl, Sue, becomes. As a bicultural girl with streetwise skills, she's able to communicate effectively to both groups, and things change as a result of her efforts.

Preaching on marriage in the twenty-first century is an increasing challenge because a similar mutual incomprehension is taking place. The "old-fashioned Bible people" cannot understand why the newer generation has little regard for traditional marriage. Meanwhile, the newer generation is perplexed by the rigidity of their old-fashioned predecessors. What's needed today, perhaps more than ever in America, are effective, bridge-building, preacher-communicators.

## The Preacher as Bridge Builder

One of my top five books on preaching is John Stott's 1982 classic *Between Two Worlds*. Stott compares preaching to bridge building. On one side the preacher must understand the biblical world. On the other side he must also understand the contemporary world. The preacher's goal is connecting these worlds to each other in a meaningful way for the hearers.

In describing the biblical side of preaching, Stott underscores New Testament metaphors describing it. The preacher is a *herald*, a *sower*, an *ambassador*, a *shepherd*, and a *workman*—each term expressing the "givenness" of the message."[1] That is to say, faithful preachers do not invent the message; they simply deliver the message given to them.

But preachers cannot stop with simply exegeting the text. They have to exegete and apply the text *to people*. Stott says, "[We need to] relate the given message to the existential situation, or, to use modern jargon, to 'contextualize' the Word of God."[2] Stott points out contextualization skills are implied in the biblical metaphors for preaching listed above. He wrote, "The herald cannot be indifferent to those who listen to what he says, or the ambassador to the people with whom he pleads . . . a consciousness farmer is obviously concerned not only to sow the right seed but to sow it in the right soil."[3]

Commenting on Stott's bridge-building concept, Pastor Tim Keller wrote:

> Some sermons are like "a bridge to nowhere." They are grounded in solid study of the biblical text but never come down to earth on the other side. . . . Other sermons are like bridges *from nowhere.* They reflect contemporary issues, but the insights they bring to bear on modern problems and felt needs don't actually arise out of the biblical text. Proper contextualization is the act of bringing sound biblical doctrine all the way over the bridge by reexpressing it in terms coherent to a particular culture.[4]

Keller clearly articulates the defining challenge of the hard work of preaching. We need to understand the text, and we need to understand people to bridge the cultural gap between the biblical world and the contemporary world.

Today many have abandoned the Bible's teachings on the issue of marriage. They are preaching "bridges from nowhere" sermons. Some are aggressively defending and promoting same-sex unions. Some argue marital specifics are not clear in the Bible, so the topic should be avoided. Others hold to traditional marriage but avoid the subject because they do not want to risk offending and/or losing people. Biblical ignorance, an antiauthority spirit, and fear of man characterize these preachers.

Others, while holding to biblical standards, have little interest in understanding culture. As a result, they preach "bridges to nowhere" sermons. They get their information about marriage from the Bible, but they fail to show the relevance of it to those who disagree with them. They fail to teach about marriage in a way that is understandable, sensible, and placed within a comprehensive worldview. Such sermons are filled with assumptions, anecdotes, and insider statements. They stimulate the faithful but do not convince seekers or skeptics.

As preachers, we must be both biblical and contemporary. We must exegete Scripture and engage culture. We must improve our bridge-building skills in the pulpit.

## The Practice of Bridge Building

Here are some specific ways we can grow in the areas of biblical *faithfulness* (interpreting from the biblical worldview) and communication *effectiveness* (connecting with the today's cultural situation), making particular application to the subject of preaching on marriage today.

### The Biblical World: Preaching the Word Faithfully

*Study the Bible and the biblical story line.* Faithful preaching begins with saturating yourself with the Word of God. As a preacher, you must be intimately familiar with Holy Scripture through rigorous study. We are giving people the words of life! We must study the Bible because people desperately need to know the message of the Bible, and we must learn it before we can communicate it.

Part of thorough Bible study is studying *biblical theology* and developing the skill of integrating it into preaching. Biblical theology deals with overarching themes that progress through the biblical story line. Biblical theology benefits preaching in two key ways: helping every sermon reflect an understanding of the whole Bible and revealing some aspect of Jesus Christ through every part of the Bible.

Further, biblical theology shows issues like marriage do not simply appear randomly in Scripture. Rather, the Bible has a wonderful narrative of marriage woven throughout. The Bible begins and ends with a wedding! In between we discover references to the marriage of Yahweh and Israel and of Christ and the church. We also see numerous examples of marriage (positive and negative) and even an entire book devoted to marital romance, Song of Solomon. Focusing on just one verse, even combined with a lot of sweaty preaching, will not persuade skeptics. Showing how marriage is part of the grand narrative of Scripture (and thus important around the world) is a much more appealing approach.

*Explain what marriage is and is not.* Many conservative preachers firmly rooted in the biblical worldview are known more for what they are against than for what they value. Scripture is filled with texts on marriage. We must carefully explain all the contours of the one-flesh union between husband and wife, not a caricature of it. It's possible some people are reacting negatively to traditional marriage because they have not been taught a clear perspective of what the Bible actually says about it. Do not allow a negative spin or a one-dimensional perspective be the only message your followers hear about marriage.

Those who only see the traditional Christian view of marriage through political commercials or from one-time visits to churches where pastors speak disrespectfully and dismissively toward outsiders will naturally oppose the concept. Those with serious questions need to hear the biblical view of marriage from loving pastors who faithfully and graciously provide substantive answers, giving people a well-informed view of covenant marriage.

*Apply the text to all the issues of marriage.* Listeners also need to hear preachers apply the Bible to issues like divorce, not simply to issues like homosexuality. If pastors are not confronting the problem of divorce in their congregations but are constantly railing against homosexuality, then they are not fully applying the various texts about marriage. It's easy to yell at people who are not in the room! Divorce, pornography, cohabitation, and adultery are prevalent in many congregations or communities and must be addressed when they appear in the text. Preachers must address these matters with the same degree of burden and passion as they do with same-sex situations.

Issues related to the single adult lifestyle or delaying marriage until later in life must also be addressed when preaching on marriage today, including positive aspects and spiritual motivations for these choices. Congregations are filled with more and more single adults who are marrying later and later in life. Therefore, when a principle related to marriage appears in the text, the preacher must think carefully about how to apply it to the unmarried.

*Present a countercultural vision of singleness.* To be thoroughly biblical about marriage, we must present a countercultural vision of singleness. Some in the Corinthian church exalted singleness too much. This view clashed with the classical Jewish exaltation of marriage. Other early believers did not value marriage enough. The contemporary church needs help understanding a biblical view of singleness. Many denigrate singles—some directly, most indirectly. Few sermons or conferences are offered on biblical singleness. As a result of the lack of attention to the subject, many singles feel like second-class citizens in the church, and some hide in guilt, shame, fear, and despair. This is exacerbated when marriage is the only life model presented for genuinely committed Christians.

Some churches take this so far as to refuse to employ an unmarried pastor. While in seminary I was the guest speaker for a local congregation. I really wanted to be a pastor so I was thrilled when a lady approached me and asked if I would be open to talking to their search committee. I gladly agreed, but it was the shortest interview on record. Once they found out that I was single, it was over. While churches may have distinct concerns with employing a single pastor, we cannot categorically refuse to consider a single person for the pastorate. Paul and Jesus were certainly qualified single leaders! Our era offers many wonderful examples of single pastors/leaders, like one of my heroes who wrote the aforementioned widely used book on preaching, John Stott.

One special concern is single men are more prone to sexual temptation than married men. Is this true? No! This common negative perspective ignores the positive consideration. A single pastor has more flexibility and more time to devote to ministry. A one-sided view of marriage as a ministry requirement robs the church of meaningful leadership by models of sexual fidelity for other single adults.

Paul celebrated singleness without putting down marriage. He held it up as an honorable state with some advantages over marriage. His perspective cuts down the idol of marriage many singles have erected. His counsel reminds single Christians not to postpone their lives waiting on marriage. At the same time Paul does not encourage singles to worship autonomy and independence. The great value of singleness is ministry flexibility, not self-centered living. Follow

Paul's pattern as you make application of biblical marital principles to both singles and married people.

We must also communicate to singles the value of the local church. Singles need community. Unfortunately many go looking for it at singles bars, nightclubs, or shady chat rooms. A better option exists: the family of God. Tim Keller describes a revolutionary vision of singleness:

> Nearly all ancient religions and cultures made an absolute value of the family and of the bearing of children. . . . [But] single adults cannot be seen as somehow less fully formed or realized human beings because Jesus Christ, a single man, was a perfect man. Paul's assessment in 1 Corinthians 7 is that singleness is a good condition blessed by God, and in many circumstances, it is actually better than marriage. . . . [This was a] revolutionary attitude. . . . Single adult Christians were bearing testimony that God, not family, was their hope. God would guarantee their future, first by giving them their truest family—the church—so they never lacked for brothers and sisters, fathers and mothers, in Christ.[5]

If you are a single Christian, you can bear a powerful testimony that God (not getting married) is your hope, joy, satisfaction, and great delight. We must present this perspective on singleness as part of helping people live in the new marriage culture.

*Present a countercultural vision of sexuality.* The Corinthian church members emerged from a culture that was largely *hedonistic.* They were *pleasure seekers.* Some, however, were more *ascetic.* They were *pleasure abstainers.* One wing was open on issues of sexual matters. The other wing was restrictive in its view of sex and sexuality, promoting celibacy as the only proper approach to life. We must preach a more balanced viewpoint, a truly biblical approach to sex and sexuality.

Modern hedonists are in our audiences. They exalt expressive individualism. They want people to feel free to do whatever they choose. They are sexually permissive. A former student of mine met a sophisticated, wealthy woman in Toronto. When the conversation turned to worldview issues, she said: "If you want to go have an affair, then you should go do it. There's nothing wrong with it. And no one should tell you that it's wrong. It's your life. Do what you want." This perspective, perhaps more subtly expressed, is held by some people who come to hear you preach.

Hedonists avoid calling sin, "sin." They call it "freedom of expression." They also invent more palatable names for activities—like "gentlemen's clubs," which sounds better than "clubs for perverted men to lust and commit adultery." Courageous preachers must hold to biblical definitions of behavior and stick with labels that communicate the truth about sinful behavior.

On the other hand we also have semi-ascetics among our hearers. They may affirm heterosexual marriage, but they do not want anyone to preach about sex in corporate worship. They view sex as something dirty, rather than a gift to be cultivated, enjoyed, and celebrated within marriage. This crowd fears talking about sex will only make matters worse. But does it? It's hard to imagine a biblical presentation on sex and sexuality in our current culture could possibly stir up temptation. The alternative to avoiding the subject of sex is believers, particularly younger believers, will develop their understanding of sexuality from the culture rather than the Bible. Sexuality is a God-given gift that should be studied within the community of faith, under the leadership of godly pastors who speak and teach appropriately about sensitive matters.

*Affirm the power of the gospel.* Faithful Christian preachers declare the gospel week by week. Sermons related to marriage can easily be part of this pattern. When preaching on marriage and related themes, preach the gospel as the source of spiritual change needed to live up to God's standards. Paul reminded the sexually immoral Corinthians that some "were" adulterers, homosexuals, and idolaters, but God changed them, washed them, justified them "in the name of the Lord Jesus Christ and by the Spirit of our God" (1 Cor. 6:11).

After recently preaching through Paul's instructions about marriage (Eph. 5), I then addressed other issues related to marriage from

1 Corinthians. During the first message, two men, who were living together as a couple, came to the service. I thought, *Oh, no.* The awkwardness was accentuated since our church plant is small and no one can hide in the crowd. After preaching through 1 Corinthians 6–7, I got a text from one of the men asking to talk with me. Again I thought, *Oh, no.* To my surprise, the meeting went well as the men told me they had decided to stop living together. Soon thereafter, one of them became a Christian, while the other repented of living in sinful rebellion.

Preach the Bible regardless of who's in the room! That's why you are there in the first place. Preach with humility, confidence, and love. Trust God, by His Spirit through the dynamite of the gospel, will change sinners. Preach with confidence because God's specialty is changing hearts. No person is so bad as to be beyond the reach of God's transforming grace.

*Prepare to lose your head.* The faithful expositor today must assume a "John the Baptist" posture. John the Baptist publically rebuked the Roman ruler Herod Antipas for marrying his half brother's wife, who was also his half niece. Because he called into question this illicit marriage, the enraged leaders silenced him by beheading (Matt. 14:1–12).

While we may not be killed for preaching what the Bible says about marriage, we will face opposition and rejection. We may lose respect in the community. We may lose certain privileges. We may lose some speaking opportunities. Pastors were once viewed positively as agents advocating social good (even by those who disagreed with their positions). Now, particularly on the same-sex marriage issue, support is dissipating. Preachers who take on this subject can expect to be vilified.

If you find it challenging to preach on the biblical view of marriage, you are in good company. No emotionally healthy person likes conflict or wants to be the object of criticism. But if you are looking to win a popularity contest, do not become a preacher who proclaims the Bible. People will stomach false teachers. They call for the heads of true prophets.

Being a prophet does not mean being divisive or disrespectful. It means being bold, despite anticipated criticism or rejection. The same-sex marriage issue and related LGBT-issue proponents have put preachers in a "John the Baptist" type position. When we stand as he did, we should be prepared for a response similar to the one he received.

Louie Giglio was invited to give an inaugural benediction for President Barack Obama. Two days later the invitation was withdrawn after critics dug up a sermon from the 1990s where Giglio addressed homosexuality. The contentious statement included nothing historically uncommon to Christian worship services. His statement was based on 1 Corinthians 6:9–10. Giglio said unrepentant sinners of all kinds will not inherit the kingdom of God—nothing new, preachers have said this for two thousand years. But as the opposition intensified, Giglio withdrew (was uninvited) from the event.

Giglio is an intelligent, winsome, compassionate, gracious Christian who leads people to do a lot of social good. Yet despite these positive qualities, he was ridiculed and rejected for espousing the church's historical view on marriage. His church and collegiate conference generates millions of dollars to fight sex trafficking, annually blesses thousands of children with school supplies, and he regularly speaks out in defense of the weak and powerless. But, because Giglio believes marriage is between a man and a woman, he was deemed too offensive to participate in public life. This is what will happen in the future to preachers who maintain biblical convictions about marriage.

## The Cultural World: Preaching the Word Effectively

In order to connect our message to the culture, we need to understand our audience well. We can never understand the thought processes of everyone in our audience or in today's culture, but that should not stop us from carefully considering the way people think about issues like marriage. Many people today may have the same vocabulary, but they are using a different dictionary. We must assume people have varying categories, and we must be willing to explain things on a basic level. Here are some ways you can improve your cultural understanding and sharpen your preaching.

*Read, listen, and talk to outsiders.* Preachers usually speak to people like those with whom they interact all week long. That's why seminary students often preach their worst sermons while in seminary! They address problems and answer questions that concern their fellow seminary students but are not pressing to most people. Pastors have a similar tendency. If we just talk to other church leaders, or just read blogs and books by Christian leaders, our sermons will speak to those issues and needs. We should not prepare sermons for our peers. We need to prepare to talk to everyday people.

How can we preach more effectively to ordinary people? Consider doing these three things: diversify your interactions with people, read widely, and prepare to preach to your "old self."

By diversifying with whom you interact during the week, you will have a better sense of how to make application in a sermon. You can do this in a number of ways. Go for walks in your neighborhood (and talk to people!). Coach a sports team. Volunteer for a community organization or school. Host a neighborhood cookout. Go to local events (and talk to people!). These interactions will change your preaching in positive ways.

For a preacher all of life is sermon preparation. Your weekly activities feed into your preaching. If you do not have interactions and discussions with people who disagree with you about issues like marriage, then you will not be able to preach compellingly about your positions. Your defense of biblical marriage may connect with other Christians but lack convincing answers to the genuine concerns of people who oppose it.

Do you know any homosexuals? any people in a same-sex marriage? Have you ever invited a gay neighbor over for dinner? One friend volunteered at a gay bar as a janitor in order to meet people. He eventually led a Bible study there and taught through the Gospel of Mark. Some of these individuals were converted, and a church was planted out of this study. While that may seem radical to you, it demonstrated his willingness to engage people on their terms rather than just condemn their behavior.

Jesus was a friend of sinners, and because He understood sinners, He could preach to them. He was the ultimate bridge builder. Follow His example. Counsel people during the week. Meet people in your community. Engage in regular conversations with non-Christians. If you avoid people, moving directly from desk to pulpit, you will not likely connect well with contemporary hearers.

In addition to your daily interactions, read widely as well. Spend an appropriate amount of time reading non-Christian material. Choose some resources that will give you a sense for how people think today, like a politically liberal newspaper or website. While you cannot read everything, read regular sources that help you understand how your hearers think about issues today.

Finally, preach to your "old self." This might be hard for you if you grew up in the church. But be honest. You have had and still have many of the same struggles, doubts, and questions of people in your community. Since I was converted during college, it helps me to ask the question, "Would I have understood this message as an unconverted college student?" Or this question, "Would I have understood this as a newly converted college student?" Prepare sermons you would have wanted to hear or needed to hear, not for your current ministry peers. They are not your audience.

*Assume biblical cluelessness.* As you diversify daily interactions, read widely, and preach to genuine needs, you will discover a general biblical illiteracy in American culture. Many people we are trying to win over have no categories for love, sacrifice, cross, sin, covenant, and so on. These biblically uninformed people have no scriptural reference points. In evangelism we recognize the need for "preevangelism." Many Americans have no real understanding of who God is, what the Bible is, or why Jesus died. We should not be surprised many people today do not agree with us about marriage since their views of love and relationships, God and sin, repentance and faithfulness, and Christ and salvation lack a biblical reference point.

In former years most atheists could be dubbed "Christian athe-ists"; that is, they rejected the Christian God. That's not the case today as many people do not really know much about the Christian God. Therefore, when preparing sermons, you must anticipate com-peting worldviews and general biblical cluelessness among your hearers, even about something as common as marriage. One church planter near Northwestern University in Chicago encountered many Asian students and others with no foundational Christian vocabu-lary. He now leads evangelistic Bible studies where he simply asks and answers basic doctrinal questions. Pastors addressing marriage issues must do so like international missionaries approach evange-lism, laying out foundational truth and building the case for biblical marriage before asking people to commit to those standards.

*Assume unbelievers and skeptics are present.* One weakness in con-temporary exposition is the failure of preachers to address unbeliev-ers throughout their sermons. When unbelievers are included, it's normally reserved for the last part of the message. Keller advises us to preach as if unbelievers are present and they will eventually show up. They will either come because you are addressing their questions, or more likely, they will show up because their friends invite them knowing you will address their needs in your sermons.

To include your entire audience effectively, address non-Christians in the introduction. Then mention them as you apply each point in the body of your sermon. Finally, include non-Christians at the end of the sermon as you ask them to respond to the message. This does not mean the great majority of your sermon needs to be directly aimed at unbelievers. It means you should try to get everyone on the bus during the introduction so they make the entire trip with you. As part of your application, have some "sidebars" throughout the sermon where you raise and address popular objections to the truth at hand. Finally, call unbelievers to Jesus Christ at the end of your message.

Do not create the impression sermons are just for "insiders." By addressing unbelievers, you not only speak to them, but you build an evangelistic culture in your church. Even if your normal audience is all believers, do this anyway. You will be amazed when, as a result,

God draws non-Christians to your worship services. Members will want to bring their friends, and you will be modeling how to talk with and include unbelievers. You can do this by preaching through books of the Bible or using other expository preaching plans. You do not have to choose between evangelism and edification. Even when you preach on issues like marriage, evangelize as you edify; edify as you evangelize.[6]

*Assess your community.* If you expect unbelievers and doubters from your community to attend your weekly worship gatherings, then learn to speak to the people in your community. Do you know the types of people who make up your community? What are their dominant beliefs, hopes, fears, dreams, idols, and values? Who are their heroes? What are the myths they believe? What are the traditions they practice? What are the cultural norms in your area? How specifically is your city fallen? How does it retain the image of God? How has the gospel been bad news to your community? How is the gospel good news to your community? Why do some oppose the traditional view of marriage? Why are some advocating same-sex marriage? As you think through these questions, preach to address these issues even if the people who need to hear the message are not yet present. This prepares your church to receive their community and sensitizes them to their needs. It also creates a positive climate for communication when community members do attend.

To help answer these questions, do a demographic and spiritual profile of your community and consider its ministry implications. For example, we recently created a list of characteristics of people to whom we are ministering in Raleigh, North Carolina. They are consumers; geographically, historically, and theologically rootless; multiethnic and international; tribal and segregated; and suspicious of authority.[7] While these are not characteristics of everyone in the city, they do reflect many of the people with whom we interact on a weekly basis. Focusing on these qualities definitely impacts the way I apply every biblical text and how I prepare the "sidebars" in my sermon each week—no matter the subject, including marriage-related issues.

*Ask for questions after your sermon.* One of the best ways to understand your audience is to ask for response immediately from them. This can be done a number of ways. People can e-mail questions to you for later response. They can text questions during the sermon, and you can answer them orally right after the sermon. You can host a dialogue luncheon or social gathering for nonbelievers immediately following the service. All of these are good opportunities to engage people about their concept of marriage and answer their questions and objections.

*Preach to change worldview, not just behavior.* The goal of preaching a biblical view of marriage is to change how people think, not just how they act or vote. We preach to help people learn and to think "Christianly" about all issues, including marriage. Unbelievers who oppose traditional marriage must be converted before they can truly develop a biblical viewpoint on this issue. Many Christians are regenerated but have never been taught well on issues like sexuality and marriage. In both cases preachers must preach to change worldview, not just behavior.

How are worldviews about marriage changed? First, we must empathize with people who do not share our perspective, not disrespect them. Many preachers are right in their stand on marriage but sinful in their attitude toward those who disagree with them. This is morally unacceptable and undercuts credibility, causing lost future opportunities to influence outsiders. It takes a long time for some people to "get it" when considering life-changing patterns to long-held beliefs. Be patient. Do not run them off by being a jerk in the pulpit! People may stumble over the gospel and reject biblical truth, but do not let it be because of your personality or attitude.

Second, we can affirm something about the worldview of those who do not share all our convictions, finding common ground to begin the dialogue. Often those who have competing worldviews believe something that can be affirmed. While this is a bit of a challenge on this particular issue, both of us value things like "freedom" and "identity." Affirm some of these common longings, as a sign of respect and understanding, and truly try to understand their arguments for these shared interests.

Third, show how their worldview falls flat and how the gospel offers them something infinitely better. In short, establish a *point of contact* with people (by sympathizing and affirming), and then have a *point of conflict* with them (as you unpack the gospel).[8]

*Be wise and love people.* At the heart of contextualization is wisdom and love. You need wisdom to discern what types of people are in your community and in your congregation. Be perceptive and pray for wisdom. In 1 Corinthians 9, as Paul described becoming "all things to all people" (v. 22), he's referring to the use of wisdom. Good preachers and missionaries are wise. They understand their context.

In this same passage Paul also reminds us contextualization is about loving others. He wrote, "I have made myself a *servant* to all, that I might win more of them" (9:19 ESV, emphasis added). Whom does this sound like? It sounds like Jesus, the one who left glory and took the form of a servant. In great love He made the gospel known to people in ways that they could understand it.

Every good parent contextualizes. I have five children. If I really care about them, I will be careful to explain things in such a way they get it. This means I address each of them a bit differently. I teach them all the same truths, but I have to understand how each one learns in order to communicate effectively. Why do parents do this? Because they love their children! Beyond just saying things that are meaningful, necessary, and true, I say what is meaningful, necessary, and true in a way my children can grasp it—because I love them.

If preachers really love their hearers, they will work hard at contextualizing their preaching. Returning to Stott's analogy, they will work hard at being bridge builders. We must hold firmly to the unchanging Word, but we must also know and love people. We do not just preach; we preach the Bible. And we do not just preach the Bible; we preach the Bible to people. Build a bridge as you preach on marriage today by communicating what the Bible says in ways your audience can really grasp it and apply it.

## The People as Bridge Builders

This generation must be taught from the Word, but they must also be taught by *example*. Part of the problem with people hearing us rightly and applying God's Word personally is the lack of models present before them. This generation has been called the "fatherless generation." Broken families are the norm, not the exception. Many people in congregations and neighborhoods need to see what our teaching looks like in everyday clothes. They need to have relationships with people that have healthy marriages. Young people need to see husbands honoring their wives, doing the dishes, working hard, teaching the Bible to the children, praying with their family, and so on. They need to see illustrations of our explanations.

As this relates to preaching on marriage, we should consider how we might tie various events and activities to our sermons. How can you put people together? Our church uses sermon-based small groups that meet in homes. One of our hopes is that within these meetings people will see what family looks like both in marriages and in a biblical community of brothers and sisters in Christ. Some outsiders will be attracted to Christian community before they are attracted to the Christian gospel. Christian marriages, as well as a Christian community marked by love and service, are powerful apologetics to outsiders and an enormous encouragement to struggling saints.

Holding up faithful, compelling examples of biblical marriage does not mean people need to see perfect marriages. Such marriages do not exist. Instead they need to see how couples work through conflict by using the Scriptures. They need to see how couples forgive each other after having an argument. They need to see how couples repent of sin and change their behaviors. They need to see couples apologize for their use of words and observe how couples make changes to say words that nourish and bless.

To do this, we must invite people into our lives, not just our weekly worship gatherings to hear sermons. The church is not a building we visit; rather, it's the people. Outsiders need to see the people of God living out their marriage commitments under the lordship of Jesus Christ. Encourage your people to invite friends into their lives and homes to see genuine Christian marriage lived out for the glory of God and the good of the community.

CHAPTER 8

# COUNSELING PERSONS ABOUT SAME-SEX MARRIAGE

*Heath Lambert*

Late at night Will sat in front of me, tormented. We had known each other for years. Will was one of the first people I had led to faith in Jesus as Savior and Lord. Even after coming to Jesus at age twenty-one, he had spent his young adulthood dealing with same-sex attraction. Since first experiencing sexual desires as a boy, Will's desires had been directed toward boys, not girls.

This caused a great deal of pain in Will's life. He did not grow up in a religious home but still felt distressed over his same-sex attraction. This discomfort sprang from several sources. The first was he knew it meant he was different. All of his friends liked girls, talked about girls, and fantasized about girls. Not Will, even though he longed to be the same as his friends. The second source was his family. Will had a sense that if his parents knew about his secret desires, they would be disappointed in him. Finally, Will had some sense his desires were just wrong. He did not know where that feeling came from, what it meant, or even how to talk about it; but the nagging doubts were there.

As Will grew older, during his college years he developed numerous sexual relationships with men. As a public school graduate now attending a secular university, he found few voices challenging the way he was living. When Will finally "came out" to his parents, they admitted that although they did not understand him, they ultimately wanted their son to be happy. As a young homosexual man, Will was in a family, at a school, and working a job where no one objected to his lifestyle

Then Will heard the gospel.

Will heard he was a sinner, Jesus had atoned for sin through His death on the cross, and he could be forgiven by repenting of his sins and trusting in Jesus as Savior and Lord. Will was undone. He had never heard such a message. That day he believed and committed his life to Jesus.

After his profession of faith, Will wanted to leave his homosexual lifestyle and sought help to do it. He made remarkable advances. He ended a number of sinful and destructive relationships, began attending church and studying the Bible, and developed a new set of friendships. Things seemed to be going well, but Will was more tormented than he admitted. He felt constant internal and external temptations. He still experienced strong desires for same-sex experiences and encountered many men he found attractive. While Will was quietly struggling with these temptations, he relocated to another town for his work.

After Will moved to his new location, he did not try to find another Christian community. Instead he settled into work and began meeting men. After a while Will met Brian, and the two fell in love. Eventually they moved into an apartment and settled into life together.

Two years later Will came to me for counseling. He was anguished and looked terrible. He had lost weight, was jumpy, had chewed his nails down to the bloody quick, and was an emotional and physical wreck. As we began our conversation, Will started to sob. Two strands were woven through his narrative. The first was his love for Brian. In so many ways he felt privileged to have found him. Brian claimed he loved Will, too. After living together for over a year,

Brian had expressed a desire to get married. Will was surprised and troubled by Brian's request.

The second narrative strand was Will's unhappiness. Brian broaching the subject of marriage made Will afraid. Living with Brian was one thing; getting married was another. Will wondered if he was ready to take such a step. Will had always felt if things were not working with Brian or if he wanted to go back to church, he could always just end the relationship. Marriage was much more permanent, and Will was not sure he wanted to do it.

Will had shared none of this with Brian, only maintaining he just was not ready to get married. When Brian wanted to know why, Will had not known what to say. He did not have the courage to tell the truth that this decision was causing him to reevaluate the morality of their relationship. It was also rekindling a desire to return to Jesus Christ and active church fellowship.

This uncertainty had been going on for eight months. Brian was frustrated Will would not take their relationship to the next level. Will was deeply torn over whether he should take the next step with Brian or end the relationship. They fought constantly, resulting in continuing emotional turmoil for Will. Because of the stress he had quit eating and was looking for a way out of the relationship. In desperation he reached out to me.

Will's story was moving. I cried with him and hugged him. He asked me what I thought he should do. I told him that it was not important what I thought. What mattered was what God wanted him to do. He then sobbed harder and confessed how wrong he had been to return to his former lifestyle and develop a relationship with Brian. He agreed he needed to get out of the relationship and needed help to make it happen. More than just leaving Brian, Will wanted to leave his homosexuality behind for good.

That night Will and I began what has become a years-long relationship of working together to accomplish these goals. This chapter summarizes what we have discussed in our times together. Over time we have worked through many issues as Will has progressed on the road to sexual wholeness and holy living.

## Fleeing Sexual Immorality

In those early hours Will's greatest need was to trust Jesus Christ in real and powerful ways. He needed to expose darkness to light. He needed to reconnect with a church. He needed to do many other things. The most pressing issue, however, was getting away from a harmful and destructive relationship.

The Bible tells the story of a man named Joseph who was in a situation similar to Will. Joseph had caught the eye of Potiphar's wife, who tried to seduce him into a sexual relationship. She made her intentions clear: "But one day, when he went into the house to do his work and none of the men of the house was there in the house, she caught him [Joseph] by his garment, saying, 'Lie with me.' But he left his garment in her hand and fled and got out of the house" (Gen. 39:11–12 ESV).

The obvious difference between Joseph and Will is the former involved opposite-sex attraction, and the latter involved same-sex attraction. Otherwise, their situations are similar. When faced with sexual temptation, Joseph ran away!

The apostle Paul later made a lasting principle out of Joseph's response. He wrote: "Flee from sexual immorality. Every other sin a person commits is outside the body, but the sexually immoral person sins against his own body" (1 Cor. 6:18 ESV). This biblical instruction made it an urgent priority for Will to end his relationship with Brian, including physically moving away from this temptation to sexual immorality.

Sharing this direct counsel with Will made him even more nervous. Will did not doubt this was the best course of action and was relieved to think of ending this burden. What made him nervous was the interaction with Brian that would be required to make it happen. Brian had already been very abrasive and harsh in his attempts to force a marriage. Will knew Brian's response would be much worse if he tried to end the relationship. He was scared of what would happen.

In our culture secular people often accuse Christians of being mean-spirited in their rejection of same-sex marriage and advocacy of marriage between one man and one woman. What is often ignored by these strident voices are the men and women who feel pressured by their homosexual partners to remain in those relationships. Many struggling homosexuals want out of their lifestyle but are afraid of the conflicts and complications they will face if they try to leave.

Will's concerns about facing Brian were real, and he needed my support so he would not have to take such a serious step alone. I offered to go to his apartment with him, help him clear out his things, and be there while he told Brian their relationship was over. Will was grateful for the offer but did not believe it was necessary. He wanted to tell Brian they were breaking up without other people present. Since he only planned on removing his clothes and a few other personal items, he felt he could go alone.

We talked about the clear message Will would communicate to Brian, expressing his strong desire to end the relationship and asking forgiveness for the sexual sin he committed against Brian. I cautioned Will that this conversation could be very difficult. We prayed together for God's strength to do the right thing, even though it would be hard. I encouraged Will to call me if things got more challenging than anticipated.

Did they ever!

The next night Will called me, crying very hard. In the background I could hear Brian screaming all manner of obnoxious obscenities. He was furious with Will for not wanting to be with him and for talking about their situation with a "Christian freak." He threatened violence if Will tried to leave. I assured Will that Jesus would help him and challenged him to trust the Lord through this very hard time. I told him to leave the apartment immediately while I was on the phone. I promised to call the police if Brian became violent in any way. Will made it out of the apartment and came back to my house later that night.

## Finding Christian Community

Will had been through a lot. He had lived through a tortuous few months in a relationship he wanted to end even though it was with a man he thought he loved. Relationships can be real and wrong at the same time. The wrongness of the life Brian and Will were living together did not make it any less real. Will's sense of loss was real, even as he experienced relief it was over.

Helping Will walk away from a very toxic relationship was an important first step. Will now needed to be involved in other, healthier relationships. For a Christian, those relationships should be found in their church. Paul gave crucial instructions to the church at Thessalonica about how to care for one another. He wrote:

> Now concerning brotherly love you have no need for anyone to write to you, for you yourselves have been taught by God to love one another, for that indeed is what you are doing to all the brothers throughout Macedonia. But we urge you, brothers, to do this more and more. (1 Thess. 4:9–10 ESV)

Paul's command to love is addressed to believers. The issue being addressed in these verses is the importance of community. Will needed to get away from a destructive community and be surrounded by loving Christians. He needed to escape from a community pursuing sin and join a community pursuing righteous living. Will needed to experience real love, self-sacrificing care from other Christians.

Paul urged Christians to love one another more and more as evidence of their faith in God because God teaches Christians to love. Christians love one another. Will had just spent two years in a very selfish relationship. He was pursuing Brian selfishly to fulfill his desire to be in a relationship exclusively on his terms. Brian had done the same thing. He pursued his own ends in their relationship—marriage—to the exclusion of what Will wanted. Both were engaging in a relationship God defines as sinful. This relationship had little love. It was marked by greedy lust. Will needed to learn what real love looked like, and he needed the church to show him. In the aftermath of this broken relationship, Christians showed love to Will in a variety of ways.

First, Will needed the loving care of the church in meeting some of his immediate needs. In the wake of the broken relationship and flight out of town, Will was left without a place to live. Several Christians came together to help with this. One business owner gave Will a place to work. Another family gave him a place to stay, rent-free, until he got on his feet.

Second, Will needed the loving care of the church expressed through godly relationships with all kinds of people, especially with other men where there were no risks of the relationships being sexual in nature. During his years of struggle, Will's friendships were either with women or homosexual men. Will needed to learn how to relate to men. Several godly men spent time with Will and became his friends.

Men and women struggling with same-sex attraction need to befriend others of their same gender who are not remotely tempted to engage in a sexual relationship. Some people asked to befriend a person struggling with same-sex attraction wonder whether it is a good idea to pursue a close relationship with them. They fear this might unintentionally create the temptation we are trying to remove. Such a practice is not a problem. What tempts people experiencing same-sex attraction is close relationships with other same-sex attracted people, without any accountability. To be in close relationships with persons of their same gender who do not have those struggles is actually quite positive, and even crucial, for men and women who struggle with same-sex attraction. Even if a person develops inappropriate feelings for someone not attracted to him or her, this can be an opportunity to speak in an open, honest, and redemptive way about how to handle the temptation. These kinds of relationships should be encouraged in your church.

In addition to these kinds of personal relationships, Will also needed to interact with other Christians at times when the entire church gathers, like Sunday worship or fellowship meals or events. He also needed intermediate levels of fellowship between the large gatherings and more personal ones. That is to say, he needed the kind of fellowship often found in a church's small-group ministry where a dozen or so people pray, share meals, and study the Bible together.

Third, Will needed to receive the love of the church expressed through its teaching ministry. The first way he needed to receive the ministry of the Word was in the regular, weekly ministry of preaching. He needed to sit with other believers and hear the Word of God declared by a faithful preacher. He needed to hear of God's faithfulness to countless generations of believers living before him. He needed to learn of God's strength to save and change people. He needed to learn more about Jesus who forgives sins and draws near to the broken.

Another way Will needed to receive the ministry of the Word was in the more personal setting of counseling. My counseling relationship with Will began the night he first talked with me about his relationship with Brian. The Bible informed my counseling conversations with Will. Over time we talked about how a good God allows such painful struggles, how to repent of sin, how to think through the complex and painful issues of his past, how to take lustful thoughts captive, how to understand the logic of sexuality in the Bible, whether marriage is a possibility for people who have had a struggle with same-sex attraction, and many other things. Despite all we have covered, there was far too much material for us to address in our weekly meetings together.

This reality meant the community of believers in our church needed to be marshaled in a different way. Several people in our church, both lay members and lay counselors, met with Will about very specific issues. There were so many issues to address that taking time to work on them only with me was impractical. We were already meeting for ninety minutes weekly. It would have been frustratingly slow, and we would likely never have gotten to many very important issues if I were Will's only confidant. Will met weekly with a team of people about a variety of different issues. At one point he was meeting with me and three other lay counselors about different things. I coordinated the team so we were not overloading him with work or giving him conflicting assignments. Because of this team approach, Will was able to spend hours and hours every week in intensive Bible study learning how to change and grow in a multitude of ways by the power of Jesus Christ.

One more reality about this issue of community also needs to be addressed. The 1 Thessalonians passage previously mentioned teaches believers are to love *one another.* Love is a two-way street in Christian community. We love one another. It is wrong for a person in Christian community only to receive love or only to provide love. To live in Christian community is to regularly receive the care of others and regularly extend care to others. It should always be both/and, not either/or.

To allow Will to receive such massive amounts of care without providing opportunity for him to care for others would have been detrimental to his spiritual life. This is not an issue of some sort of *quid pro quo.* Instead, it demonstrates care for Will to help him learn how to care for others. Because of this need, we connected Will with many opportunities to serve: he helped out around church, served needy members of our community, and worked around the houses of some of the people who were counseling him. These acts of servant love stitched him more deeply into the lives of those who were helping him. Being around their homes and families allowed more conversations, dinner invitations, and closer relationships to develop.

## Finding Will

Will's story raises a crucial question: During the years he lived as a homosexual, was he a Christian living a sinful lifestyle, or was he (despite his earlier profession of faith in Jesus) really not yet a Christian? The most important issue facing Will had to do with whether he had truly repented from sin and placed faith in Jesus Christ as Savior and Lord. This issue is particularly important for two reasons.

The first reason is Will's story raises questions about the legitimacy of his profession of faith. After apparently walking with the Lord for a season, Will ran away from the church, had sexual relationships with other men, and considered entering a same-sex marriage. Those are not activities an obedient Christian does. Will's behavior could have two biblical explanations. His profession of faith could have been counterfeit, meaning his status as an unbeliever had never changed. He also could have experienced genuine conversion years earlier but then succumbed to temptation and lived a backslidden life. This was a crucial issue for Will to settle and for you to consider as you counsel "Christian" men and women whose lifestyle choices raise similar questions.

This issue is crucial because of its eternal consequences. But it was also important because Will was being asked to do some significantly challenging things. He had to take the deeply painful step of breaking off a complicated relationship. He had to walk away from a life to which he had become accustomed and into a strange new situation filled with unknown variables. In addition he had to develop counseling relationships with several people where he was learning about Jesus, reading the Bible, and learning the Word of God. Will also needed to flee from sexual immorality, be in Christian community, learn to serve, and continue his counseling program.

While all of these activities and disciplines were important, none had the power to solve Will's problems. Even learning about Jesus, while critical, could not change Will. Only trusting Jesus personally could empower Will to do the things needed to accomplish life change over the long haul. This meant the central issue to address with Will was whether he was a Christian, depending on the grace of Jesus to inform and transform his life. To sort out this issue, Will and I spent significant time talking about, thinking through, memorizing, and applying Ephesians 1:3–14. Several themes in this passage turned out to be particularly significant for Will as he determined the status of his relationship with Jesus.

### Redeemed by the Blood of Jesus

In Ephesians 1:7, Paul wrote, "In him [Christ] we have redemption through his blood, the forgiveness of our trespasses, according to the riches of his grace" (ESV). Three powerful realities from this verse transformed Will's life. First, there is something Will *had*, namely, "redemption through his blood," the blood of Jesus. Paul defined this transaction as the forgiveness of sins. The good news of the gospel is Will was forgiven for all the sins he had committed in his life. This includes his homosexual lust and behavior, as well as everything else.

Second, redemption comes "according to the riches of his grace." Jesus Christ has rich grace, which He showers on people. The redemption and forgiveness of sin available to Will did not come to him because he deserved it but because Jesus Christ overflows with rich and abundant grace to save sinners.

Third, Will has redemption and abundant grace "in him [Christ]." The forgiving grace of God is not universal. Not everyone receives this forgiveness. The rich grace of redemption comes only to those who repent of their sins and trust *in Christ* to make the payment for their sin.

Will, just like any other person, must be in Christ to receive the overflowing riches of the gospel. As mentioned above, it was crucial for Will to know if his previous profession of faith was a genuine conversion. If it was not a genuine conversion, it would be necessary for him to repent and place faith in Jesus before he could realize God's resources for change. Over time, through careful Bible study and too many other factors to enumerate here, Will concluded his conversion from years earlier was genuine. He came to believe his time with Brian was a period of serious rebellion and flagrant sin he committed as a believer. I ultimately agreed with this appraisal.

In the early weeks of counseling Will, however, I did not overly concentrate on determining the legitimacy of his conversion experience from years past. Instead, I concentrated on passages like Ephesians 1:7 and urged Will to trust in the work of Jesus described in this verse. What Will believed about Jesus years earlier may have been interesting but was relatively academic and tangential to the counseling currently happening. What was most important was Will trusted Jesus in the present. If Will had a present relationship with Jesus, we could hold the investigation about his prior religious experience until another, less urgent time. I took Will at his word he was trusting in Jesus Christ for salvation and counseled him with confidence, knowing if his faith was genuine it would eventually bear fruit.

## Adopted as a Son

Ephesians 1:5 says, "[The Father] predestined us for adoption as sons through Jesus Christ, according to the purpose of his will" (ESV). This was wonderful news for Will and is wonderful news for everyone else as well! In Christ, Will is more than a forgiven sinner. He has received the exalted status of a son. This verse makes a definitive statement about the nature, character, and status of Christian people. These realities are significant for helping men like Will leave the temptations of their homosexual lifestyle.

Nature and identity are hugely important categories in the homosexual community. In that community people do not merely engage in homosexual acts. They *are* homosexual. Homosexuality is a defining reality for them. It is common to hear advocates for homosexuality and same-sex marriage equate objections to their sexuality with objections to their right to exist as human beings. Homosexuals center their identity and status as persons in their sexual behavior.

Will struggled profoundly with this issue. For his entire life almost every sexual thought had been about other men. Will struggled with sexual impulses in his adolescent years the same way most boys do. The difference between Will and others, however, was most boys experience normal kinds of heterosexual temptations, whereas Will's were much different. Adolescent boys identify with one another's sexual issues in their growing-up years and thus normalize their sexuality (even when it is characterized by sinful lust). Will, unlike most young men who struggle with heterosexual lust, did not have an outlet to normalize his sexuality. It began to take on a certain immensity most men with heterosexual temptations do not experience.

This meant Will was tempted to understand himself as gay. Will needed to be reoriented by Paul's message in Ephesians. Will was not defined by his homosexual lust and behavior any more than other people are defined by heterosexual lust and behavior. In Christ he came to know himself as a new creation—a *son*—with a corresponding new identity established by God.

This is a significant issue. How we understand our fundamental nature dictates how we think and act. I have three children who understand they are *my* children. When they see me, they run up to me, jump in my arms, and give me hugs and kisses. The children who live next door do not treat me this way. They like me and hopefully think I am a nice guy, but they are much more reserved around me. The difference is my children know they are *mine*, and neighborhood children know they are not. How we understand our identity informs how we think and act.

When persons define their nature, identity, and character as being "gay," they will most likely think and act like someone who is gay. When persons embrace the truth, however, then their most critical reality becomes their relationship with God. They then define their nature, identity, and character as being a "son," "daughter," or "child" of God. When they define their status this way, they will likely begin to think and act out of who they have become, not who they once thought they were.

## Holy and Blameless

Ephesians 1:4 says, "He chose us in him before the foundation of the world, that we should be holy and blameless before him" (ESV). Christians receive an enormous number of spiritual blessings at their conversion. In fact, we have received every single spiritual blessing it is possible to receive (Eph. 1:3). One of those many blessings is God's choosing to make Christians "holy and blameless."

This truth was significant for Will and is for anyone struggling against any persistent sin, including homosexuality. Will was not merely concerned about his life; he was without hope. He believed he would never be any different than he was at that moment he first came to me for help. He believed the feeling of being "stuck" with his struggles and relationships would always characterize his existence.

The truth he learned from Ephesians shattered this hopelessness with Christ-centered encouragement. Jesus gave Will the blessings of holiness and blamelessness. In Christ these realities became his through conversion and, through counseling and discipleship, became living realities for him. Will started and sustained his journey toward change with the conviction that in Jesus change is not only possible; it is required. Change is something a loving, holy, and sovereign Father has chosen, secured, and made practically possible for him in Jesus.

This issue of change is crucial when it comes to homosexuality. There are two extremes to avoid, which Ephesians 1 corrects. On the one hand, many people believe change is impossible. They teach homosexuality is innate and immutable. Gay is something you *are*, and you cannot change your nature. Paul begs to differ. He says change is required in the Christian life because people defined by sinfulness (of which, homosexuality is just one manifestation) are called to be holy and blameless. Based on Ephesians 1 (and multiple other passages), the Bible argues strongly and persuasively that every person, including homosexuals, can change.

On the other hand, some people have misunderstood the nature of this change. Some argue, for change to be genuine, persons struggling against homosexual desires must become heterosexual and get married. Change therefore becomes tantamount to having opposite-sex attraction and a desire for marriage. The Bible does not teach this. The Bible never teaches heterosexual desires are a virtue in and of themselves. The Bible always commends sex within heterosexual marriage (cf. 1 Cor. 7:1–5). Heterosexual desires are never praised in abstract. Furthermore, the Bible describes singleness as a blessing allowing one to serve the Lord wholeheartedly (1 Cor. 7:25–40). The kind of change that leads to heterosexual attraction and marriage is certainly possible and is a reality for many. It goes beyond the Bible's message, however, to *require* this understanding of change.

Ephesians 1 defines the kind of change people can expect as being "holy." The change we should all pursue and expect is holiness in our desires and behavior. Will needed to pursue holiness in his desires by putting off lust and demonstrating genuine love and holiness in his actions by putting off fornication and practicing chastity.

Nearly ten years after first meeting Will, he has developed sexual attractions for women and is pursuing marriage. He is thankful for this, and so am I, even though heterosexuality and heterosexual marriage were never the goals of our counseling. Holy living was always the goal.

## Sealed with the Spirit

Paul concludes this passage with this profound thought, "In him you also, when you heard the word of truth, the gospel of your salvation, and believed in him, were sealed with the promised Holy Spirit, who is the guarantee of our inheritance until we acquire possession of it, to the praise of his glory" (Eph. 1:13–14 ESV).

Earlier, I addressed Will's need to be in a Christian community. Will needed to extend loving service to others in a church context. He also needed a loving community to come alongside him and help him through significant change and temptation. These verses from Ephesians describe an even more profound element of community. Paul teaches believers, including men like Will, are given the powerful Holy Spirit to be with them and in them.

The mind-blowing reality that God the Holy Spirit indwells believers had two significant implications for Will. First, it meant God was with him always. Even when he felt lonely and isolated, even when loving members of the Christian community were unable to be with him, and even when he was discouraged with his slow progress, the powerful presence of Christ was dwelling within him. Will was never alone. No believer ever is.

Because of the indwelling Holy Spirit, Will had infinitely powerful resources for change. The Christian community surrounding Will has a lot of resources. We can provide wisdom, accountability, support, prayer, guidance, and more. We can *help* him change. The Spirit Will has dwelling within him, however, will *make* him change. The Holy Spirit relentlessly pursues the character of Jesus formed in us—a powerful, life-changing, hope-filling reality. No believer is ever truly alone but is indwelt by God the Holy Spirit who empowers and motivates new life.

Studying, memorizing, and meditating on Ephesians 1:3–14 changed Will's life. If you were to ask him about it, he would tell you he found his true self by renewing his mind with this passage of Scripture. All his life he had defined himself by his sinful sexual desires. Cultural influences conspired to reinforce his warped thinking. Over a prolonged period of time, Will learned that in Jesus Christ he was so much more than a person defined by same-sex attraction. Will learned he was redeemed by Jesus, adopted into God's family, enabled to live a holy and blameless life, and empowered by the indwelling Holy Spirit. Truth set him free. He will never be the same again.

## Concluding Reflections

The new marriage culture will make the kind of counseling I did with Will more and more common. Being equipped to use the Bible to counsel people struggling with same-sex attraction and considering same-sex marriage will be a required skill for contemporary pastors. Ministers of the gospel in previous generations likely could not have imagined a culture that would embrace homosexuality, much less same-sex marriage. Because of that it is hard for past generations of leaders to envision the urgency of counseling someone like Will away from such a decision. Unfortunately such urgency is our reality in American culture today.

As I reflect on my experience with Will, two things stand out. First, Will did not require much persuasion that marrying Brian would be sinful. His guilty conscience had been accusing him, and he already knew it. Will needed support to do the right thing more than he needed convincing what the right decision was. Other people may not have such a sensitive conscience and will require more persuasion of the truthfulness and authority of Scripture on these matters. Pastors and counselors must be bold, yet compassionate, to confront people as needed.

Second, improved and intentional counseling ministries are the need of the hour. As faithful churches proclaim the biblical teaching on the ethics of homosexuality, they must match that message with a commitment to help people with the process of living out those biblical principles. It will not be enough in the new marriage culture to tell the "Wills" we meet their choices are wrong. We must also be able to help them change while providing the patient counsel and loving church community necessary to sustain them through the process.

## CHAPTER 9

# COUNSELING PERSONS AFFECTED BY SAME-SEX MARRIAGE

## *Debbie Steele*

Nancy Heche, a Christian mother, author, and speaker, is a healthy example of someone dealing with the reality of a family member in a same-sex marriage. She has written clearly and honestly about her experience in coping with her famous actress daughter's much-publicized lesbian relationship. Nancy recognized her journey would involve obedience to God's gentle and persistent leadership as He revealed His truth about the situation. She learned her journey was not about changing others but rather about God changing her. Nancy realized through this experience it was undeniably God's desire to bring her into a deeper level of submission to Jesus Christ. It was also God's desire to bring those who struggle with same-sex attraction into a new life of surrender and pursuit of a life-altering relationship with Jesus Christ.[1]

As current cultural attitudes toward sexuality raise new challenges for the church, pastors and ministry leaders will encounter family members seeking answers about how to respond to their adult child or spouse's same-sex attraction. For most ministry leaders today, it is just a matter of time before they will encounter this predicament. This challenging dilemma will be phrased something like this, "What do I do now since my child (or niece, nephew, brother, sister, or even a spouse) has told me he/she is gay?" Many Christians will face overwhelming negative emotions when this reality hits home. But when the shock has worn off, the hard work of hammering out a newly defined relationship must be done. Pastors and other ministry leaders will find themselves front and center in caring for families going through these kinds of difficulties.

## Foundations for Pastoral Counseling

Pastors, counselors, and other ministry leaders are first responders to families with questions about sexuality, gender-based moral dilemmas, and issues related to same-sex marriage. At the outset it is important to lay out some parameters for what pastoral leaders can accomplish in these situations. While definitive counsel from the Bible is available and appropriate, most veteran ministry leaders know they cannot control what their counselees think or do. In preparing to intervene and respond to these issues, keep the following goals and guidelines in mind as a framework for effective counseling.

First, allow Christian family members to share their story, providing empathic listening and comfort. Do not judge or condemn individuals for their negative feelings, anger they feel toward their child or spouse, or any frustration they express toward God and His perceived failures in the situation. Allowing, even facilitating, this kind of open expression is an important first step forward.

Second, normalize the Christian family members' feelings by providing context for what they are expressing. Helping them understand how their response is normal in the situation goes a long way toward keeping them open to working on their feelings and changing their perspective as needed.

Third, help Christian family members focus on what they can control. They can control their emotions (with God's help and support from others), their actions, and their attitudes. They cannot control the beliefs and actions of their homosexual family member. They cannot stop a same-sex marriage from happening. Helping them to sort out the difference between what they can control and what they cannot is foundational to their ability to move forward.

Fourth, help Christian family members learn to cope with their situation in God-inspired ways. God is at work in their situation, but they may have trouble discerning how that is true when so much seems so out of control. As a pastoral counselor, your responsibility is to help your counselees center on God, His Word, and His activity in their situation.

Fifth, help Christian family members develop greater self-awareness, manage guilt and shame, and then move them through the process of grief, forgiveness, and reconciliation. These are spiritual processes; pastoral leaders are uniquely suited to help people with these problems. A personal relationship with God provides adequate resources to resolve all these issues.

Finally, lead your church to be a supportive fellowship that reaches out to all people, including the homosexual community. Make sure your church tells the truth, but in a way all people can hear it and respond accordingly. As we move through the rest of this chapter, these foundational statements will be amplified and interwoven through the presentation.

## Pastoral Care for Family Members

The focus of this chapter is insight and instruction to pastors and ministry leaders for helping Christians cope more effectively with their response to homosexual family members, including those who enter into a same-sex marriage. The previous chapter focused on counseling a person considering or involved in a same-sex marriage. This chapter focuses on everyone else impacted by that decision.

The ultimate goal for family members relating to homosexuals or those involved in a same-sex marriage is to love them, while at the same time sharing biblical truth with them. Generally speaking, adults who disclose their homosexuality to their parents or spouse are more likely making a declaration regarding same-sex attraction than actually asking for some type of approval.[2] They have usually wrestled long and hard for many years with the decision to confess their homosexuality to family members, bracing themselves for the long-awaited judgment and rejection. Yet, when adult loved ones "come out of the closet," they often bring a bewildered and heart-broken family right along with them.

In response to a disclosure like this, Christian family members usually face overwhelming emotions like shame and guilt. When confronted with the reality of a homosexual child or spouse, they often wonder what they did wrong, what they could have done differently, or more devastatingly, what is fundamentally broken in their child or spouse? Christian parents and spouses worry about what their family, friends, and church family are going to think. They may feel their reputation will be tarnished and that they will be judged by Christians and non-Christians alike. They are going to be concerned about their testimony and about sullying the name of their church. In short, when they come to you for counseling, they will come frustrated, broken, and in need of a tremendous amount of comfort and care (2 Cor. 1:3–7).

Comfort through pastoral counseling begins with allowing Christian family members to share their fears and concerns about their loved one's homosexuality in an open and honest environment. When sacred and deeply held Christian beliefs and values are disrespected by the homosexual loved one, strong emotions are likely to surface. Therefore, it is essential to normalize and validate a Christian parent's or spouse's overwhelming emotions. These feelings are not necessarily right or wrong in the moment but simply a normal outcome associated with the painful news of a loved one's "coming out." So, the first goal of pastoral counseling in this situation is helping family members of someone who announces his or her homosexuality to cope with their erratic emotions. Pastors and ministry leaders can do this in such a way it brings a sense of calm to the situation. This first step often includes supportive affirmation and prayer for the hurting family, the homosexual child or spouse, and the watching community.

## Focusing On What Can Be Controlled

Throughout the counseling process, Christian parents and spouses must continually be reminded to focus on those things under their control. The typical reaction for most Christians dealing with the shock of homosexuality in their family will be a desperate out-cry for God to change their gay loved one. A logical conclusion is to believe God desires the gay individual to change; therefore, the Christian is just praying according to God's will (1 John 5:14). While this thought process is accurate and helpful when used in the proper context, a bigger picture looms on the horizon. Paradoxically, this type of prayer could be construed as self-serving rather than having an altruistic purpose. This flawed thinking concludes that if God were to change the homosexual orientation of the child or spouse, then all painful emotions would be resolved or evaporate.

This singular strategy—praying until the homosexual person changes—is not generally effective for dealing with ongoing real-life situations. Prayer provides a vital foundation for the overall process, beginning first with personal prayer and reflective engagement with God and self. Christian parents or spouses may find themselves con-fused in terms of their relationship with God, wondering how God would allow this to happen to their family. Pastors can assure family members it is acceptable to be honest with God about how they are feeling and thinking. They can bring their fears and concerns for their loved ones to Him. Expressions of despair directed toward God can be construed as an act of turning toward Him. They can result in being drawn to God out of desperation, out of the vague need to experience a higher power. No matter the motivation, when a hurt-ing Christian turns to God, He will manifest His presence. God will reveal His grace and mercy in surprising and miraculous ways. Once Christian parents or spouses begin the process of appropriate prayer that reflects their own tried and tested life, they will be better prepared and equipped to pray for their child or spouse with same-sex attraction. They will recognize God will release His power to bring about change that results in relational, emotional, and spiritual healing for the entire family—not just for the homosexual family member.

Closely linked with praying is managing one's thought processes, which must be controlled and guarded (2 Cor. 10:3–5). Pastoral counseling sessions should be geared toward helping Christian family members understand the process of transforming their nonproductive thoughts through God's truth. Specifically, ministers must counsel Christian parents and spouses on how to deal with their naturally negative thoughts, as well as their unhealthy emotions and actions. Counselors can convey that simply thinking about a homosexual loved one may naturally cause a Christian to be "triggered," which results in an automatic release of powerful, albeit, negative emotions (like anger, rage, guilt, shame, betrayal, sadness, anxiety). Typically, these potent emotions are followed by nonproductive, harmful reactions such as verbal outbursts, self-righteous condemnation, and emotional withdrawal. Accompanying destructive behaviors may include crying, begging, pleading, manipulating, avoiding, rejecting, and/or cutting off all contact with their homosexual family member. Unintentionally, these nonproductive reactions do even more damage to family relationships, leading to defensiveness and further disengagement. Christian parents or spouses need to think through their long-term goals rather than reacting inappropriately based on their immediate distress.

One of the best ways to circumvent the nonproductive, negative cycle, which only results in the gay person's feeling punished, can be found in Scripture; specifically: "The fruit of the Spirit is love, joy, peace, patience, kindness, goodness, faithfulness, gentleness, self-control" (Gal. 5:22–23 ESV). At first most Christian parents and spouses who find out about their loved one's same-sex attraction are likely to feel a disconnect with the fruit of the Spirit in the midst of their painful, personal anguish. Partnered with supportive counsel and proper pastoral care, the Holy Spirit can produce the fruit of the Spirit among Christian family members, particularly the fruit of self-control. Unless the parent or spouse does something to break their destructive thought patterns, the cycle of disconnect will continue, causing further damage to family relationships. Counseling sessions can be used to work toward a healthy alternative, helping the family members achieve reconciliation and restoration of the distanced relationship resulting from hurtful attitudes, words, and actions among family members.

## Dealing with Shame and Guilt

In the context of ministering to followers of Jesus Christ, effective family counseling focuses on helping Christian parents or spouses govern *their* emotions, thoughts, and behavior, not the behavior of the homosexual family member. All three of these areas can be resolved in a healthy way as God intervenes in their lives. Romans 12:2 references "renewing of the mind." Since a transformation or renewing of thoughts is at the heart of change, application of this verse will result in a more Spirit-led approach to life's difficult issues. In particular, emotions like guilt and shame often plague Christian parents and spouses dealing with homosexuality in their family. Pastors can counsel and inform them about these primary emotions, recognizing that illegitimate guilt and shame emerge from a line of thinking inconsistent with transformed thinking. Romans 8:1 states, "There is therefore now no condemnation for those who are in Christ Jesus" (ESV). Christians who decide to live in shame and guilt are needlessly condemning themselves. This kind of shame and guilt results from a worldview inconsistent with God's truth, originating from a flawed, unbiblical perspective of the redeemed self.

Even so Christian parents and spouses often feel a certain amount of guilt or shame emerging from their presumed responsibility for their homosexual loved one's same-sex attraction. Some may believe they inadvertently played a role in their child's or spouse's choosing or endorsing a homosexual lifestyle, regardless of evidence to the contrary. By virtue of being a part of fallen humanity, mistakes have inevitably been made by all parties involved, which can lead to feelings of guilt and regret. How then do Christians deal with these feelings?

A clear exposition of Scripture is helpful. When confronting sinful lifestyles among the Corinthians, Paul differentiated between a godly grief (conviction) and a worldly grief (self-pity). He wrote, "For godly grief produces a repentance not to be regretted and leading to salvation, but worldly grief produces death" (2 Cor. 7:10). Godly grief is performed in a believer's life by the Holy Spirit. He convinces Christian parents and spouses of their own sins; He does not condemn them for the sins of others. Godly grief is followed by repentance leading to a change of attitudes, emotions, and behavior based on God's perspective. On the contrary, worldly grief arises from a self-preserving will, the dictates of a natural conscience, and/or a fear of loss or condemnation. Typically, worldly grief does not lead to true repentance, only an overbearing sense of condemnation. It may produce short-term changes but without lasting transformational change produced by the Holy Spirit. Without the Spirit's producing real change, the person will return to habitual, ungodly attitudes, emotions, and behaviors resulting in further damage to relationships within his or her family.

Oftentimes a lack of self-awareness and the inability to accept personal shortcomings are connected to feelings of guilt and shame. Christian parents must pray for God's perspective, seizing the opportunity for both personal growth and healing. As personal wholeness is experienced, it spills over into the family relationships in multiple, positive ways. The Holy Spirit often speaks distinctly and works powerfully through pain and heartache. Pastoral leaders must teach Christian parents or spouses their godly grief is real and a part of their healing process. While they may be focusing on their losses or perceived losses (lifelong relationships, potential grandchildren, public rejection, etc.), God wants them to focus on deepening their trust in Him. Therefore, pastors can play a central role in helping

Christian parents or spouses process their grief and come to a place of acceptance related to their perceived and real losses. Parents and spouses cannot undo or redo the past, but these counseling strategies will promote opportunities to restructure the present that will result in a more favorable future.

Along with guilt, shame is a prominent emotion Christian family members may experience when confronted with a loved one's homosexuality. Shame is an emotion chronicled from earliest times in the garden of Eden. The story of Adam and Eve (Gen. 2—3) includes the first couple hiding from God after disobeying Him by eating the forbidden fruit. An overwhelming awareness of inadequacy and a sense of deep lacking, as a direct result of their real guilt, produced their shame. Shame brings with it a feeling of humiliation, exposing the person's unworthiness and fear of rejection.[3] Shame results when guilt is perceived, either legitimate or illegitimate. The reality of a family member's homosexuality elicits the crushing fear of what others will think. Similar to the Genesis narrative, a Christian parent's or spouse's first response may be to hide the secret and quietly endure the shame. A second response may be to try to reverse the child's or spouse's homosexuality to alleviate the feelings of shame. Pastoral counselors must help family members change this perspective. For their sense of worth, they must shift their focus from changing their wayward family member or protecting themselves. They must turn fully to God and find fulfillment based on the knowledge and acceptance of their relationship with Jesus Christ and His righteousness (Rom. 4:22–25).

## Communicating Healthy Boundaries

A major concern parents or spouses may verbalize is whether they will be expected to compromise their biblical convictions regarding homosexuality to preserve family relationships. The answer is decidedly and unequivocally no. Although family members will disagree regarding the rightness and wrongness of a homosexual lifestyle, family members can agree to disagree on the issue with the underlying hope of restoring and rebuilding healthy relationships. Rather than focusing on the differences of beliefs among family members, pastors can provide valuable assistance helping Christian parents or spouses clarify appropriate boundaries with a homosexual child or spouse. Boundaries represent the "rules" that must be processed and articulated in light of the changing dynamics in relationships. Christians should clearly communicate where they stand on various family issues and what they can and cannot accept. This can be done while also reassuring a homosexual family member of their love and support. Building or restoring a healthy relationship should be based on well-articulated boundaries.

In relationships among mature people each person has to decide for himself or herself what he or she will or will not believe and/or do. Parents and spouses need to communicate what they are able to tolerate and what they are unwilling to compromise when it comes to behavior in their own home, as well as other family activities. For example, what kind of relational involvement can a daughter expect from her parents if she decides to marry another woman?

The answer to this question is not clear-cut. The foundation to the answer lies in this agreement: Christian parents and homosexual children both agree neither will be expected to violate his or her beliefs and values. Each individual's decisions should clearly respect the boundaries of the other, never pushing one's own agenda at the expense of the other's personal views. The development of sensitivity to each person's beliefs and values increases the capacity to maintain contact in these difficult situations. In addition, establishing parameters about family events takes the guesswork out of what both parties expect from each other. Whether Christian parents attend their child's same-sex wedding or invite their child's partner over for Christmas dinner does not necessarily translate into a blanket statement of approval of their lifestyle. Decisions such as these will depend on the level of comfort versus the tension between parent and child. Ultimately the response of Christian parents and spouses should be a reflection of God's relationship with His creation. Although God demonstrates unconditional acceptance of His beloved, He also clearly opposes certain behavior and allows consequences of sinful actions to play out in the lives of believers and unbelievers alike.

Relating well requires open dialogue and communicative relationships, which means talking honestly about family situations likely to be faced because of a child's lifestyle choices. This includes how and when to tell other family members (like small children or aging grandparents) about a family member's homosexuality. The responsibility, ultimately, for sharing this information rests with the homosexual person but must be shared appropriately and in a timely manner. Once one family member is told, the information should be shared in appropriate ways to all other affected family members.

Other specific and important issues to resolve might include displays of affection at family get-togethers and ways of publicly acknowledging any romantic relationship (including a same-sex union). Just as with heterosexual relationships, boundaries of modesty and decorum should be observed, meaning an agreed–upon consensus about things like holding hands, embracing, and sleeping in separate rooms when visiting a parent's home. A line in Robert Frost's poem "Mending Wall" says it well, "Good fences make good neighbors."

Just as with Christian parents, a Christian spouse faces a variety of unique issues when forced to navigate the quagmire of his or her marriage partner's "coming out." For example, when a spouse confesses to a homosexual affair, the couple will need specialized counseling to deal with the tension and uncertainty of their present and future relationship. The Christian spouse may want answers related to why the gay spouse married him or her in the first place. There is no simple or singular answer for why a person who has same-sex attraction marries and keeps his or her homosexuality hidden. Cultural and religious taboos against homosexuality are still largely intact among evangelicals in America. Ironically, viewing homosexuality as being incompatible with their spiritual beliefs may lead some to enter into a heterosexual marital relationship in hopes of eliminating or at least limiting their homosexual proclivity. Many individuals with same-sex attraction may marry because of their God-given need for attachment and connection and out of a sincere love and respect for their opposite-sex spouse.

Just as with a heterosexual affair, a homosexual affair requires both partners to reexamine their marital relationship. They need to examine some important questions. The spouse who has an affair will have to make a decision about what he or she wants to do with his or her sexual feelings. If both partners decide to reconcile their marital relationship, the couple will need help developing the terms under which they will continue to live together. This includes a commitment to fidelity, as well as ongoing individual and marriage counseling to solve the many problems and issues creating and resulting from their actions.

The initial shock of discovering a spouse's homosexuality can lead to extremely troubling emotions, thoughts, and actions. A pastor can be instrumental in helping a couple make wise decisions early in the process that will greatly benefit them in the long run. For example, a planned separation for a few weeks or months may provide time for individual counseling and personal reflection to prepare the way for effectual, godly transformation. A pastor can provide perspective, helping a couple understand their situation and realize healing will take time.

When pastors counsel couples who have separated or who are considering divorce as a result of a same-sex affair, they need to be aware of the similarities as well as the differences compared to counseling heterosexual couples who are impacted by adultery. Just as with heterosexual adultery, a couple coping with a homosexual affair will need assistance to determine how they will handle matters like discipline of their children, division of household responsibilities, providing child care, managing finances, and managing their conflict behavior in front of their children. Generally speaking, children experience extreme turmoil in the midst of their parent's acrimonious marital conflict. Whenever ongoing conflict occurs between spouses, children live in the emotional tension, no matter its source. Oftentimes children feel as if they must take sides with one parent over another. Feeling pulled between parents prevents children from maintaining healthy relationships with both parents, which for the sake of the children should be the goal. The well-being of dependent children will be a reflection of the love, caring, and maturity of parents who are navigating through the whirlwind of one partner's homosexual behavior.

## Reconciling Relationships

We were created with a deep desire to live in a loving and attached relationship with God and others, particularly family members. Pastors have the opportunity to help distressed family members focus on the importance and value of relationships within their family system. Emotional engagement is crucial in maintaining and restoring the connection between loved ones. Reconciliation of relationships involves emotional accessibility and responsibility. Therefore, it is essential to approach the homosexual behavior of a family member from a relational perspective versus a behavioral one. In short, the focus must be on learning to relate to a homosexual family member, not just trying to change his or her behavior.

Relational problems require relational solutions.[4] The idea that homosexual loved ones must "get their act together" before there can be a genuine reconnection is counterproductive to their healing. Speaking out angrily or using harsh words to correct or change a person's mind and behavior is usually unproductive. Talking to gay family members about homosexuality from a biblical perspective with the hope of convincing them they are wrong will most likely result in further disconnection. In many cases the person may have already tried to change or asked God to change his or her same-sex attraction. More often than not homosexuals assume they already know what their Christian parents or spouse believe about their lifestyle. Hearing their parents or spouse reiterate their Christian beliefs time and time again only leads to feelings of repetitive disappointment and persistent alienation. Adult children especially have difficulty hearing disapproval from their parents. The homosexual loved one may conclude his or her parent's Christian beliefs about homosexuality relegate him or her to a future without physical inti-macy.[5] These types of misunderstanding oftentimes result in even further estrangement within the relationship.

As part of providing counsel, one important area a pastor is uniquely qualified to help family members work through is the struggle to give and receive forgiveness. This is foundational to building or rebuilding family relationships. As mentioned previously, godly conviction leads to repentance, which then leads to forgiveness, reconciliation, and restoration. Boundaries that are not associated with ultimatums, but with grace and mercy, are part of a long and often trying process that can lead to building of connections between family members. The establishment of trust within the forgiveness process will more likely occur as a Christian parent or spouse con-sistently responds in godly ways, both emotionally and behaviorally.

A by-product of the ensuing trust between family members is the opportunity for forgiveness of past hurts and grievances. Forgiveness can be defined by a variety of metaphors and descriptors such as a "letting go" of something, wiping the slate clean, marking "can-celed" on the debt, or "paid in full" on the bill. Forgiveness means a Christian will not allow shame and guilt to separate family members from one another. As Christian parents or spouses fully understand the forgiveness they have received from God in Christ (Eph. 4:32), they are better prepared to relate to a homosexual family member. In addition, pastors unveil God's grace in the restorative power of Jesus Christ's work on the cross. Pastors must continually point families struggling with same-sex attraction issues to Jesus Christ's forgiveness, healing, and example of loving all people, no matter how difficult it might be.

Pastors can also help Christians understand sexual sin from a relational standpoint. They can assist Christian family members to understand better the dynamics of how to address this topic in a gra-cious and loving way, aiding the process of repentance and forgive-ness by teaching them how to dialogue with a loved one endorsing a homosexual lifestyle. For example, the use of well-formulated ques-tions (rather than repeated lectures) can enhance communication and increase significant contact. Asking an individual struggling with same-sex attraction to share feelings, hopes, fears, and key points of his or her journey are all good ways to open up communication and connection. As Christian family members learn to listen carefully and respectfully to those answers, they will communicate they are genuinely seeking to understand the other person's experience. Both parties need reciprocal understanding, which is an essential, yet absent dynamic in many relationships. This process serves to increase awareness and insight, which will further advance positive connections between family members. Empathic listening decreases fears and facilitates the deep need for attachment. Once healthy communication is restored, then a Christian parent or spouse has a much better opportunity to be a conduit of communicating biblical truth. Helping a person open his or her heart to hear God's truth is the ultimate goal of building and maintaining meaningful family relationships.

In the quest to reconcile with a homosexual family member, Christian parents and spouses should remain faithful, praying God is at work in their loved one's life. An important relational dynamic to keep this faith alive is for Christian parents and spouses to participate actively in a Christ-centered, Bible-teaching church. Maintaining Christian fellowship helps keep them emotionally stable and overcomes their inevitable discouragement.

Good churches also encourage their members to invite homosexual friends and family members to take part in church activities. Churches that are serious about helping families with homosexual members will be welcoming to all, providing ministry to the specific needs of the individual struggling with homosexual tendencies. Homosexuals have observed conservative, evangelical churches open themselves up to alcoholics, divorced people, murderers, and other people who have made lifestyle choices contrary to biblical truths. Despite the presence of churches who minister effectively in this arena, they may have also witnessed homosexuals treated in less acceptable—even abusive—ways.

Because an increasing percentage of homosexuals believe they were born with their same-sex orientation, as they understand it, confronting their behavior is tantamount to rejecting their person-hood. When churches present their position on homosexuality by being argumentative and condemning, their point comes across as offensive and hinders effective sharing of the gospel. People who do not profess to be Christians and therefore do not hold to the moral teachings of the Bible may not feel remorse for breaking the moral codes of Scripture (1 Cor. 2:14). Can the church with integrity and scriptural support expect an individual to resist same-sex attraction before coming to faith in Jesus Christ? Since the Holy Spirit produces godly transformation, conversion must precede sanctification. Pastors must lead churches to make sure their message to the homosexual community is clear: we love you, but we cannot normalize your behavior. The church's message is everyone, no matter their sexuality, is welcome to come to church, to hear the gospel, and to be transformed into the likeness of Jesus Christ.

Because of the importance of the church as an intermediary of preaching and teaching God's Word, churches must practice proactive ministries directed toward reaching the homosexual community for Christ. A church should begin its focused ministry activities to homosexuals by discussing pertinent issues with their leadership teams, as well as with the congregation. If necessary, outside consultants or trainers can be invited to help the church develop its plans. These might include seminary faculty, parachurch specialists, or denominational leaders who can educate and equip the congregation. The goal is to provide ministry both to homosexuals and to those whose lives have been impacted by homosexuality, sexual sin, emotional brokenness, and/or same-sex marriage (i.e., Charlene Hios, from Bridging the Gaps Ministries).[6] Churches can also offer support groups (Homosexuals Anonymous, Celebrate Recovery, Parents and Friends of Lesbians and Gays, etc.) for those dealing with same-sex attraction, as well as for family members who are coping with a loved one who has openly embraced a homosexual lifestyle or same-sex marriage. As a result of these efforts, bridges can be built among those struggling with the effects of same-sex relationships.

God wants to reconcile all people to Himself. The gospel invitation is not conversion to heterosexuality but conversion to Jesus Christ. The church should supply compassionate ministries to those involved in a homosexual lifestyle by walking alongside them and disciplining them as they would any other person who is pursuing a relationship with Jesus Christ.[7] These ministries must address the issues and struggles of those who fail to live in the fullness of all God intends. Mature, heterosexual Christian believers are essential in coming alongside and mentoring those struggling with or leaving a homosexual lifestyle. As they are learning to live in obedience to absolute truth, instruction and guidance are required as they apply biblical principles in their relationships with God, themselves, and others.

# CHAPTER 10

# YOUTH MINISTRY IN THE NEW MARRIAGE CULTURE

*Paul Kelly*

The school bell rings. Teenagers push their way toward first-period class. The camera zooms in on the banal conversation of three friends. Suddenly an unseen student splashes blue slushie in the faces of the unsuspecting trio. Maniacal laughter erupts from the teenage jock that just "slushied" his classmates. He and his buddies watch the spectacle as they stroll down the hallway. The famous name of the teenage drama is sung to us: *Glee!*

*Glee* drew a large audience among adolescents as it focused not on the popular high school kids but on teenagers who were picked on or teased. The show highlighted the value of all students and the need for people to be accepted whether they were antisocial, disabled, had homosexual parents, or felt same-gender attractions. *Glee* has been one of the most-watched shows of recent television seasons, targeting adolescents with a strong message affirming openly homosexual teenagers. The show characterized those who view homosexuality as sinful as mean and ignorant.

The values of youth culture concerning homosexuality have changed dramatically in recent years. In some ways this is a positive development. Years ago teenage males who did not exemplify stereotypical manliness were ridiculed, called queer, and sometimes physically attacked. Teaching teenagers to stand up to those who bully others has been good.

But beyond this, youth culture has also migrated to accepting homosexuality as normative behavior. Teenagers now explain a peer's same-sex attraction by saying, "That's just the way he or she is." This relabeling of sinful behavior as identity choice is confusing at best, disastrous at worst. Leading youth ministry will become more challenging as the current trend of legalization and normalization of same-sex marriage continues in American culture.

## Unique Challenges for Adolescents in the New Marriage Culture

Imagine Jeremy visits your youth group. One of his school friends, who attends your church, invited him. He seems happy and engaged in the Bible study. He gets along well with the other students. Before the youth meeting is over, one of the kids tells you Jeremy has two moms, his birth mother and her female partner. Does that change the way you view Jeremy? Does it change the way you minister to him and his family?

Now imagine you are leading a Bible study on a passage that touches on the sin of homosexuality. You try to be sensitive to the kids in the room, but Mandy leaves the room in tears. You were unaware she has a lesbian aunt. Mandy has a close relationship with her aunt and plans to be her maid of honor in her upcoming wedding to another woman. How do you balance truth with grace as you care for Mandy?

Or consider this scenario. A teenage boy asks to talk to you . . . alone. You sit down with him in an empty classroom, and he blurts out, "I think I'm gay." He confesses having romantic feelings for other guys. "I know our church doesn't believe in people being gay," he says, "so do I have to leave our youth group since I feel this way?" How do you respond to the questions this young man is asking . . . and to the questions he isn't asking?

Adolescence is a unique time of life. It's a time of seismic changes. Outward signs of the changes are obvious—like the size and shape of bodies, complexion changes, and maturation of reproductive organs. Less visible changes are happening as well. Teenagers are developing the capacity to think more abstractly, hypothetically, logically, and introspectively. Social roles are also changing within their families, in their peer group, and in the marketplace. Adolescents are on a road of self-discovery. They are thinking more deeply about themselves, questioning who they are, and trying out a variety of roles to determine where they fit in society. Because of their unique life stage, adolescents are more vulnerable than adults to shifts in culture, particularly shifts that challenge their sexual identity. Youth ministry in the new marriage culture will have unique challenges because of adolescent stage-of-life issues.

## Adolescents Live in Families

When teenagers grow up in a family with two moms or two dads, they do not view their family as a cultural issue, an anathema to God, or a social experiment. To adolescents their family is simply family. Families led by same-sex partners give teenagers love and support. They help them with their homework, encourage their success in sports or music, set curfews, and argue with them about cleaning their room. These adolescents do not view their families as having something wrong with them. For the most part adolescents love their families and seek to protect their parents, no matter their lifestyle choices.

Adolescents growing up with same-sex parents fare about as well as their peers in terms of academic success, peer interaction, and antisocial behavior.[1] This does not mean growing up in a family headed by same-sex partners is equivalent to growing up in a family with a mother and a father.[2] But, so far, little research on the distinct outcomes for adolescents with same-sex partners has been conducted.

Specific long-term outcomes for adolescents from these families are not yet clear.

Of course, no adolescent is naturally conceived in a same-sex union. The most common families with same-sex partners might include a mother, her child(ren) from a previous relationship, and her same-sex partner. Another similar family constellation might be a father, a child(ren), and the father's same-sex partner. Other options might be a parent, an adopted child(ren), and a same-sex partner; or a same-sex couple who adopts a child(ren). One or both lesbian partners might conceive a child through in vitro fertilization. Same-sex couples (of either gender) can have a child through a surrogate mother. These are just a few of the family formations found in same-sex relationships.

Regardless of how adolescents end up in a family with same-sex parents, to them the constellation is simply "their family." When their family is attacked, they are likely to defend it. They resist the notion they are being raised in a sinful situation. They are likely to defend their living situation and describe their family as loving and warm.

Unique problems surface when engaging students with homosexual parents. Students may be defensive concerning teachings from the Bible concerning homosexuality. These youth may engage in arguments or remove themselves from the youth group (the latter may be more likely). Same-sex parents may be concerned about their adolescent children attending a church that teaches homosexuality is a sinful practice. Since students are minors, their parents will have a significant influence on their participation in the youth ministry.

When working with adolescents, churches also have the responsibility of working with their parents. Adolescent children of same-sex families may attend youth camp, mission trips, or retreats. They may make a profession of faith and request baptism. Same-sex parents may ask difficult questions about the church's teachings on homosexuality. They may be restrictive in what they allow their students to do in church. Youth ministry in the new marriage culture will be different because we must navigate the waters of changing family dynamics to care for youth in those families.

## Adolescents Are Defining Their Identity

Erik Erikson wrote, while human beings work on identity forma-tion throughout their lifetime, determining who they are is a major focus during adolescence. He defined developing identity as the pri-mary task of adolescence.[3] Teenagers are in the process of building a sense of personhood, determining how they will function within society, and differentiating themselves from the people around them. This process includes both a discovery aspect (finding out who they are, what they are good at, what feels right to them) and a construc-tion aspect (determining who they plan to be, how they choose to interact, what contributions they desire to make).

Identity development is largely influenced by environment. Adolescents take their cues from family, school, society, and church as to what kind of person they should be. In American culture ado-lescents are pummeled with a plethora of messages about who they should be. Everything from Google ads to billboards scream at them: you must be attractive, you must be wealthy, or you must be true to yourself! Society presents a variety of identity choices to adolescents, and while there is value in adolescents having freedom to shape their identity, the mixed messages teenagers receive can be confusing.

Identity development operates on several levels at the same time. Teenagers are evaluating their own preferences, tastes, and personal characteristics. They are working out the kind of person they will be: compliant, rebellious, serious, playful, industrious, or spontaneous. They are also discovering their sexuality and hammering out what it will mean for them to be a sexual person.

Sexual identity is a significant aspect of who we are. Adolescents are determining what it means for them to be male or female. The new marriage culture introduces a new wrinkle for teenagers in the development of their sexual identity. More than forty years ago, Erikson discussed the impact of things like lines of dress, behavior, and how the outlook of males and females were growing less distinct. He commented, more than a generation ago, it was difficult to imme-diately recognize boys from girls in a group of adolescents. While he insisted the adolescents could navigate the changes in gender typing, he noted challenges to the development of a healthy sexual identity given such issues.[4]

The new marriage culture expands those difficulties exponentially. Adolescents are now receiving mixed messages from their culture about sexual identity. They must not only identify what it means to be a man or a woman and what kind of man or woman they choose to be but whether their attractions are actually toward the opposite sex or the same sex. The identity confusion creates increasing difficulties for teenagers as they seek to resolve identity conflicts.

## Adolescents Are Developing Critical-Thinking Skills

Because of the rapid development of the adolescent brain, teenagers begin thinking in new ways. They think more logically and begin to challenge the conventional thinking of their parents. They are more focused on ideals, on what should be. They become better at self-reflection and begin analyzing motives. Often adolescents will argue with parents, teachers, and peers as a way of trying out their newfound cognitive abilities and shaping ideas.

All of these processes are new (and exciting) for adolescents. But they lack the life experiences to make effective use of all this new information. Even though their cognitive abilities are broadening like never before, they are still vulnerable to making poor choices based on limited knowledge or experience.

Adolescents are also vulnerable to competing emotional messages. They have a strong desire for social acceptance, which often leads them to faulty thinking and evaluation of potential decision outcomes. Because of the cognitive changes and challenges of adolescence, Christian teenagers may not evaluate the cultural messages related to homosexuality and same-sex marriage in light of their faith. Teenagers have a strong capacity for empathy and may confuse caring for someone with accepting everything that person does.

The new marriage culture is affecting the values of teenagers—even Christian teenagers—concerning their view of homosexuality and marriage. American culture tends to take the Jerry Seinfeld line seriously: "Not that there's anything wrong with it." When you ask a teenager who has grown up in church what he thinks about homosexuality, he or she will likely crumple up his or her forehead and make a statement like: "I guess it is probably a sin, but I'm not sure I can really say what is right for another person."

The approach Jesus took with sinners is instructive in helping teenagers learn to answer this question more effectively. Jesus was hardest on religious leaders who looked down their noses at sinners, condemning their spiritual pride. In contrast, He met humility with mercy. The church must not respond to sinful behavior like the Pharisees but rather with the attitude of Jesus. Teenagers must be taught to process information and respond as Jesus did, confronting sin while loving sinners.

Today the church is producing a generation of young people without this type of spiritual discernment. We have often replaced God's standards with cultural norms. Like the Old Testament Israelites who kept building pagan altars, Christians today keep slipping into the belief systems around them. Current cultural influences are doing a good job communicating secular values. Movies, television shows, websites, and novels are venues for cultural persuasion. Teenagers often lack the spiritual discernment and critical-thinking skills enabling them to challenge these influences. Rather than seeing same-sex marriage as a misuse of God's plan for intimate companionship, they embrace the idea people should have the right to love whom they choose. Churches must train teenagers to think more insightfully and biblically about these issues.

## Adolescents Explore Sexual Feelings

With the onset of puberty, adolescents are ushered into a world of sexual feelings that is both exciting and confusing. Production of androgens for both boys and girls increases sex drive during the teenage years.[5] In addition, sexual behavior of adolescents is greatly influenced by their environment. Parents who talk to their teenagers about sexuality have a greater influence on their decisions than they might suspect. Still, only about half of American adolescents report receiving information about sex from their parents.[6] So, where do students get information about sex? They mostly find it from friends, books and magazines, television, and websites.[7] Youth culture expert Walt Mueller reports, "Two-thirds of all [television] shows include talk about sex and 35 percent of all shows include sexual behaviors."[8] This is especially troubling because studies have shown exposure to sexual content on television tends to predict teenage sexual behavior.[9]

According to Jeffrey Arnett, "Sex cannot be understood apart from its cultural context."[10] The cultural values and messages about sex determine the context in which adolescents experience their sexual nature. The sexual scripts teenagers learn largely determine their understanding of the meaning of sex and how sexual relationships should develop. Sexual scripts also suggest the meaning of relationships to gay, lesbian, and bisexual teenagers although it is not as prevalent as the culture makes it seem. In a study cited by Arnett, less than one-fourth of adolescents who reported an attraction to same-sex peers ever participated in same-sex behavior.[11] Even fewer identified themselves as gay or lesbian.[12]

The new marriage culture encourages adolescents to explore sexual orientation as part of developing their sexual identity. Hormonal changes, discomfort and confusion related to their sexual feelings, and lack of parental input, along with cultural scripts validating homosexual expressions of sexuality, are a potent mixture of sexual confusion for teenagers. Churches must acknowledge emerging sexuality among young believers and guide them to embrace a Christian perspective on these issues.

## Adolescents Experience Same-Sex Attraction

One researcher claims 10 percent of American high school-age youth self-identify as gay, lesbian, or bisexual.[13] Other studies suggest this number is between 4 and 7 percent.[14] There are many reasons for these feelings. While exploring those reasons may be helpful for counselors, it seems more profitable for churches to equip teenagers to address the temptation, rather than analyze its many causes.

How can teenagers experiencing same-sex attraction resolve these issues? Mark Yarhouse describes the inner narrative often heard by a teenager who experiences same-sex attraction: "The reason you are experiencing attraction to members of your same sex is because you ARE homosexual. The only way you can be true to who you really are, is to embrace those feelings, admit who you are, and act on those feelings with members of your gender. Attraction equals identity equals behavior."[15]

That is not an appropriate narrative given the way the Bible presents homosexuality. Paul wrote to the Corinthians:

> Or do you not know that the unrighteous will not inherit the kingdom of God? Do not be deceived: neither the sexually immoral, nor idolaters, nor adulterers, nor men who practice homosexuality, nor thieves, nor the greedy, nor drunkards, nor revilers, nor swindlers will inherit the kingdom of God. And such were some of you. But you were washed, you were sanctified, you were justified in the name of the Lord Jesus Christ and by the Spirit of our God. (1 Cor. 6:9–11 ESV)

The Bible clearly condemns the sin of homosexuality. While some Corinthian believers had formerly engaged in homosexual practices, those sins did not define their current identity. Rather, they were cleansed from sin by the power of Jesus Christ and found their identity in Him. Did that mean they never felt temptation again? That's doubtful! Former coveters are still tempted by greed. Former adulterers are still tempted by illicit sex. Those who have committed homosexual sin will likely continue to experience temptation to commit those sins again. Helping adolescents overcome same-sex attraction involves teaching them to separate attraction from identity and temptation from behavior.

In the new marriage culture, more teenagers will openly discuss issues concerning same-sex attraction with youth leaders. We need to communicate a better narrative than the one offered by our culture. We need to separate attraction/temptation from identity/behavior and teach adolescents to manage their sexuality, including same-sex attraction, in a healthy manner.

# Changes for Youth Ministry in the New Marriage Culture

Recently, while leading a discussion among adult youth leaders, I asked, "In the new marriage culture, what changes do you foresee in youth ministry?" A long silence followed the question. Then one woman in the back of the room said, "I really don't see any change. Our calling is to love teenagers and to lead them to faith in Christ. That really doesn't change if their parents are of the same sex."

While at first her answer surprised me, ultimately, she was right. When Jesus told us to go into all the world and make disciples, He knew the people we would encounter would be from all kinds of sinful backgrounds. Jesus promised to empower us for this difficult task (Acts 1:8). The call to make disciples includes reaching out to everyone including homosexual teenagers or straight kids with same-sex parents.

Still, how we reach and teach young people must be adapted to cultural surroundings. The current rush toward normalization of same-sex marriage is creating a huge cultural shift which impacts youth ministry. Effective youth leaders need three core pastoral skills: caring, leading, and teaching. While these skills are timeless, expanding and adapting them is necessary in every generation. The new marriage culture is simply the latest cultural anomaly demanding we adjust how youth leaders care, lead, and teach.

## Caring for Youth in the New Marriage Culture

Because of some unique issues, caring for teenagers is different from pastoral care for adults. Twenty-four percent of American high school students say they have considered suicide, and 3 percent have actually attempted it.[16] Most teenagers have at least one sexual partner by the time they finish high school, and many have had several.[17] Mueller reported, "By the time they reach their senior year in high school, more than half of all teenagers have used an illicit drug (53.5 percent), 47 percent have used marijuana, three-quarters have used alcohol (75.1 percent), and half have used cigarettes (50 percent)."[18]

Pastoral care of teenagers requires youth leaders to develop a high level of empathy, listening skills, and crisis-management skills.

The new marriage culture does not change the pastoral skills needed by youth leaders, but it does present a new set of challenges. My consultations with youth ministers across the country reveals these trends: more teenagers are self-identifying as gay or lesbian, more are experimenting with homosexual behavior, and most now affirm the culture's approval of same-sex marriage.

Today you may encounter a teenage girl who tells you she is sexually active with her girlfriend. You may find two teenage boys making out in a dark room in the church. You may have a teenager refuse to visit your church because she has two moms. These new situations demand new applications of traditional pastoral skill sets. How do you provide pastoral care to youth in situations like these? Here are five suggestions.

*Deal with your sense of discomfort about homosexuality.* One youth minister asked me how to deal with students coming to his youth group because of their attraction *to him.* Their homosexual advances were discomforting, and the situation seemed overwhelming. As a youth leader you may feel repulsed by the behavior of some young people. You may need to adjust your attitude to see troubled teenagers as people Jesus loves.

*Know when to refer someone for specialized counseling.* As a youth leader, your goals should include building a team of people who can help with any problem you encounter. Realizing you are not the best person to help each teenager does not reveal a lack of compassion or competence. Rather, it indicates you are aware of your limitations and value the skills of others. You are committed to pastoral care for every person, no matter who gives it or receives the credit.

*Communicate with compassion.* Teenagers need to know they can talk honestly with you about their problems and concerns. They need to know you will not turn your back on them because they discuss a taboo subject with you. When you respond with compassion, you encourage them to face their fears and confront inappropriate behavior, knowing they have your support rather than condemnation.

*Be clear about the biblical teachings related to homosexuality.* The Bible clearly identifies homosexual behavior as sinful, but it also provides hope for overcoming it. People can be forgiven any past sin and sanctified from any current sinful pattern by Jesus (1 Cor. 6:9–11).

*Provide hope.* So many teenagers have bought into the cultural script, "You experience same-sex feelings because you are homosexual, and the only way to be true to yourself is to act on your feelings." As a pastoral leader, help teenagers establish their identity in Jesus and what He says about them. While this process may be a prolonged struggle, hold out consistent hope that change is possible.

## Leading Youth Ministry in the New Marriage Culture

Many leadership issues in youth ministry are similar to leadership needs in other ministries: modeling, vision-casting, strategic planning, and so forth. Some issues, however, are unique to youth ministry leadership. Teenagers are minors, and because of their level of energy and excitement, the need for oversight is much greater. Youth ministry events often involve arranging transportation, collecting permission slips, securing medical releases, and providing appropriate protocols for safety and security.

The new marriage culture adds some additional issues to this list for youth ministry leaders. Some of these issues include:

*Make logistical plans to account for teenagers experiencing same-sex attraction.* For example, a typical youth mission trip includes multiple teenagers of the same gender sharing a hotel room. Previously the biggest concern has been about those teenagers sneaking out of their rooms at night and getting into trouble. Today a new concern is managing same-sex attraction and experimentation among teenagers. As a youth ministry leader, you may have confidential information about same-sex attraction temptations among some under your care. Managing this, without calling undue attention to it, is a new leadership challenge for youth ministers.

*Make your youth group safe for teenagers with same-sex attraction.* Bullying is alive and well in many youth groups. Clearly it is unacceptable to make fun of or intimidate anyone. Teenagers must be taught how to love and accept homosexual peers while walking the fine line between accepting them into the group without condoning their behavior. To reach sexually confused teenagers with the gospel, we have to accommodate them at events where the gospel is preached and lived.

*Make careful decisions about sponsor issues.* It is now necessary for more than one adult to be with any group of teenagers. Adults must be more careful about issues like dressing in front of teenagers, sharing sleeping quarters on youth trips, and being alone with any youth group member, even a person of the same gender. These policies for adult sponsors accomplish several goals: protecting sponsors from false accusations, assuring the safety and well-being of youth participants, and absolving the church of any question about its integrity in making its ministry available to all people.

*Plan to accommodate single homosexual parents or same-sex parental couples who attend youth activities.* A youth ministry should have an open-door policy with parents—all parents. Parents are always welcome to observe a Bible study or event in which their adolescent children are participating. Parents often want to know, and need to know, what their children are experiencing at church. Homosexual single parents or same-sex parental couples are no different. Your youth ministry must plan to include them, in appropriate ways, as parents with youth in your program. The same limitations should apply to all parents who want to observe the youth ministry.

## Teaching Youth in the New Marriage Culture

The auditorium was packed full of teenagers. The preacher was addressing the fall of humanity, the story of Adam and Eve. As an aside he remarked, "And remember, God created Adam and Eve, not Adam and Steve." Most of the Christian audience nodded; a few snickered. After the service one young man made a beeline for the preacher. "I need to talk to you about your comment concerning gay people," he said. "I disagree with you. We are supposed to love all people, even homosexuals. It's wrong to ridicule them." The ensuing dialogue did not solve the problem!

Too often Christians boil our theology down to bumper-sticker slogans. Particularly related to new marriage culture issues, we often use cute phrases to curry favor with an audience we assume already supports our perspective. Youth leaders who approach teaching on homosexuality, gender issues, or other aspects of the new marriage culture in this way will find increasing resistance to their message. Many common approaches need to be avoided or revamped.

For example, some youth leaders rail against homosexuality. They ignore all other kinds of sin, from gluttony to gossip to adultery, and are unwilling even to engage in conversations with those who practice homosexuality. Their attitude communicates disdain for gay teenagers who conclude all Christians must hate them. This teaching approach encourages bullying or verbally ridiculing people who struggle with same-sex temptations or who may be living out homosexual behaviors.

On the other extreme some youth leaders now teach homosexual behavior is an acceptable alternative to heterosexuality. They have bought into the cultural myth homosexuality is a God-given sexual preference. They equate sexuality with ethnicity and make practicing sexuality a civil right. This kind of reckless approach to teaching the Bible must be avoided. Teach the truth no matter how difficult it may be.

In some cases youth leaders avoid these two extremes by simply ignoring the subject all together. This is unconscionable today. Homosexuality, same-sex marriage, and related issues are pressing social realities. Teenagers are being bombarded with erroneous information about these matters. Youth ministry leaders must teach the truth about these issues. The current cultural shift on these issues means the church cannot be silent in the future. Teenagers are still developing their set of moral beliefs. We must teach them what the Bible says and guide them to Scripture for their standard. Youth leaders can focus on the following core truths as foundational to teaching about sexuality in the new marriage culture:

*God loves all people.* Jesus died on the cross for everyone, and every sin can be forgiven. This includes those tempted by same-sex attraction, teenagers experimenting with same-sex practices, and people who identify as gay or lesbian.

*God calls all people to repent of their sin.* All of us are tempted, though not all in the same manner. Temptation does not determine identity. Temptation is a distraction from the fulfilled person God has called us to be. When we succumb to temptation, we sin. All of us, including but not limited to those who sin sexually, are called to repent from our sin.

*God labels homosexual behavior a sin.* While sexual temptation is not sin, acting on that temptation—either by lust or by action—is sinful. Homosexual behavior is clearly called sinful in multiple passages throughout the Bible (Lev. 18:22; 20:13; 1 Cor. 6:9–10; and 1 Tim. 1:8–11).

*God expects His people to love and care for everyone, including homosexuals.* We are responsible to show the love of God to every person, not just the kinds of people we like. While overcoming cultural prejudice is difficult, it is still essential. The first-century church was full of people who formerly practiced all sorts of wickedness (1 Cor. 6:9–11). The church today should be the same.

*God assigns us the task of making disciples.* When individuals embrace Jesus, we are responsible to disciple them (Matt. 28:18–20). They must be taught to overcome their past lifestyle choices including their sexual practices. If and when they fall into the same sins again, we restore them gently, motivated and humbled by remembering our sinful leanings (Gal. 6:1).

## Relating to Families of Teenagers in the New Marriage Culture

Healthy youth ministry is always family ministry. Teenagers live in families and are largely dependent on their parents for everything from emotional support to a ride to youth group meetings. Parents are charged with the spiritual growth and nurture of their children. Jewish parents were called to make a high investment in the spiritual lives of their children (Deut. 6:4–9). The New Testament echoes the same teaching for Christian parents. For example, Paul instructed fathers to "bring [your children] up in the discipline and instruction of the Lord" (Eph. 6:4 ESV).

Jewish children stepped into adulthood as they entered their teenage years; however, parents still exercised authority and influence in their lives as adolescents. Parents are still significant in shaping the attitudes and behavior of their teenage children. Based on the "Sticky Faith" research conducted by the Fuller Youth Institute, Kara Powell and her associates have concluded, "Parents are usually the most important influence in their kids' lives."[19] The spiritual lives of teenagers usually end up much like the spiritual lives of their parents.[20]

Working with families may be dramatically affected in the new marriage culture. Jim Burns and Mike DeVries have suggested four pillars necessary for effective work with parents of adolescents: communicate, encourage and equip, involve, and reach out.[21]

*Communicate.* Better communication systems for parents will be essential in the new marriage culture. Youth leaders who work with children of single homosexual or same-sex couples will need to develop appropriate relationships with those parents. They not only need to communicate clearly the goals of the youth ministry, the events taking place, and the safety protocols used in the ministry but also specialized information about the beliefs taught and standards upheld through the ministry.

*Encourage and equip.* Equipping homosexual parents or those in a same-sex relationship may be tricky. Many of the questions and concerns of traditional parents will be shared by homosexual parents (and should be addressed accordingly). For example, training on setting limits, understanding teenagers, guiding career or college choices, and many other topics are of interest to almost all parents. Inviting same-sex parents to this kind of training may be much appreciated and provide entrée into relating in a healthy way to them as a couple. On the other hand, it may be difficult to equip these parents with spiritual skills to guide their teenagers if they reject or resist your teaching on biblical standards on morality, sexuality, and marriage.

*Involve.* Involving same-sex parents may be a challenging aspect of working with families in the new marriage culture. Generally, parental involvement is an expected and desired part of developing a youth ministry. Many parents provide the volunteer sponsors, drivers, and support workers needed to make youth ministry work. Participation of gay parents in Bible studies, as sponsors, or in other capacities may present unique challenges. Youth leaders must weigh carefully the outreach potential for involving these parents against the potential confusion their presence can create regarding the ministry's behavioral standards. Policies for parental participation may recognize different levels of involvement and leadership, including the requirement that church membership be essential for some youth leadership positions.

*Reach out.* Reaching out to gay or lesbian parents of teenagers should include intentional efforts to share the message of Jesus Christ with them. Be willing to enter into spiritual conversations with all parents of all members of your youth group. Talk about the spiritual development of their teenagers and connect it to their spiritual development/leadership in their family. The call to youth ministry in the new marriage culture includes the call to share Jesus Christ with parents—traditional couples, same-sex couples, homosexual single parents, and straight single parents.

## Conclusion

Youth ministry is essential to the health of a church. Churches that do not have a strategy for reaching teenagers with the gospel will soon become irrelevant. God has called the church to embrace everyone, including teenagers, with the love of Jesus. That love extends to teenagers who struggle with problems like homosexuality. Effective ministry in the new marriage culture calls for us to deal with our discomfort, our frustrations, and our failures. We must address those affected by the new marriage culture with love, humility, grace, and redemption. May God give us the strength to do it!

## CHAPTER 11

# CHILDREN'S MINISTRY IN THE NEW MARRIAGE CULTURE

*Ann Iorg*

Caring for and training children is an important responsibility for adults. When children are not given what they need to mature adequately, they carry those shortcomings into adulthood. As adults, when they live out those inadequacies, society spirals downward. This is happening today and will only intensify if the church does not accelerate its efforts at teaching children about family, gender, and marriage issues.

## Churches Are Primary Training Centers

Church leaders must continually emphasize love for children and their training, lest churches forget the significance of this task. Every child must learn basic concepts to be a productive part of society. These are best learned from someone who cares for them on a consistent basis—first at home, then church, school, and other training venues. Parents, grandparents, other relatives, pastors, teachers, coaches, and mentors are crucial to ensure children grow into mature, productive, caring adults who make a positive contribution to society.

In our culture (and many churches), we are not giving children the training they need in the area of personal identity and family relationships. Therefore, children are growing into adulthood without a strong sense of who they are in God's eyes, their purpose in life, and the proper role and significance of the family. Left to their own understanding (and intensified by media influences), they do what comes naturally, which is to be completely self-absorbed. Instead of copying what Jesus said, "Not as *I will*, but as *You will*" (Matt. 26:39, emphasis added), they say, "Not as *You will*, but *my will* be done."

In the area of identity and marriage relationships, some think, *I don't care how God created me, so I will redefine myself to suit my own ideas.* They also conclude, *I don't care what God says about the family, so I will redefine my family to satisfy myself.* Some simply think, *I don't know what's right about marriage and family, so I will just do what seems best.* Lest we be too judgmental, we must admit much of this confused thinking is a product of the church's neglect to teach children foundational truths about these issues. We have not done the hard work of communicating to the next generation. We are now reaping cultural weeds among adults because we neglected to sow biblical seeds of truth in their lives as children.

The church cannot neglect its responsibility to train all ages in godly living, particularly what it means to be a family. This includes teaching children, even the youngest preschoolers who can be learning foundational concepts. Children will develop beliefs about themselves and the family whether we consciously teach them one or not. When we neglect to teach children, they make up their own beliefs about themselves and the family based on what they observe in the culture, hear through the media, or learn from secular teachers. We can be sure these influences will not teach a biblical viewpoint or reach a suitable theological conclusion.

The home and church are primarily assigned this teaching task by God, not schools or the government. The training must be a mutual effort both at home and at church. The best scenario is when a common message is heard and reinforced in both settings. But since some children grow up in families where sound teaching is neglected, the church must make it possible for every child to receive godly instruction. The church cannot leave the entire teaching responsibility to the family, lest many children be left out all together.

When adults tell me they grew up in church but never learned anything about the Bible, I am deeply saddened. How can this be? We cannot be so spiritually self-centered at church we forget the task of teaching others, especially children. Jesus said the greatest commandment is to love God, and the second is to love our neighbor as ourselves (Matt. 22:37–39). Being a church member means loving others by serving them, not just going to church to get our needs met. Not everyone is gifted to teach children, but everyone can share the responsibility to ensure a quality teaching program for children. Those who cannot teach can assist by keeping things organized, recorded, supplied, and funded so teachers can do the important work of training little ones.

We must redouble our commitment to training children as a priority in the church. What we plant in a child's life from birth through age twelve, we will later reap in society. Ways of thinking and relating about marriage and family, developed in childhood, will definitely carry over into adulthood. Adults can and do change, but change is much more difficult as a person gets older. Better to teach the right perspective when a person is young and pliable. Therefore, parents and adults in church must consistently teach children not only for their individual benefit but for society as a whole. What the next generation will believe about gender issues, sexuality, marriage, and the family depends on these efforts.

Even though what a child learns at church is important, the greatest influence in a child's life is still his or her immediate family. The church has a primary role, not only of teaching children but of helping parents learn to model and teach truth at home. Since many Christian parents did not grow up in church or have good examples of parenting at home, the church must intentionally train them how to teach their children. Doing this is an important component of a good children's ministry and helps parents partner with their church in training their children.

Churches also have the opportunity to be the "family of God" to many children who have little or no Christian influence in their homes. It can model being a big family where children see many examples of godly relationships. This also helps strengthen Christian families, for when children doubt mom and dad, the larger church family reaffirms what is right. Children need many good influences to help them learn. They definitely need teachers—but also mentors, examples, and encouragers—to help them grow. The current cultural confusion about marriage will only be overcome in the next generation by a concerted effort from all of us. It begins with addressing key issues in teaching children to navigate issues raised by the new marriage culture.

## Foundational Issues for Teaching Children

Every culture has strayed from the biblical ideal in some way. The new marriage culture is just the latest deviation. Christian adults who know Scripture must diligently teach children, being careful to emphasize certain points when the culture is swaying people in a different direction. Helping children understand what the Bible says and *how* and *why* it is different from what culture says are both important.

### Teach God-Given Identity, Not Individual Rights

In teaching children, we must emphasize biblical concepts of identity in Jesus Christ and God's purposes for them. We teach children God is all-powerful and allows us to be a small part of His plan because He loves us. One important method for teaching children these truths is helping them learn through Bible stories. Moses led the Israelites out of Egypt not because it was his plan but because that was God's purpose for his life (Exod. 2—3). Joseph was sold into slavery and spent time in prison only to conclude ultimately this was all part of God's purpose for him. Joseph told his brothers, "You intended to harm me, but God intended it all for good. He brought me to this position so I could save the lives of many people" (Gen. 50:20 NLT).

God has a purpose for every person He creates, "Your eyes saw me when I was formless; all my days were written in Your book and planned before a single one of them began" (Ps. 139:16). God makes each person exactly as he or she is for His purposes. In America we often tell our children, "You can be whatever you want to be." This may be the American dream, but it is not biblically correct. We should teach, "You can be whatever *God wants you to be.*" By emphasizing God-given identity and purpose in life, we lay the foundation to counteract the cultural emphasis on changing gender or defining family roles to suit ourselves.

In the new marriage culture, we are reaping the results of an extreme focus on individualism and personal rights. Americans customarily are told to "have it your way." Taken to the extreme, people believe they can decide their gender and definition of family, no matter how this affects society. We have lost our sense of community and sharing life together. Preserving families and children are critical in building a strong civilization. This does not mean everyone should marry and raise children, but it does mean everyone works together to support and protect the family. Paul and Miriam are biblical examples of people who used their influence to protect the institution of the family, even though they were not married. Paul wrote extensively on the family (Col. 3:18–21; Eph. 5:22—6:4; 1 Cor. 7:1–7), and Miriam wisely protected her baby brother, Moses (Exod. 2:4–8). Jesus also highly valued marriage, family, and children (Matt. 5:31–32; 19:3–9, 13–15; Mark 10:2–16). Jesus' disciples, not Jesus, neglected to bless the children (Matt. 19:13–15; Mark 10:13–16; Luke 18:15–17). We must not make the same mistake today.

## Teach Personal Growth, Not Altered Identity

As we establish our identity in God's purpose, we must eventually come to grips with our imperfections and the imperfections of others. If what God makes is good, then why are we so flawed, and how do we manage those shortcomings? Part of helping children establish their identity is teaching them to understand weaknesses within God's purposes. Rejecting those real or perceived weaknesses leading to an altered identity (like through gender-altering behavior or gender-change surgery) is not the solution. God wants us to be shaped by the process of overcoming weaknesses leading to self-improvement, not to becoming someone we are not. If we do not see value in our total being, including our weaknesses, we will ultimately reject our identity rather than attempt to develop our God-given identity.

We must teach and model for children how to value flaws and weaknesses as opportunities for personal growth, not as indicators we need to become someone we are not. We all have things we do not like about ourselves, but these are areas to improve, not signs God made a mistake when making us. We should be free to become the best version of ourselves without changing our identity and rejecting God's best in our lives.

I want to be the best possible version of Ann Iorg. I work on my weaknesses and depend on God to help me. But I am not trying to become someone else. We teach children to improve themselves but only after accepting God made them, weaknesses and all. Bible stories are terrific teaching tools to help children understand this concept. Moses had a speech impediment. Joseph was cocky. Jacob was a deceiver. Paul had poor eyesight. The Bible points out these weaknesses so we can identify with them, not idolize them. We must teach children to accept their identity, see value in their imperfections, and focus on personal growth instead of rejecting who God made them to be. Our imperfections cause us to depend on God and are therefore a necessary part of our relationship to Him.

## Teach about the Family

"The family" is a subject churches often teach adults but not children. To counteract the new marriage culture, we must teach children the biblical ideal of the family and how to deal with the reality of less than ideal family life today. This can be a sticky problem. Children do not usually get to choose their family. They are either born into a family or chosen by adults and placed in a family. When teaching children about the family, be sensitive to the family dynamics of the children in your class. They may represent a variety of family backgrounds and have many questions, concerns, or doubts, especially if you only present the "ideal" family without teaching about the reality of family life today.

Even though families are flawed, do not hesitate to teach biblical ideals. Children will someday be family leaders and can later make different and better choices about family life. They can strive for what God has planned as they grow older. While I was teaching on the family in a fifth-grade Sunday school class, a girl from a rough background told me, "After I have been married and divorced a few times, then I will look for a really great guy." She had no other model from her home except repeated divorce and remarriage. We had to help her see she could look for a really great guy the first time around!

As part of teaching on the family, we must help children see how God takes care of them in an imperfect world. Just because family dynamics are not according to God's ideal does not mean a person cannot have a full and meaningful life. The Bible gives us many examples. God provided for Ruth and Naomi as they cared for each other (Ruth 1–4). God preserved Moses' life while he was raised by Pharaoh's daughter (Exod. 2:9–10). God protected Joseph during his teenage years as a slave (Gen. 37:18–28; 39:1–6). God guided King Josiah after his father died when he was only eight years old (2 Kings 22—23; 2 Chron. 34—35). Daniel stayed close to God even when he was taken into captivity as a teenager (Dan. 1:3–6). These stories are good examples of God's caring for children in less than ideal family circumstances. We teach ideals and acknowledge imperfections. By doing so honestly, we help children learn to trust God through the family chaos they may currently be experiencing.

My father died when I was twelve. The rest of my life has been lived without an earthly father. God put many men in my life to compensate for my loss; uncles, friends, pastors, and teachers affirmed me and showed me a father's love and a father's image. Many children come from less than ideal families for any number of reasons, usually not the child's fault or responsibility. Teach children that God loves them and will sustain them through the challenges their family life may present.

Another aspect of countermanding the new marriage culture is teaching children the value of gender roles and differences. God did not create just one kind of person. He created two distinct genders, male and female (Gen. 1:27; 2:18–24). He then created great variety within those two genders—multiple ethnicities, personalities, cultures, and languages. Why? The answer: God is a relational being. He created humankind ultimately as a reflection of the kind of relational being He is (Gen. 1.26). He wants to relate to us. That is humbling! He also wants us to relate well to one another, celebrating our differences and being enriched by them.

Sadly, we often fall short of God's relational ideal. Too many people today belittle gender role differences instead of celebrating and appreciating them. We want everyone to be like us, think like us, act like us, or look like us. Yet God loves variety. Think of the diversity in the animal kingdom alone. An elephant is completely different from a shrimp! God delights in making unique creatures and partnering them for the common good. Humankind is the ultimate expression of God's desire for compatibility in relationships (Gen. 2:24–25).

Children must be taught to value their gender, celebrate its uniqueness, value the opposite gender, and appreciate the opposite gender's uniqueness. Each person, of each gender, can contribute to making other people whole. As adult men and women, we must teach and model affirming gender roles, differences, and positive features. Ridiculing the opposite sex and trying to make them act like us is counterproductive. Children must be shown the value of their gender and that there is value in every person of both genders. One of the reasons for same-sex attraction is a misguided belief it is easier and more fulfilling to relate intimately to someone of the same gender. Teaching children to value gender differences, as well as teaching them how gender differences can enrich their lives, are important steps toward helping them achieve wholeness in who they were created to be. Those who embrace male/female differences and learn from them enjoy a much more balanced life.

## Teach a Comprehensive Curriculum

Finally, as we teach children, we need to be sure we are teaching a well-rounded curriculum that integrates a comprehensive biblical worldview. This may seem like a formidable goal for children's curriculum, but fortunately many good options are available to assist churches of every size. Children need to learn how God intersects every area of our lives. We need to help children understand how God is at work in their family, in the church, in their community, in themselves, and even in the natural world.

Some churches make a serious error by simply pulling together videos, Bible stories, and activities in a haphazard way to keep children entertained. They lack a cohesive curriculum plan for developing children through their teaching program. A careful curriculum design has been developed by LifeWay Christian Resources and is described in materials like "Levels of Biblical Learning" and "Learning as They Grow." Both of these resources list eight topics every child needs to learn as part of foundational training: (1) God (God the Father), (2) Jesus (God the Son), (3) Bible, (4) creation, (5) self, (6) family, (7) church, and (8) community. Then, as children get a bit older, two other topics are added: Holy Spirit (God the Spirit) and salvation.

LifeWay's children's curriculum is based on communicating these topics thoroughly and in age-appropriate ways. A child who consistently goes to Bible study in a church that effectively uses this curriculum (or one with a similar strategic design) will, over time, receive comprehensive biblical worldview training. This helps children grow up with a solid, general understanding of God and prepares them for more specific studies later in life.

There are lots of options among curriculum suppliers, but whatever your church chooses, insist it has a sound curriculum design. Be sure your children's teaching program is not focusing on narrow topics or designed primarily to entertain. Insist your church lays a thorough foundation of truth about God and life through a teaching ministry for children. Whatever gaps are left in the theological development of children will have to be repaired later through intense study as teenagers and adults. Sadly, the life damage done in the meantime, particularly in poor choices about gender and marriage issues, may be difficult to overcome.

# Training Volunteers to Minister to Children

Few churches are large enough to have paid children's ministry leaders, and even then the bulk of the direct ministry to children will still be done by volunteers. Developing a strong children's ministry, centered on a quality teaching program, is a challenging but essential labor of love for every church. Here are four key areas of emphasis when training volunteers to teach children about gender, marriage, and family issues today.

## 1. Train Volunteers How to Teach Children

One misconception adults have is training children can only be done by those who are called just to this task. In reality not enough adults with this kind of special calling are found in most churches to adequately teach and minister to children. We need an all-church effort with many hands sharing the task. Even adults who do not feel "called" just to children's ministry can learn how to effectively help with children's ministry as substitute teachers, assistant teachers, greeters, sponsors, drivers, or other tasks.

Even among willing adults, the reality is most adults are not trained to work with children. They have not been taught about child development or learning styles. They have never studied human development or life-span development. Curriculum design is a foreign language! Teaching children requires training and experience to do well. When volunteers are trained, children are happier (and so are the adults!) and learn far more. The high stakes of teaching children about marriage and family issues today mandates teachers and other workers be trained to improve their skills. The stakes are too high for child care or busywork to be substituted for sound teaching.

Many resources are available to train volunteers for your church's children's ministry. Some user-friendly examples are *Teaching*

*Preschoolers: First Steps Toward Faith, Teaching Children: Building Foundations of Faith,* and *Kids Ministry 101.* Besides these how-to training resources, we must also teach adults what the Bible says about children so they understand how valuable children are to God and how much He wants to serve them. Some important passages are Deuteronomy 6:4–9; Psalm 78:3–8; Proverbs 22:6; 29:17; Matthew 10:42; 18:2–5; 21:15–16; Mark 10:13–16; Luke 2:52; Ephesians 6:1–4; Colossians 3:20–21.

## 2. Train Volunteers to Be Culturally Sensitive

When it comes to teaching children about family issues, we must constantly remember children come from a wide variety of family backgrounds and are hearing competing messages about marriage and family from people in authority (like schoolteachers and popular personalities).

We must teach volunteers to be culturally aware of the situations they may encounter among their students. They must learn to treat everyone with respect, even if they completely disagree with their lifestyle. We also need to help teachers not jump to the wrong conclusions. For instance, in some cultures a wife does not take the husband's last name. This is common among many people who attend our church, for example. If a child does not have the same last name as his mother, that does not mean the parents are divorced or cohabitating. Children's workers cannot make this assumption.

Similarly, if a child comes to church with two mothers, two fathers, or any other unbiblical parenting relationship, we must care for the child and teach him or her as we would every child. Remember, children have no control over the choices their parents make. Our job is to help children make the best of their situation. If we see indication of any child abuse, we must contact authorities. Otherwise, no matter how distasteful or frustrating we may find a particular family situation, we need to include their children in our ministry. We must also keep an open relationship with the parents in hopes we may influence them in their relationship with God at some point.

Many people live the way they live because they do not know it is wrong. As adults, people become set in their thinking and habits. Most are not going to change their minds upon hearing truth about their behavioral choices for the first time. We have to keep relating to them as long as they are open to hearing the truth, even if they are not changing as fast as we would like. We must keep an open relationship with children and their parents, no matter the choices the parents are making, until we have exhausted all possibility of reaching them for Christ.

### 3. Train Both Men and Women as Volunteers

Like never before, we need both men and women teaching children at church. Children need to see men in leadership roles so they appreciate their gender distinctives and contributions. When both genders are present in ministry leadership, children learn to accept and appreciate all kinds of people. When married couples work together in ministry, they model and teach positive family relationships simply by working cooperatively together. If men are slow to commit to a teaching ministry among children, include them in the ministry as greeters or administrators. Simply having them present communicates, both to children and their parents, the value your church puts on children's ministry.

Many adult friends have told me about men and women who taught them as children. When telling me these stories, they usually remember the people and the love they sensed from them more than the Bible lessons. But the fact they are such solid adult believers indicates the Bible stories were also "sticking" and making an eternal difference in their lives.

### 4. Train Volunteers How to Answer Difficult Questions

Children ask challenging questions. Their questions often point out areas we have never considered. This is unnerving to adults who think they should know everything! When children ask difficult questions, we need to answer what we know but also be willing to admit we do not know everything. Particularly on questions about themselves and their family, we need to know what the Bible says and how it applies to everyday life. When a child asks, "Why does Johnny have two daddies?" we have to be ready to answer carefully but honestly. We need to answer honestly that God's plan is for a child to have a mother and a father. We also need to consider why the question is being asked and whether "Johnny" is present for the conversation. There is no formula to memorize for every one of these situations. God will help you explain that while relationships are not always what they should be, God still cares for us and provides for us.

In personal questions about gender identity, we must affirm a child's God-given identity. We must also help children learn to relate to their friends who are experiencing gender confusion. A boy in our community dressed in girl's clothing each day and was encouraged by his mother to live out his "gender choice" at school and be a girl. The girls did not want to play with him because he was a boy. The boys did not want to play with him because he dressed like a girl. Christian parents (and his teachers at church) were faced with teaching their sons how to treat this boy. We encouraged them to treat this boy like God made him, as a boy, regardless of how he dressed. A Christian family, including their children, prayed for this young man and tried to build a relationship with his mother.

Another question raised at a church came from a child who moved to a new school only to discover one of the new teachers had gender-reassignment surgery during the previous summer. Miss White had become Mr. White. The challenge the parents had was explaining this to their second-grader! We responded by reinforcing God's creative plan (Ps. 139), talking about how God made each of us who we are, and how good it is to know God has done this for us. We also helped the child understand some people who do not know the importance of God's plan feel the need to change themselves. They thought they would be happier as someone different than God designed, but that is never true. We can only be truly happy when we live God's plan for our lives the way He created us. Remember the previous section of this chapter—God facilitates personal growth, not gender alteration—when answering these kinds of questions.

## Training Parents to Minister to Their Children

Another important way a church can minister to children is training parents to be primary teachers for their children. This can be done in a variety of ways including having a yearly parent training event, inviting a guest speaker on child training, organizing a book study about teaching children at home, hosting a parenting conference, or developing a parental mentoring program (where older parents coach new parents). No matter the method chosen, here are four key aspects of training parents to teach their children to thrive in the new marriage culture.

### 1. Train Parents to Affirm Their Child's Identity

Teach parents to affirm their child's identity—early and often! Teach parents to speak positively about gender distinctives and differences. Help them develop a greater comfort level in discussing gender issues with younger children and answering sexuality-related questions as children get a little older. Ultimately, provide some healthy tools to fully educate older children about their emerging sexuality as puberty nears.

Encourage parents to participate with their children in gender-based events like mother-daughter parties or father-son campouts. These are helpful to build a sense of belonging with one's own gender. They are also helpful for presenting different models of women and men to girls and boys; so they observe a variety of healthy expressions of their gender. Creating strong gender identity will make it less likely a child will feel the need to change identity later in life.

Opposite gender events, like a father-daughter activity or a mother-son outing can also be helpful. These are opportunities for parents to celebrate their opposite-gender child and affirm their child for who he or she is and is becoming. This can be helpful in overcoming cultural stereotypes. Being a woman is not about being frilly or weak but about using God-given relational skills to be a helper to humanity. Being a man is not about being bossy and controlling but about using God-given drive and strength to provide and protect.

Making sure your child experiences various expressions of these gender strengths from different models helps reinforce their gender identity.

## 2. Train Parents to Model Biblical Family Relationships

We must help parents understand what the Bible says about family relationships so they can teach and model these truths at home. Hopefully this will reinforce what is also being taught at church. Most parents want to be good parents and good spouses, but many do not know how to teach these concepts to their own children. Many parents have never had any training in child development and need help knowing what is appropriate for each stage of development. We can help parents by providing some of the training opportunities mentioned in the introduction to this section. We can also reinforce for parents their "on the way" role of teaching children as life happens. In some cases the church must provide biblical counseling for parents so they can be emotionally healthy and thus give their children an emotionally healthy home.

## 3. Train Parents to Answer Tough Questions

God planned for every child to start out safe and protected in his/her mother's womb. But as parents soon learn, every child quickly grows up and has to live in a chaotic, imperfect world. Too many Christian parents react by trying to overprotect their children. A better strategy is preparing to answer tough questions and providing consistent teaching to equip children to thrive in this environment.

Helping our children move from a safe home environment to the broader sinful world where they will make their impact for Christ is difficult. Children need to come gradually to understand our imperfect world and how to keep it in perspective. As part of this process, they need someone to answer their tough questions and help them make sense out of the messiness of our world. The best strategy for helping children survive this transition is steadily, patiently, and honestly answering their questions and addressing their concerns.

Teaching children biblical ideals is not enough without also helping them process the hard reality that the world is far from ideal. Likewise, if we just show them the problems and not the ideals, they accept the problems as normal. When we fail to help children process difficult experiences, we short-circuit their spiritual development and limit their ability to cope with the difficulties of life as adults. We need to let children experience life, talk with them about the everyday problems they are experiencing, and help them put things into perspective based on the Christian worldview we are trying to develop within them.

## Special Considerations in the New Marriage Culture

Ministering to children at church is more difficult than ever and getting even more difficult by the day. As our culture is changing, here are three key security issues your church will need to address related to the new marriage culture.

### 1. Develop an Adequate Check-in System

Every church, no matter how small or large, needs some type of security check-in system for every child under age twelve. These systems range from expensive electronic devices to simple numbered stickers or wristbands. Choose the system that works best in your situation, but make sure you have a secure way to accept and release children from your care.

The new marriage culture presents an infinite number of family constellations. When an adult brings a child to church, it is reasonable to assume he or she has custody and permission to do so. That adult, therefore, is the only person who should be allowed to pick up a child. Children should be released only to the parent or guardian who brought them and checked them into the children's ministry activity or class. Whether it's a custody battle between heterosexual divorcees or a tug-of-war between same-sex partners, no church's children's workers should be arbiters of such conflicts. Accept and release children to the person who checks them into your program, not to anyone else. If the person who brings the child cannot pick up the child, he or she needs to make prior written arrangements for the child to be released to another person. This way workers have proof of permission to release the child to someone else. Only the person who brought the child can give this permission and only by doing so in advance and in writing.

## 2. Screen Volunteers Carefully

Volunteers staff most children's ministries. The difficulty of finding them makes it easy to compromise the standards for their recruitment. The stakes are too high to continue this practice. Volunteers should be screened in two key ways.

First, do a legal background check on every potential volunteer. A church has multiple ways to do this from elaborate/expensive to simple/inexpensive. If you are unsure how to do this, check with larger churches in your area to see what system they use. Lifeway Christian Resources offers an online system many churches use. While it may seem too strict, the best policy is any person who cannot pass the background check cannot work with children. A church cannot compromise on this point.

Second, set some basic biblical knowledge and behavioral standards for children's ministry volunteers and require them to be met by every potential worker. These standards should not be unreasonable but should ensure your children's ministry volunteers will cooperate to provide a consistent message and witness to the children in your programs. You may have higher standards for teachers and perhaps some less stringent standards for greeters, helpers, or other support workers in your program. Setting standards will not make it harder to recruit your team. People are actually drawn more to organizations with high standards than those with lax standards.

## 3. Keep Accurate Records

Record-keeping forms may need to be reworked to include all types of families being reached through your children's ministry. The old categories of "mother" or "father" may not be applicable. "Guardian" or "aunt" or "foster parent" or "father and father" may be more common. Acknowledging these categories does not endorse these family situations but simply creates an accurate record of a child's family dynamic. An inclusive term like *primary caregiver* or *secondary caregiver* may need to be used (with a space to designate what kind of relationship that person has to the child). The form should also record a child's legal guardian. These days children are being brought to church by grandparents, aunts, uncles, child-care providers, and family friends. Families today can consist of any number of relational situations—single parent, stepparent, grandparent, guardian, adoptive parent, foster parent, same-sex parents, or single parent with a live-in partner (just to name a few!). Listing all of these options on a form is impossible, but we need to know who is legally responsible for a child left in our care at church.

## Conclusion

We have a lot of work to do! As a church, we must be consistent in teaching children, training adults, and helping families. The results will be far-reaching into society. God is faithful, however, and will give us the wisdom we need to deal with whatever comes our way.

Training children about gender and family issues in the new marriage culture is challenging. But doing it effectively is essential to assure healthy homes in the coming generations.

## CHAPTER 12

# THE NEW MARRIAGE CULTURE MOVEMENT AND THE CIVIL RIGHTS MOVEMENT: A COMPARATIVE ANALYSIS

*Leroy Gainey*

The new marriage culture movement has positioned itself as a civil rights movement, borrowing the language and strategies of those efforts to legitimize homosexuality and same-sex marriage. As an African-American pastor and faculty member living near San Francisco, California, for almost thirty years, my perspective allows me to compare and contrast these movements. The purpose of my comparison is to uncover the similarities and differences of these two movements and then to make judgments about the civil rights claims of those who advocate same-sex marriage.

## A Personal Perspective

As a multicultural ministry practitioner-theologian, civil rights issues and same-sex marriage issues are more than theoretical problems for me. As a church planter, pastor, speaker, writer, and teacher, my ministry field has included all kinds of people. This diversity has included being pastor of a multicultural church for more than twenty-five years, which has consistently shared the gospel with Hispanics, Asians, and African-Americans (and many others) including people who identified as gay or lesbian. The love of Jesus leaves no room to play favorites! Jesus does not discriminate based on race, ethnicity, culture, or gender (John 4:1–26).

People who are born one way sometimes decide to live another way. In the 1950–60s many African-Americans put formula in their hair to make it straight or used bleaching cream to lighten their skin. They perceived these changes made them more desirable and favorable in society at large. They wanted to be more accepted. These practices illustrate how far people have gone (and still go today) to meet two primary needs only God can fulfill: acceptance and identity. In my ministry experience persons attempting to legitimize homosexuality and same-sex marriage are doing a similar thing, looking for acceptance and resolving identity issues. Perhaps it is even seen in choosing titles like *gay* or *lesbian* to define themselves, looking for acceptance and identity for their lifestyle among others who use the same descriptors. These identity and acceptance issues are part of what is driving the same-sex marriage issue as people want the acceptance and identity being married brings in our culture. My ministry field has been "ripe unto harvest" with people struggling with these issues.

## A Historical Perspective

When America was founded, laws were enacted among the thirteen colonies that defined marriage.[1] Those laws were based on Puritanical biblical interpretation.[2] People who came to America as indentured servants had the right to marry.[3] With the introduction of African slavery into the thirteen colonies in 1619, a dilemma arose concerning the legality of their marriages. In some states African slaves were considered three-fifths of a human. Therefore, legal marriage was not possible since it could only happen between "full" males and females. Since in most states African slaves were not considered full humans, they were thought of as the property of their owners. Slave owners could do whatever they wanted to with their slaves, including breeding them with other slaves, with their masters, or breaking up families for capital gains.[4] Federal and state laws prohibited marriage between whites and blacks (slave or free). This was not true for other races.[5]

African slaves in southern states received rights as full human beings in 1863 by the passage of the Emancipation Proclamation. Though this federal mandate gave African-Americans equal protections under federal laws, southern states enacted laws depriving them of equal rights, including forbidding marriage to whites.[6] Jim Crow laws in the South allowed harsh punishment of anyone crossing the white-black marriage line.[7] This continued until 1957 when the laws against miscegenation were first toppled in Virginia, the first southern state to legalize marriage between Anglos and African-Americans.[8] In the early 1950s California decriminalized all marriages between Anglos and other races.[9] After the change in Virginia, one by one other southern states granted legal status to marriage between Anglos and African-Americans.

Historically the most significant change in American marriage laws has been the legal status of Anglos marrying outside the Anglo race. The main issues of the African-American civil rights movement have always been centered on political, economic, social, and educational equality—not marriage as a means to equal rights.[10] After the Civil War the marriages of all African-Americans to African-Americans were recognized and given legal status, eliminating the dreadful three-fifths rule. Because of this the African-American civil rights movement never centered around African-American marriage rights, either to marry other African-Americans or persons of other races. The civil rights movement did not include a movement related to marital rights.

Same-sex marriage in the U.S. is a recent phenomenon. The first attempt at a same-sex marriage occurred in 1970 in Minnesota. This prompted many states to amend their constitutions specifically to forbid marriage between the same sexes. Not until 2004, when the legal status of same-sex marriage was accepted in Massachusetts, did this social change reach an apex of acceptance that had historically been rejected by both federal and state laws.[11] When President Barak Obama endorsed same-sex marriage in 2008, the floodgates opened, and change has been pouring through as judges now hold same-sex marriage to be a constitutional right. This has happened despite federal laws and state constitutional amendments defining marriage as only legal between one man and one woman.

These legal changes have had a chilling effect; many Americans now have a feeling of hopelessness about their power to vote on and decide legal positions on social issues. "Power to the people" was a popular slogan of the civil rights movement in the 1960s. African-Americans believed in enacting social change by voting. Homosexuals also have a slogan summarizing their agenda: "We're here, we're queer, get used to it."[12] Their preferred candidates have lost many elections, but they push their goals forward through judicial action.

Same-sex marriage is only the tip of the iceberg of the LGBT (lesbian, gay, bisexual, transgender) social agenda. Their agenda encompasses cultural changes radically different from any other in American history. Laws approving same-sex marriage will radically reshape American culture and change the course of history. In the civil rights era the two laws that made the most sweeping changes concerning the racial balance of power were the Civil Rights Act and the Immigration Act.[13] These two laws changed the balance of societal power, taking it out of the hands of Anglos and distributing it to multicultural constituencies. These acts opened the door for the debate and successfully challenged the idea that some previously unacceptable behavior (like recognizing full humanity of African-Americans) was now culturally acceptable. Changing laws eventually changes the culture, as the effects of these two laws illustrate.

The problem with the current legal changes being promoted by the LGBT community is they are happening in the context of a postmodern worldview. The civil rights movement appealed to absolute truth (often espoused by African-American pastors using the Bible). The homosexual movement is based on relativism, meaning whatever is true for you is equal to whatever is true for me. This relativistic advocacy has not produced tolerance (in the correct sense of the word) but rather ungodliness as all behaviors are sanctioned. Now laws are being enacted to enshrine those behaviors as culturally normal. This relativism is not historically connected to the struggles of African-Americans to achieve personhood, fulfill their civil rights, or enact laws that define and defend behaviors based on absolute truth.

Up until 2004 same-sex marriage was rarely considered a serious or valid option due primarily to the Bible's expressed disdain of this type of union.[14] The historical biblical interpretation of marriage has always rested on the notion it was a union between a male and a female. One obvious point stands out. One of the purposes of biblical marriage is procreation (Gen. 2:24–25). Same-sex marriage may be a new concept, but it is also a concept diametrically opposed to the biblical ideal of marriage because—for just one of many reasons—procreation is impossible.

No other racial group in America has had the conspicuous legal restrictions on marriage that were placed on African-Americans. Because of this historical reality, it would seem the African-American community's experience would engender support for the current same-sex marriage movement. While some African-Americans may choose to do so, there is no valid historical precedent or parallel between the two experiences based on the civil rights movement.

## A Comparison of Root Causes

The causes of the African-American civil rights movement were rooted in the disenfranchisement of African-Americans. This began in 1619 when the first Africans were stolen from their homes in Africa and brought here as slaves. The resulting sociopolitical-economic challenges to African-Americans over the past four hundred years can

easily be documented with credible evidence. Throughout this struggle the African-American church and its leaders have been a prominent voice for reform, based on timeless truth revealed in Scripture.

The present climate for African-Americans is much improved,
though achieving full equality is a continuing struggle. For all due
purposes equal opportunity is available for African-Americans who
want to seize it and are willing to work for personal advancement.
Racism has not been eradicated, and the hearts of all Americans are
not in full accord on racial issues. Discord erupts when race is considered part of a cultural conflict (like police profiling) or the unfair
treatment of any person (like unfair hiring practices). While these
incidents can have a ripple effect, scraping open old wounds, the
improvement in race relations as a result of the civil rights movement
is easily seen throughout our culture.

The causes of the same-sex marriage movement are different.
The primary goal seems to be societal acceptance of homosexuality, including teaching it in schools, advocating for it in public life,
and even finding blessing for it from pastors or churches. The goal
of advocates is not gaining equal human rights but advocating for
redefinition of the institution of marriage itself. Civil rights available
to married couples are equally available to same-sex couples through
civil unions. But that is not enough for same-sex marriage advocates
because it does not satisfy their true cause. Their real goal is legiti-
mization of their lifestyle choices by normalizing their behavior in
American culture.

The rapid cultural change on this issue is mind-boggling. When
same-sex marriage was first proposed, it was inconceivable it could
ever really take hold in a "Christian nation." Those who thought this
underestimated the power of postmodernism to undermine societal
commitments to absolute truth. The general sentiment in America
today is all behavior is permissible because what any person considers
right must be tolerated by all as right. The result is a growing acceptance of sexual behavior previously considered wrong or deviant.

In contrast to the civil rights movement, same-sex marriage
advocates have been opposed by most Christian leaders. But recently

this has been changing. Same-sex leaders are looking for pastors and other leaders who will reinterpret thousands of years of biblical understanding to validate their choices. The LGBT community is now borrowing this practice from the civil rights movement, getting the religious community to advocate for them as part of "God's rainbow family."

## A Brief Biblical Perspective

Since same-sex marriage advocates are now appealing to the Bible for support and since the civil rights movement was largely led by pastors (with a Bible in their hand), it is appropriate to summarize some core scriptural insights on this issue.

First, every time homosexuality is mentioned in the Bible, it is addressed as sin or in an ungodly context.[15]

Second, some Christians in the Bible were former homosexuals (1 Cor. 6:11). All people, regardless of their past sins, can be accepted into Christian fellowship after they have renounced their sins.

Third, Jesus forgave sins but also said, "Go and sin no more" (John 8:11 NLT). All LGBT persons can be forgiven of past actions but are mandated to change their future behavior (which is the same for every person, no matter the sin).

Fourth, being tempted or "oriented" to any behavior is not sin. Being tempted and surrendering to temptation are different. Sexual temptations are real and strong. Jesus empowers us to resist temptation (1 Cor. 10:13).

Fifth, no matter how some churches may define marriage, the biblical definition is clear—one man married to one woman for life. Many Christian denominations still hold this position.[16] Those that do not, tamper with God's standard to their peril.

## Goals for the Movements

The goals of the civil rights movement were always about equal rights denied because of color. Federal and state laws have been changed. There are no longer any legal barriers to advancement. Affirmative-action policies are even being challenged by some African-American leaders who no longer believe they are helpful to African-Americans. African-Americans are now considered competent in any field from medicine to politics. These changes resulted from the success of the civil rights movement.

But even when advocating for these changes, many in the movement taught full actualization could only come through spiritual transformation. Even during slavery African-Americans relied on Jesus to survive their dire circumstances. They believed their most important needs—love, acceptance, identity, security, and purpose—could only be met through a relationship with God through Jesus Christ. African-Americans have achieved much through legal changes but were always sustained by spiritual strength. We have come a long way since we got off those slave ships!

The goals of those who promote same sex-marriage come from a different perspective, leading to different outcomes. Those who consider themselves "gay" (statistically a small percentage) have the goal of changing culture to gain social acceptance of their lifestyle.[17] In contrast to the civil rights movement, they want more than equal rights. They want cultural advocacy. They have attempted to make "gay" a synonym for the new "black."[18] Identifying gay individuals as a new race of people is a new concept. "Gay" or any aspect of "LGBT" has never been part of the world's understanding of race.[19] This concept is conspicuous by its absence in earlier research fields like sociology, psychology, and psychiatry. The "gay" race is not found in any world history books. Homosexuality, until the past few years, has never been referred to as a disenfranchised race of people.

The goal of the LGBT community is advocacy, not equality. They are not satisfied with enjoying human rights (like civil unions). They are intent on redefining society to fit their sexual practices. As we are already observing, this is showing up in everything from "gender choice" bathrooms in public schools to public shaming of any person who dares to speak out on the immorality of their behavior.

## Methods for the Movements

The methods of the civil rights movement were marches, sit-ins, demonstrations, voter registration drives, and demands the judiciary uphold the law. These were nonviolent methods used and advocated by Dr. Martin Luther King Jr. While other groups used more strident, even violent approaches, by far the best results were achieved through nonviolence.[20]

The methods of advocating same-sex marriage have been similar, with one major difference. Voter registration, demonstrations, and passing laws have reshaped the culture's treatment of homosexuals. Some of these, like laws preventing bullying and assault of LGBT persons have been needed.[21] Other laws have been enacted that have gone far beyond protecting individuals. They are designed to change cultural mores. The most visible of these laws relate to approving same-sex marriage.

Using marriage as a wedge to push the gay agenda is still a relatively new tactic, having its beginnings in 1975 when the first same-sex marriage case was thrown out of court. From 1975 to 2004, little public effort was devoted to this tactic. It has, however, gained traction since the first same-sex marriage law was approved in Massachusetts in 2004. Since then, more than thirty states have had laws prohibiting same-sex marriage repealed.[22] While this repealing occasionally has been done by the electorate, more often it has been done by judges. This is the major difference between the same-sex marriage movement and the civil rights movement. The later depended on elections; the former depends on activist judges.

In California, although voters twice made clear they did not approve same-sex marriages, judges have overruled the electorate in favor of same-sex marriages.[23] Since 2004, openly gay politicians (some in same-sex marriages) have ascended to high offices and are pushing the agenda of same-sex marriage.[24] President Obama is the first sitting president to advocate for this position. While the same-sex advocates have won their major victories in the courts, it now seems political leaders will reinforce those decisions by statute.

The legal activity involved in both the civil rights and same-sex marriage movements is similar. Both groups have been socially and legally stigmatized and have solicited governmental acts to provide them equal protection under the law. The means and methods for achieving these similar outcomes came about because laws had to be challenged and changed. In the instance of African-American civil rights, the offensive laws prohibited behaviors that should be available to all persons (like voting or attending public school). The same-sex marriage movement is different. It wants to pass laws that grant special privileges to a select few, those persons who choose to practice a homosexual lifestyle. Advocates of same-sex marriage do not admit this, but it seems the freedom to marry is a tactic to promote LGBT rights as a whole, not simply to secure the rights of marriage in and of itself.

## Time Line of Significant Events

Summarizing time lines is difficult because of the scope of these two movements. But highlighting points of demarcation is helpful in conceptualizing how the movements have developed.

### The Civil Rights Movement

1857—The Supreme Court denied citizenship and constitutional rights to all black people in the Dred Scott decision.

1863—The Emancipation Proclamation was issued by President Abraham Lincoln, which freed African-American slaves in the Confederacy.

1865, 1868, and 1870—Passage of the thirteenth, fourteenth, and fifteenth amendments to the constitution marked significant progress for former African-American slaves (including the due process, equal protection, and the right to vote).

1954—The Supreme Court unanimously ruled in *Brown vs. the Board of Education* that public schools segregation was unconstitutional. "Separate but equal" was abolished as a legal standard.

1957—Dr. Martin Luther King Jr. became the first president of the newly organized Southern Christian Leadership Conference, bringing his conviction about nonviolent social change to the forefront.

1960—President John F. Kennedy issued Executive Order 10925, prohibiting discrimination in federal government hiring on the basis of race.

1963—More than 250,000 people of all races participated in the March on Washington where Dr. King gave his famous "I Have a Dream" speech.

1964—President Lyndon B. Johnson signed the Civil Rights Act of 1964, prohibiting discrimination of all kinds based on race, color, religion, or national origin.

1965—President Johnson issued Executive Order 11246 to enforce affirmative action.

1967—The Supreme Court ruled prohibiting interracial marriage was unconstitutional, and sixteen states were forced to revise their laws.

1988—Congress passed the Civil Rights Restoration Act, which expanded the reach of nondiscrimination laws within private institutions receiving federal funds.

1992—The Supreme Court upheld the policy of the University of Michigan's Law School, which indicated race could be one of the factors colleges consider when selecting students.[25]

## The Same-Sex Marriage Movement

1970s—The LGBT movement focused on gaining equal protection, stopping job discrimination, and ending social stigma. Redefining marriage was not a prominent theme. A traditional values movement recognized the power of this emerging movement and voiced opposition to gay rights, feminism, and nontraditional roles in marriage.[26]

1980s—The homosexual movement was defined by the AIDS epidemic. Those who became ill or died (and their families) had to deal with institutions like hospitals, probate courts, funeral homes, adoption agencies, etc. Many treated gay partners and other family members as legally disenfranchised.[27] They could not consult about treatment, use their health insurance to cover their gay partner, make suitable funeral arrangements, or deal with postdeath legal and financial matters. All of this put homosexuality more in the public eye and, in many cases, in a sympathetic light. It also made clearer some of the benefits of marriage and prompted a shift in the LGBT community away from civil unions to gaining approval for their marriages.

2010—The Supreme Court struck down the Defense of Marriage Act. (In my opinion, striking down this law was the landmark "civil rights act" moment for the same-sex movement.)

2011—President Obama declared his administration would no longer defend DOMA or implement its policies.

2012—President Obama became the first sitting president to affirm that same-sex couples should be able to get married.[28] The National Association for the Advancement of Colored People (NAACP) gave its formal support for same-sex marriage. Later that year the Democratic Party became the first major political party to endorse "freedom to marry" in their national platform. Recognition of same-sex marriage was embraced as a political, social, human, civil, and religious issue.[29]

## Outcomes and Implications of These Movements

The success of the African-American civil rights movement is remarkable and too vast for this chapter to summarize adequately. Personally, without this movement—given the racial history of the Southern Baptist Convention—I would not have been the first African-American professor of educational leadership elected to the faculty of a Southern Baptist Seminary (1987). I would not have had the opportunity to become one of the first African-American pastors to lead a predominantly Anglo Southern Baptist church (more than twenty-five years at First Baptist Church, Vacaville, California). Beyond these personal outcomes, the civil rights movement overcame apartheid in the United States, removed barriers to African-American education at the highest levels, ended housing discrimination, assured fair hiring practices without racial considerations, mandated minority contracting and business development through public works, out-lawed marriage discrimination by race, and stopped public segrega-tion on the basis of race (no separate but equal allowed).

The full significance of the same-sex marriage movement is yet to be seen. Certainly LGBT individuals now have the right to marry in all states. The social stigma of same-sex relationships is lessening, particularly among younger adults. The change in marriage laws has had profound impact on how many people view the gay lifestyle. More people than ever believe homosexuality is an inborn trait. Many people now affirm homosexuality as a badge of tolerance to show how progressive they have become.

Social structures are being forced to change, aided by the judi-ciary in many cases. Thus the divide between the popular mind-set and judicial mandates continues to grow. It will be interesting to see how this plays out. There is a significant counterrebellion among the electorate who are dissatisfied with activist judges overturning their votes. How same-sex marriage was pushed on the general population may have serious repercussions in the years to come. All of us, no matter how we perceive theses changes, have been impacted by the civil rights movement and will be impacted by same-sex marriage for years to come. Here is a summary contrasting some of the implica-tions of these two movements.

## Sociological Implications

For a people brought to America on slave ships, having an African-American president is quite an accomplishment. This achievement took four hundred years, but those hardships have been worth it. Slavery, as a social evil, was wrong in the seventeenth century, and it is wrong wherever it exists today. The civil rights movement helped make this change. In American culture this is no longer a debatable point. Control and dominance of humans by other humans is unacceptable. It deprives society of the best all people have to offer. Racism and prejudice cause one group falsely to feel they are superior to another group, causing the other group to feel inherently devalued. Now widespread conviction among most people confirms this is not only sociologically unacceptable but also detrimental to society's benefit.

The social pressures of identifying as LGBT are diminishing in many places. Although many still have a negative opinion, acceptance of same-sex marriage is growing. In popular culture, opposition is seldom heard except from a minority of church leaders who still espouse a traditional position on marriage. Marches, picketing, or public protests of same-sex marriage are infrequent. The larger community seems conspicuously silent on the issue, which means the mind-set of people has changed, they have given up their fight, or they do not want to engage in arguments with others. Many people may have strong feelings against same-sex marriage, but societal pressures have largely silenced them. There does not seem to be any prognosis for change in this pattern. Same-sex marriage will probably become a more socially acceptable part of society (hence the need for this book on how to minister in this day).

## Psychological Implications

America is healthier when the protections in the Declaration of Independence are afforded to all its constituencies. This is foundational to the document itself. The inalienable rights it enumerates were not afforded to all people (before or after it was written) for about four hundred years. Seeing all people as fully human, afforded certain human rights, is paramount to the psychological well-being of the American constituency. America is stronger, both internally and on the global stage, because of the civil rights movement. The whole world watched the struggle and development of the African-American civil rights movement, inspiring similar events like what took place in South Africa. In both instances what started out as civil rights issues turned into human rights issues. The well-being of people everywhere was improved by the success of the civil rights movement. People in many more places are now being treated equally and humanely with pressure building for change in still-oppressed places in the world.

Before 2000, few people thought about same-sex marriage as something that would contribute to the health of the nation or to the emotional health of homosexuals. Homosexuality was a clinically treatable problem until 2011.[30] Same-sex marriage now appears to be a contributing factor to people investigating the gay lifestyle who would otherwise not have considered it acceptable. Some of this attitude rests on the postmodern idea there is no universal truth or timeless values. As a result, the "human narrative" (however you tell your story) is above all other human standards for carrying out life. Americans are inventing new ways of undoing what has historically been part of the bedrock of psychological health—the traditional home. For centuries societies have believed psychologically healthy people were produced best in a home with a father and a mother, but this is no longer the case.

## Theological Implications

The civil rights movement drew its inspiration, its metaphors, and its sustaining power from the Bible. Preachers taught the truth from Scripture and applied it to political and governmental structures. This was a natural process, based squarely in historic, orthodox Christianity.

The same-sex marriage movement is trying to find religious justification for its efforts. For example, in the case of Matthew Vines' work, *God and the Gay Christian: The Biblical Case in Support of Same-Sex Relationships,* Vines presents, to some, a convincing argument in support of same-sex relationships and marriage, using the biblical text. As previously mentioned, several churches and denominations are taking this position. The problem against this argument is there are no biblical books, chapters, or verses in the Bible where God supports same-sex marriage or homosexual behavior.[31] The Southern Baptist Convention, the largest non-Catholic American denomination, still clearly calls same-sex marriage and homosexual behavior sinful.[32] This has placed Southern Baptists in opposition to their government, taking a decidedly "politically incorrect" position. The former president of the Southern Baptist Convention (and first African-American so elected), Dr. Fred Luter, famously said, "What is biblically wrong cannot be politically correct." He received scorn and rebuke from several groups but continued to stand courageously for the Bible.[33]

Sound theology does not carry much weight in public life today. Voices from other humanistic disciplines (psychology, sociology, philosophy, etc.) have a more acceptable perspective for same-sex marriage proponents, as they have continually changed with the times. LGBT lifestyles, including same-sex marriage, are no longer seen as moral issues but are now viewed only as human rights issues. That is, humans have the right to behave in whatever manner they decide as long as no direct harm is done to another person. And, if someone is hurt in the process, it is still permissible if the law has been followed. Personal preference is the first determiner of behavior and then the law, with no regard for the Word of God.

## Concluding Personal Observations

As an African-American, evangelical, Baptist, Christian, I view life through the lens of the Bible and make no apology for doing so. I am not bigoted, prejudiced, ethnocentric, or homophobic. My personal assessment of all things is determined from seeing life through the lens of Scripture. This is my only standard of righteousness, and all things—including sexual matters—must be judged by the plain meaning of the Bible.

African-Americans, like all people, were created in the image of God (Gen. 1:26–27) with potential to become godlier by adopting the character of Jesus Christ (Rom. 8:29). African-Americans were once legally classified as second-class citizens, three-fifths human, slaves with masters, etc., but African-Americans have always been people created by God to reach the highest human potential possible— physically, mentally, and spiritually. Once African-Americans were liberated from slavery, participation in educational systems and other training has proven our potential.

This pattern will not be repeated in the homosexual community, even with the "blessing" of same-sex marriage. While homosexuals are also created in the image of God, they will not fulfill their potential by actualizing their behavior. Their lifestyle does not contribute to their quality of human life, nor does it contribute to the attainment of the image of God. Medical crises, psychological turmoil, and spiritual wandering will mark those who share homosexual lifestyles.

This conclusion and warning is not popular today. By basing their conclusions on human reasoning, the LGBT community has rejected any semblance of absolute moral standards. They make up rules to justify their behavior, tearing up biblical standards as they go along. The blind are leading the blind, where the smartest or glibbest humans in leadership roles determine what is best and right for the rest of us. This does not change what the Bible says, for the wages of sin is still death (Rom. 6:23). The repercussions of going against God's Word always reveal themselves and eventually demonstrate what is right. These consequences may include disease, pestilence, destructive weather, economic disaster, or even attack from other countries God allows to rise up as enemies.

God's Word warns of a way that seems right but leads to destruction (Prov. 14:12). This destruction is not so much an event but a downward spiral way of life. When we go the route of sin, individually or culturally, we choose to go against God in a fight no human can possibly win. Empires have fallen because they went against the Word of God in their moral practices. Arrogant people think history is on the side of whoever is winning at the time. But in reality history is on the side of the Word of God (Rev. 22:7). May God give us the wisdom to live like we believe this!

## CHAPTER 13

# NAVIGATING LEGAL CHALLENGES TO CHURCHES

## *Brad Dacus*

The changing cultural climate regarding homosexuality, transgender people, and same-sex marriage (and even sex offenders) is becoming more and more challenging to churches today. Churches must address these issues with both defensive and offensive strategies. A *defensive* strategy—that is, policy statements a church should adopt to minimize risks to the church—is helpful. But an effective game plan for churches must also have an *offensive* strategy to maintain relevance in ever-changing communities. In this chapter, after discussing bylaw changes and protective policies for churches, we will focus on an example of a church that has successfully managed to thrive while impacting a community some might otherwise presume as difficult to reach with the gospel.

## Defensive Strategies: Preemptive Policies to Protect Your Church Legally

Newly enacted laws, as well as recent court decisions, offer new challenges to churches regarding how they define and address issues surrounding sexual behavior and gender orientation. Consequently churches should take precautionary steps to protect themselves from legal challenges to their theology, governance, and activities. Such precautionary steps involve a wide range of issues like church employees, marriage ceremonies, facility usage, counseling, and other church-related ministries. While all of this can seem overwhelming, churches must not become preoccupied or be immobilized in their ministry endeavors by the "what-ifs" of potential legal challenges.

Pacific Justice Institute has prepared a number of generic documents to assist churches with managing the growing number of today's legal challenges. For example, suggested language for bylaws dealing with marriage and human sexuality is provided as part of this chapter. This type of documentation needs to be added to a church's statement of faith (sometimes called church tenets, articles of faith, declaration of faith, fundamental truths, etc.) and inserted into the church bylaws. Additionally, a model marriage policy covering applicants, clergy, and facility usage is also included below. This kind of document is an administrative policy and, as a stand-alone document, should not be inserted into the bylaws. Finally, a suggested policy for use of facilities or premises is included.

All of these suggested policy statements should be considered models and reviewed by an attorney familiar with a church's mode of government, legal status in its state, and other pertinent local legal issues. As you consider these policies, Pacific Justice Institute is also available to consult about legal questions or concerns (free of charge) to churches and religious organizations.

It is also important to note these policies are by no means intended to create barriers to reaching out to those seeking redemptive help. Rather, they are necessary in assisting a church to deal with those who are opposed to church doctrine, do not respect church authority, and are willing to use legal means to challenge the church's ability to minister to those struggling with sexual orientation and gender identity issues.

The following section will propose bylaw language for a church to add to its statement of faith related to several issues concerning marriage and human sexuality.

## Bylaw Statements on Marriage Issues

In the past, churches and church leaders have not needed to give much thought to defining marriage in their church bylaws. Pastors would have previously thought, "After all, doesn't *everyone* know what marriage is? Marriage has been around longer than governments or laws of men. The Bible clearly defines marriage. Isn't that enough?"

Unfortunately, the laws of nature and nature's God have been thrust aside by many secular humanists, pushing the envelope on attempting to *redefine* marriage. The courts have historically been hesitant to search *theologically* through the Scriptures to determine *legally* the sincerely held religious beliefs of a church. Without a clear statement of such beliefs about marriage, the courts are now questioning, for example, why a church would deny a same-sex couple the opportunity to rent their facility to have a wedding. Consequently, with judicial activism striking down the traditional definition of marriage, churches are becoming more and more vulnerable to civil litigation if they do not have an explicit definition of marriage in their bylaws.

The United States Supreme Court decision to redefine marriage to include same-sex marriages makes it imperative for virtually every church in America to clearly articulate their biblical definition of marriage. Here is a recommended definition of marriage that should be inserted into the church's bylaws as part of its statement of faith.

*Definition of Marriage:* Marriage is a sacrament (or ordinance or rite) of the church. [Alternative: Marriage has been instituted by God.] This church defines "marriage" as the exclusive covenantal union of a man and a woman in which such union is a lifetime commitment. A civil government's sanction of a union will be recognized as a legitimate marriage by the church only to the extent that it is consistent with the definition of "marriage" found in these Articles.

Part of maintaining a biblical or traditional standard of marriage is being explicit about what acceptable forms of marriage can be solemnized at weddings on church premises. Churches must be explicit about what constitutes an acceptable marriage ceremony and the kind of marriage relationship the church will condone. During counseling of a person or couple seeking to be married at a church facility, a pastor may discover their perception of a healthy marriage relationship is different from that permitted by the church's bylaws. In such circumstances that pastor must be able to discontinue the counseling and, even more important, terminate any plans for the couple to be married by the pastor or have the wedding held at the church. A clear statement on human sexuality, also added to the church's statement of faith, can be helpful in clarifying these issues. Here is suggested wording for such a statement.

> *Human Sexuality:* Legitimate sexual relations are exercised solely within marriage as defined in our statement of faith. Hence, sexual relations outside of marriage (referred to in the New Testament as *porneia*, πορνεια) including but not limited to adultery, premarital sex, homosexuality, and pedophilia are inconsistent with the teachings of the Bible and this church. Further, lascivious conduct, transgender behavior, and the creation and/or distribution and/or viewing of pornography are incompatible with the biblical witness about healthy sexuality.

Another important aspect of maintaining these standards is making sure all ministerial staff the church employs share the church's convictions about marriage. Occasionally a church will hire an employee or affirm a board member who later reveals a different philosophy about marriage. One of the first cases taken on by attorney John W. Whitehead, the founder of the postmodern religious freedom movement in America, involved such a situation. The worship leader of a church had decided to "come out" by declaring his homosexuality. When the church terminated him for violating church teachings, he sued the church for discrimination.

Fortunately the church won the lawsuit by proving such conduct was a violation of the church's religious doctrine. By adopting the following requirement for employee qualifications, a church will be in a stronger position to defend itself in the event an employee engages in unacceptable conduct (e.g., conducts a same-sex wedding) that clearly deviates from church bylaws regarding marriage. For employees (as opposed to volunteer leaders), it is also recommended this statement be included in any written employment agreement.

Here is some suggested wording for a statement on employee qualifications.

> *Staff Qualifications:* All ministers, board members, and employees shall affirm their agreement with the articles of faith and shall conduct themselves in a manner that is consistent therewith. This shall be a prerequisite and continual condition for these positions.

While many churches today do not have formal church membership, those that do should adopt bylaw language that makes clear prospective members are in agreement with church doctrine. The affirmation of agreement may be in writing. While lawyers (like me) prefer written affirmations, many church members are uneasy about "signing on the dotted line" when it comes to spiritual commitments. If this is true, a church can still have this language as a part of their verbal confession and request for membership in front of the church. In this form of church government and practice, the congregation will provide plenty of witnesses, if needed, to verify the admission of agreement with the doctrinal statement. A church would also be wise to make sure new prospective members actually receive a copy of the church bylaws *before* affirming a written or verbal commitment to membership. This ensures they had the opportunity to read the bylaws and know what they were affirming, and it reinforces a church's position on holding members accountable to the church's statement of faith.

Churches without formal membership should still take some steps to define participation and protect themselves regarding their definition of marriage. In those situations, churches can adopt similar language for qualifying attendees for different levels of service (e.g., Sunday school teacher, elder, deacon, persons permitted to serve Communion, etc.). Churches that do not have formal membership as part of their ecclesiology should consider revising this aspect of their practice to strengthen their ability to maintain doctrinal standards among those who identify with the church.

Here is suggested language for a church's bylaws related to membership qualifications.

*Member Qualifications:* Every member shall affirm their agreement with the statement of faith and behave in a manner consistent therewith. This shall be a prerequisite and continual condition for membership.

## Policy Statements on Marriage Issues

As mentioned earlier, churches cannot assume a judge in a civil lawsuit will know what the Bible says about marriage or even if the church believes what the Bible says about marriage. That is why the church should spell out, in its own words, exactly what it believes about marriage and specifically what it believes the Bible mandates regarding marriage. The more theological the definition, the more difficult it will be for a judge to argue with it. Courts are not allowed to disagree with a church's beliefs in their decisions. They are only permitted to decide the sincerity of those beliefs. Churches are encouraged to express a definition that is spiritual and yet understandable to a potentially nonchurched, nonbelieving judge.

While the suggested policy statements below dealing with clergy, applicants, and church premises are boilerplate, the first paragraph explaining marriage should be customized to specifically parallel the theology and doctrine of the church. Such customization makes it easier to prove legally the sincerity of those beliefs. Consequently a church is encouraged not to adopt the first paragraph below word for word. Instead, use it as an example of the kinds of affirmations a church might want to make in constructing its administrative policy on the matter.

Here is suggested language for an administrative policy on marriage:

> Marriage is a union ordained by God. It was first instituted by God as recorded in Genesis and codified in the Levitical law. The Old Testament prophets compared it to a relationship between God and His people, examples of it are in biblical historical narratives, and the wisdom literature discusses the unique unity of this relationship. Jesus explained the original intention and core elements of marriage, and several New Testament epistles give explicit instructions on this union. Marriage is a typology of Christ and the church. As such, the church views marriage as a profound spiritual institution established by God. Due to the importance of marriage in the biblical witness, our church has adopted the following policies.

### Clergy Policies on Marriage

1. Only duly ordained clergy shall officiate at marriage ceremonies conducted on church property.

2. Clergy employed by the church shall be subject to dismissal and/or loss of ordination for officiating a marriage ceremony inconsistent with the definition of marriage in the statement of faith.

## Applicants for Marriage

1. Applicants wishing to have a ceremony performed by a member of the clergy employed by the church or to use the church facilities for a ceremony must be entering into a marriage within the definition of marriage in the statement of faith.

2. Applicants shall receive ___ hours of required premarital counseling by clergy or counselors employed by the church or other persons who, in the sole opinion of the pastoral staff of the church, have appropriate training, experience, and spiritual understanding to provide such counseling.

## Use of Premises for Weddings

1. Any marriage performed on church premises shall be officiated by a member of the clergy employed by or approved by this church.

2. Clergy officiating marriage ceremonies on church premises, whether or not employed by the church, shall affirm their agreement with the statement of faith and shall conduct themselves in a manner that is consistent therewith.

3. The clergy assigned by the church to implement the procedures contained in this marriage policy may, in the minister's sole discretion, decline to make church facilities available for, and/or decline to officiate at, a ceremony when, in the minister's judgment, there are significant concerns that one or both of the applicants may not be qualified to enter into the sacred bond of marriage for doctrinal, moral, or legal reasons.

Some may wonder about the overlap between some of the earlier language to be included in the church's bylaws and these policy statements. The reason for the overlap is because the prior language is intended to be adopted in the church bylaws. The language above addressing marriage theology, clergy participation, applicants, and church premises is solely intended for church policy purposes, not for bylaws purposes. Policy statements apply to a wider audience than church bylaws and can usually be changed more quickly; thus additional issues are addressed in this format.

## Special Situations Regarding Church Facilities

What if a building is *not* owned by a church and is rented out for marriage ceremonies?

Privately owned facilities have already been successfully sued for denying wedding services on their private property. A couple in Schaghticoke, New York, had a large barn-like structure on their property, which they rented out for wedding ceremonies. When approached by two homosexuals wanting to rent the facility, the couple refused, citing their sincere religious convictions against same-sex marriages. The homosexuals sued under New York's public accommodation law and won. Even though the property was privately owned and the couple had sincere religious convictions, the administrative court found the facility to be a place of public accommodation, which required them to provide services for same-sex wedding ceremonies without discrimination.[1]

Many clergy may not think much about this court decision, assuming all "church property" is actually owned by the church. However, such is not always the case. For example, the pastor of a church (or some other individual) may own a property used by the church but is nonetheless owned in the name of the pastor or another person. This can become problematic, leaving the pastor or private owner open for a civil lawsuit if he or she denies homosexuals the opportunity to rent the property for a wedding and the litigants are able to show the property had been rented out in the past.

How can these problems be prevented? Here are several options to limit litigation and increase protections for individuals or churches related to the use of their facilities. First, the owners can sell or give their privately owned property to their church. Some people may find this financially difficult to do, especially if they are holding the property as an investment or perhaps planning on later selling the property to fund retirement.

Second, the owner can stop allowing privately owned property from being used for weddings in the future. If this option is selected, the owner should post the decision so he can adequately validate the policy change was made well before any inquiring homosexual couple is denied.

Third, owners could rent their private property to the church for any dollar amount. It would then be up to the church to make sure it has adopted the proper bylaws to protect the church from litigation.

Fourth, the owner can form a separate religious nonprofit 501(c)3 organization and then rent the property to the organization. Once again the new nonprofit organization should adopt the protective bylaws just like the church and must be able to comply with state and federal 501(c)3 requirements.

The above are by no means all the options an individual or church might use to solve this problem. Other contractual, trust, and/or title arrangements may be considered and applied. Before choosing any of these options, it is highly recommended the property owner seek the advice of a tax attorney and certified public accountant specializing in nonprofit tax law and facility use.

## Proper Exclusion from Certain Church Activities

Clearly not all church activities are for everyone. For example, adults are not invited to be students in a first-grade Sunday school class! Churches can legally exclude persons from some church-sponsored activities. Here are some less obvious, albeit proper and pertinent exclusions churches might consider related to marriage issues.

### Marriage Retreats

Churches sponsor marriage retreats for all married couples who simply sign up and pay the registration fees. But this method of publicizing a retreat can become problematic. For example, what if a legally married, same-sex couple signs up for the retreat, pays the registration fees, and then shows up early Saturday morning to board the church bus for the retreat? What if the retreat coordinator discovers this and tells the couple, in front of other people, they cannot attend because the church only recognizes married couples who are monogamous and heterosexual? The result: the offended couple files a lawsuit against the church for damages due to the humiliation and emotional distress they endured. How does a church prevent this from happening?

In addition to the previously recommended bylaws and policies, a church should have an application form couples complete as part of event registration. This defines beforehand whether a couple qualifies to attend a retreat or other activity for married couples. The application should also clearly state that the determination of who will be allowed to attend the retreat will be made by church leaders in accordance with the church's policies and bylaws. In the event a couple is disqualified from attending, they should be notified before the event to avoid any unnecessary hardship or embarrassment.

## Sunday School Teachers/Church Camp Counselors

Like all employees or paid staff, volunteers working with children should be properly screened. A church should conduct criminal background checks, personal interviews, etc., to ensure potential workers are compatible for the position in question. Generally, when dealing with babies or toddlers, it is recommended male workers not teach or provide care without a female being present as well. And while some women may not appreciate this, only female workers should be allowed to change diapers. Why? There is a much higher probability that suspicions or accusations of child sexual abuse will be lodged against men. Churches should take all reasonable precautions necessary to prevent such risks, even the risk of baseless accusations. Remember, however, in the event there is even a reasonable suspicion child abuse has occurred on church property or at a church-sponsored event, the church is required by law to report it to local law enforcement.

These are just two common situations where a church could and should wisely exclude persons from participating in activities. Other situations are also legitimate expressions of this principle and should be determined with local legal guidance.

## Establishing Appropriate Boundaries or Conditions for Attendees

Churches generally want all who are sincere in their search to know or learn about God to feel welcome to attend their activities. But some attendees, though thoroughly welcome, still need special considerations.

### Registered Sex Offenders

A registered sex offender is someone who has been convicted of committing, at some time in the past, a sexual act with a minor (person under age seventeen). For example, a sex offender could be someone who sexually molested a five-year-old boy. Or it could be someone who, at the age of eighteen, had sexual intercourse with a sixteen-year-old girl—even if he thought at the time she was eighteen as well. Consequently, the church needs to *assess the risk* in deciding what constraints are proper.

As part of this assessment, note the issue of *time* should also be taken into consideration. Generally, the more time that has passed since the sex offender's incident, the less risk exists. However, if an attendee was guilty of sex offender behavior with a child (versus an older teenager with a younger teenager like the eighteen-year-old mentioned above), a church should maintain tight constraints, no matter the amount of time that has passed since the occurrence. This may seem heavy-handed to someone not familiar with such perpetrators. The temptation for sexual actions with a child, however, almost *always* continues to be present in such individuals. Helping to limit that temptation with proper constraints is for the benefit of the entire church, including the sex offender.

Based on the level of risk assessed, a church might also establish clear boundaries on church property of acceptable places (e.g., sanctuary, adult Sunday school classes) and unacceptable places (e.g., children play areas and Sunday school classes) for a sex offender to visit or occupy. A sex offender should also have someone appointed to be with him *wherever* he might go on church grounds. That accountability partner should meet the offender when he arrives at the church and walk with him out to his car (or other transportation) when he leaves. While it may seem uncomfortable for males, the accountability partner should accompany him to the restroom or make arrangements for him to use a separate one-person restroom. A sex offender needs to understand why this is being done—both for his protection from unfounded accusations as well as for the protection of others.

## Transgender Persons Attendance Policies

A church may take a number of directions when it comes to transgender persons participating in their church. Here is a summary of optional policies churches have adopted in the past (and should consider for the future), although some do not seem effective in addressing the issues. Care must be given to balance the need to manage transgender participation with the need to invite all persons to participate in church activities to hear the gospel and be changed.

*Not allowed unless dressed appropriately.* This policy requires all transgender persons to dress like their actual birth biological gender. The concern addressed by churches with this policy involves the protection of children from encountering a man dressed like a woman or a woman dressed like a man. Unfortunately this policy effectively ensures most transgender people simply will not attend a church. If they do not attend church, they will be less likely to experience the transforming love, truth, and counseling a church has to offer.

*Allowed only if no one or no children know.* This "don't ask, don't tell" approach may seem convenient in addressing a valid concern. Attendees can attend as long as no one really knows who they are (or were). This approach may fly in the face of the kind of transparency many churches may strive to maintain. Also, many transgender people still look like their biological gender even after full transition, making this policy effectively moot.

*Acceptance only if postsurgery.* Accepting only post-sex-change-surgery transgender people has a number of problems. First, it excludes those who have not had surgery. Surgery only occurs after the person has had hormone therapy and dresses to solidify the new gender identity, effectively making it difficult for him or her to attend most churches. Second, this policy implies acceptance by the church of the newly professed gender identity if the person has gone all the way with surgery, effectively affirming an identity most churches do not intend to affirm.

*Acceptance only if presurgery.* This approach takes the position if a person has yet to have the gender-modification surgery, there may still be hope to convince him or her to turn away from the decision. This implicitly communicates that some (e.g., postsurgery transgender people) are to be given up, a difficult position to argue from the historic Christian position of hope for all to come to repentance and faith.

*Acceptance only if they stay away from children areas.* This policy intends to minimize exposure of children to something many would struggle to understand, or worse, be influenced to accept. If this policy is adopted, a church needs to make clear they understand transgender persons are not the same as sex offenders. Since this policy is similar to the one which might be in place for sex offenders, it must be made clear the church is not assuming or communicating the transgender person is a sex offender.

*Accept all transgender people as they are.* This policy treats all transgender people the same as all other church attendees. Loving them as they are, without diluting what the Bible teaches about dressing like the opposite gender. This approach will be uncomfortable for some church members, particularly those with children, and may well result in some church members leaving or not participating in church events where transgender people are present.

*No policy.* This approach works only if no transgender person ever visits or attends a church, an approach less likely to work in view of the growing rise in transgender persons.

### Transgender Restroom Policies

Separate from the question of church attendance is the issue of a transgender person's use of church restrooms or changing facilities. Transgender persons see themselves differently from how others see them. Consequently, requiring a transgender biological male or female to use the restroom of one's biological gender can be extremely awkward and unacceptable to the person. If the individual actually looks like the opposite sex, this can be problematic for other users as well.

To resolve this issue, and prevent potential resulting liabilities, churches can establish a unisex restroom designated only for use by a transgender person. These restrooms can be converted to being one-person-at-a-time restrooms. If a church is unable to adopt this alternative, they may simply discuss their situation with transgender persons and ask them not to use church restrooms at all. A more reasonable approach may be to arrange to have them use a restroom when no one else is using it. In order to implement this, the church could have someone standing outside the restroom and/or place an "in use" sign outside the restroom when being used by a transgender person.

# Offensive Strategies:
# A Church Model for Effectively Connecting with the LGBT Community

Now that we have examined a number of *defensive* measures for churches to consider implementing, do not wrongly conclude your church should be solely satisfied with protecting itself. The next significant decision for every church to make is determining the measures that should be taken to effectively evangelize and minister in the LGBT (lesbian, gay, bisexual, transgender) and same-sex marriage subcultures. Rather than a legal summary, a better way to assess how something applies in a real-life ministry setting is hearing from a pastor in the middle of a community where these subcultures are prevalent. One such church is Calvary Chapel of Signal, California. Recently I interviewed Pastor James Kaddis on *The Dacus Report* (a national radio show). Pastor Kaddis was interviewed because he exhibits a fruitful balance of effectively reaching out to these subcultures without compromising the teachings of Scripture. Below is a paraphrased transcript of this interview.

**Dacus:** Pastor James, are there many homosexuals or transgender persons in your community?

**Pastor:** Oh yes. In fact, our church is located in the middle of the homosexual epicenter for Long Beach, California, which as you know, is a bastion for LGBT subcultures.

**Dacus:** Do you ever have homosexuals or transsexuals visit your church; and, if so, how do you deal with them?

**Pastor:** Yes, we have them visit all the time. We start by remembering we are *all* sinners. Churches should yearn to draw *all* sinners to come to Christ. And if you don't allow some sinners to come to church, you have greatly limited the possibility of them hearing the gospel. So we welcome all homosexuals and transgender persons to attend our church the same way we do everyone else. My attitude is simply this: Iif Jesus wouldn't turn someone away, then why should I turn them away?

**Dacus:** Do you have any conditions for those attendees?

**Pastor:** With the exception of boundaries limiting registered sex offenders interacting with children, we are otherwise very much consistent across the board in how we implement conditions for attendees. For example, we don't want anyone in our church exchanging kisses on the lips in our facility. That expectation applies to heterosexuals and homosexuals alike. Attendees must dress with reasonable modesty, and that applies to everyone—to transgender persons as well.

**Dacus:** I know you preach primarily expository messages. So what do you do when you reach a verse applicable to homosexuality or transgender persons? Do you just skip it?

**Pastor:** No, no! It's my obligation to preach the *whole* Word of God so that is exactly what I do. I don't sugarcoat any of it. I also don't go out of my way to highlight one sin over another. Sins have different destructive impacts, but the Word of God teaches *all* sin is detestable in the eyes of God.

**Dacus:** Have you ever had a homosexual or transgender person disagree with you after you mentioned their sin in a sermon, and how did you respond?

**Pastor:** I simply make this clear: it is not about what I say. It is about what God's Word says. I also make clear they have the freedom to disagree with me. I will still love them and welcome them to continue to attend our church.

**Dacus:** Then what usually happens?

**Pastor:** Sometimes they will stop attending. But other times they stay. In fact, in our church right now we have a homosexual couple attending regularly. We love them unconditionally. We also have ex-homosexuals attending our church whose lives have been changed by coming to know Christ.

**Dacus:** Do you try to address their homosexual sin soon after they attend your church, or do you wait awhile?

**Pastor:** We don't focus on their sin anymore than we focus on any other person's sin. Our focus is on everyone's need for Jesus and specifically leading them into a real, personal relationship with Jesus. We have seen that, as someone grows toward the Lord, it's only a matter of time before the Holy Spirit, with the study of God's Word, eventually convicts them, and they turn from that lifestyle. But it's important to remember that Jesus must always come first if there is to be any hope of real transformation.

**Dacus:** Have you had any demonstrations against your church, and does the homosexual community know what you teach?

**Pastor:** While we have not had any violence or demonstrations, we have adopted the model policies provided by Pacific Justice Institute to help legally protect us should something adverse happen. One reason, perhaps, why we haven't had hostile confrontations thus far is our church's involvement with the local community. We continually strive to connect with the community in different ways, like our annual alternative to Halloween celebration. Our last one had over three thousand attendees!

**Dacus:** Do you have any other examples of connecting with the community?

**Pastor:** We also make an effort to develop real relationships in this community. For example, one of our assistant pastors was invited by the chairman of the Gay and Lesbian Center to put his art on display at the Center for three months. He did so, and team members of our church attended, developed relationships, and several people were saved as a result. They even allowed us to have a stack of Bibles in the Center for those who might want one! If people see that you love and respect them unconditionally, it goes a long way, one person at a time.

## Conclusion

Churches in America today cannot be blind to the growing legal challenges resulting from the expanding influence of the LGBT movement and legal redefinition of marriage by the United States Supreme Court. Churches need to adopt the proper defensive policies to help ensure they do not end up losing a legal battle, possibly costing them their facilities, resources, identity, and ministry in the their community. Taking such measures is all a part of being wise as serpents but gentle as doves (Matt. 10:16).

But a healthy church cannot thrive by letting fear and caution become the driving force determining church operations. A healthy church must be fundamentally driven by the love of Jesus Christ for all persons. While different churches may vary with different perspectives on how they deal with their employees and attendees, the overall position of a church should be love and respect for all, faithfully teaching the full, unqualified truth of the Word, with the endgame always centered on leading every person into a genuine, maturing relationship with God through faith in Jesus Christ. In the end, changing culture is all about changing one life at a time through one relationship at time—person to person and every person related to Jesus.

# CHAPTER 14

# A PASTORAL MODEL FOR ENGAGING COMMUNITY

## *Jim L. Wilson*

With the window open, the sounds of the city fill the room. There's the repetitive thumping from the cars racing down Highway 101, the occasional blast of a horn from an irate driver, and the scream of emergency vehicle sirens. Pastor Phil Busbee did not seem to notice. It was as if he had learned to sway with the pulsating rhythm of the city and its disquieting clamor.

Or it might be a trade-off he made, a comfort compromise. He put up with the noise to feel the invigorating saltwater breeze that slips into the room through his open window. Looking outside, some might only see a city with streets, public transportation, buildings, indigents, vendors, and tourists. Busbee saw more, much more. Directly across the street from his church building is the home of the San Francisco Lesbian Gay Bisexual Transgender (LGBT) Community Center in the middle of a city known as "the gateway to the gay community."[1]

Some would close the window, pull the blinds, ignore the needs, and condemn the hurting. But not Pastor Busbee. His window was open and so was his heart.

## Location, Location, Location

As its name suggests, First Baptist Church, San Francisco, was the first Baptist church built in San Francisco. It was also the first Protestant church built in California. Founded in 1849, the church has met in four locations, three of them during its first fifty years. The great earthquake of 1906 destroyed their building on Eddy Street, causing them to find a new location. Within two years they had selected their current site on the corner of Market and Octavia Streets where three sections of the city meet. It's a strategic location. Within a four-block radius sits city hall, theaters, hospitals, and a public library. The church building is in the center of the city. To the west is the Castro district, to the east is Downtown, the Mission district is to the south, and Pacific Heights lies to the north.

Directly across the street in the city known as "the gateway to the gay community" is the multistory LGBT community center. Busbee told his congregation, "We must accept the fact that God has given us a seat at the gate."

The church believes it has always had a strategic location, positioned at the gateway of the city, offering hope to all who pass by. The opening of the center was just more recent confirmation of this reality. Some churches would have turned out in full force to picket the opening of an LGBT center. First Baptist Church chose to serve them instead.

About six months after Pastor Busbee arrived at the church, he was shown an architectural model for a new building going up across the street. That's when he found out who his church's new neighbor would be. "I remember thinking that I wanted to have a presence at the groundbreaking ceremony that didn't violate our convictions but at the same time would communicate to them that we were open for a relationship," Busbee recounted. But what could they do? A face-painting booth or an invitation to have coffee and doughnuts in the church's fellowship hall didn't seem appropriate. But Busbee knew the church needed to do something.

## Insert Cliché Here

"Hate the sin and love the sinner," that's what we always say. Easier said than done when someone builds an LGBT center practically on your church's front porch! Pastor Busbee did not want to put a stamp of approval on the sinful lifestyle the city was celebrating, and neither did he want to join in on the celebration. Yet ignoring a major civic event in the church's neighborhood did not seem right either.

The key to loving the sinner and hating the sin is approaching life as Jesus did, in grace and in truth. The apostle John wrote, "The Word became flesh and took up residence among us. We observed His glory, the glory as the One and Only Son from the Father, full of grace and truth" (John 1:14).

Jesus was Truth. John referred to Jesus as the Logos, a familiar word to the Greeks or Hellenized Jews of His day. Aristotle identified three artistic proofs—ethos, pathos, and logos. *Ethos* is the overall impression an observer has about another person's honesty and integrity. Though ethos is unquantifiable, it is persuasive. We tend to believe believable people. The second of Aristotle's trilogy is *pathos*. It's a gut feeling about the rightness of something. It's persuasion from within. The last word Aristotle used was *logos*, the word John used in John 1:14. *Logos* meant the final word, the truth that convinces beyond a shadow of a doubt. It is indisputable, logical evidence.

Jesus is the final Word, the Truth, that was from the beginning. In another passage John called Jesus "the true One" (1 John 5:20), and in Revelation he called Him "Faithful and True" (Rev. 19:11). Jesus called Himself "the truth" (John 14:6).

When He came into the world, Jesus was full of truth, but He was also full of grace. John wrote, "Indeed, we have all received grace after grace from His fullness" (John 1:16). How gracious was Jesus? John acknowledged receiving "grace after grace" from Him. The apostle Paul wrote, "The grace of our Lord was more than abundant, with the faith and love which are found in Christ Jesus" (1 Tim. 1:14 NASB).

How gracious was Jesus? According to Paul, His grace was "more than abundant."

Pastor Busbee knew the secret to a suitable response to the LGBT center was communicating the truth about Jesus and the truth Jesus taught but in the spirit of grace which marked His life and ministry. Doing so would require living out those qualities, putting them into practice through visible acts of service coupled with clear communication.

## Incarnational Ministry

Jesus incarnate was full of grace and truth. Those two characteristics mutually coexisted in Jesus' life and ministry. In God's economy grace and truth are not to be separated. They are complementary extremes. In John 1:14, John wrote that the Logos was "full of grace and truth," and a few verses later he explains the relationship of the two: "For the law was given through Moses, grace and truth came through Jesus Christ" (John 1:17). The contrast is important to note. Moses' law had truth but no grace, and it led to guilt (Gal. 3:19). Truth without grace exposes guilt. At the worst truth without grace creates animosity.

The mission of the incarnation was straightforward: "to save sinners" (1 Tim. 1:15). Jesus was not born for any lesser purpose than showering His mercy upon sinful people who believe in Him and then immersing them in His grace, resulting in their salvation.

The key to accepting and loving people without compromising theological convictions is leading with compassion. "The front of Jesus' presence to unbelievers was compassion. The front of His presence to the hypocrites was harsh. We tend to reverse that," Busbee observed. "To me, the church largely missed the 'mercy opportunity' of the last century—the AIDS crisis. We took a position of condemnation and judgment, as opposed to seeing AIDS as an illness. How a person got it shouldn't have changed our response to it."

Homosexuality is a detestable sin (Rom. 1:24–32). It is also a controversial sin, but it is not the only sin that plagues society. Divorce creates many societal problems; yet most people are able to minister to divorced persons without having to go repeatedly on the record that they are "against divorce." Perhaps if the church had taken the same approach to the AIDS crisis, the gay community would have seen our grace and would have been more interested in our truth. James wrote,

> The wisdom that comes from God is first utterly pure, then peace-loving, gentle, approachable, full of tolerant thoughts and kindly actions, with no breath of favouritism or hint of hypocrisy. And the wise are peace-makers who go on quietly sowing for a harvest of righteousness—in other people and in themselves. (James 3:17 PHILLIPS)

Leading with grace is a wise approach that produces a harvest. It is practicing the words of Jesus, "See, I send you out as sheep among wolves. Be then as wise as snakes, and as gentle as doves" (Matt. 10:16 BBE). Not only is joining grace with truth a biblical approach; it is the wisest strategy.

Incarnational ministry is coming in grace and truth. It leads with grace, but truth follows as its companion. In His exchange with the woman caught in adultery (John 8:2–12), Jesus was gracious, encouraging others not to judge her harshly. But after her accusers dropped their stones and walked away, Jesus called her to live righteously. "When Jesus stood up, He said to her, 'Woman, where are they? Has no one condemned you?' 'No one, Lord,' she answered. 'Neither do I condemn you,' said Jesus. 'Go, and from now on do not sin any more'" (John 8:10–11). Jesus said clearly, "I don't condemn you, but stop your immoral actions." He led with compassion, but He did not compromise the truth. It is never enough to say, "Neither do I condemn you." It must always be followed with, "Go and sin no more" (NLT).

Pastor Busbee wanted to express the same message, a message filled with grace and truth. He did not want to approach his neighbors with a self-righteous, condemning posture. He wanted to come with a redemptive spirit that expressed grace and truth. After consulting with other church leaders, as an act of Christian love and service, Busbee offered the church parking lot for the visiting dignitaries to use during the groundbreaking ceremony. This may seem like a small gesture, but in "parking challenged" San Francisco, it was sharing one of the church's most precious commodities. When Busbee made the offer, he was surprised by the reaction of the LGBT center director. The man's jaw literally dropped open.

On the other hand, he was not surprised by the reaction of some Christians who thought he was sending the wrong signal. They did not understand grace is not the opposite of truth; it complements it. Parking is always a problem in the city and it did not serve the neighborhood to increase congestion by double-parking cars on the streets. Opening up the church parking lot to the governor of California, the mayor of San Francisco, and other dignitaries was not a theological compromise. It was simply a neighborly act that opened the door for an amicable relationship and the opportunity to proclaim the gospel at a later time.

Grace never replaces truth; it complements it. Grace is to truth as mercy is to justice. They are inextricably entwined. Extending genuine grace is never compromising truth. Busbee's gracious act was an extension of the truth he believed and taught. It was an attempt at incarnational ministry in the twenty-first century. It was also an acknowledgement that times have changed. The American church no longer ministers from a position of cultural, philosophical, or pragmatic dominance. It must find practical ways to communicate grace, love, and truth in ministry situations unthinkable just a generation ago.

The church will not compete in the marketplace of ideas by adopting new techniques, programs, or methods. An attitude adjustment is what is really required. Christians must meet the needs of the people in their community, looking for opportunities to lead with grace and speak truth in love. Speaking truth isn't enough, and neither is only leading with grace. We must lead with grace and speak the truth in love.

## Regaining Lost Influence

The church may no longer be dominant in American culture, but that does not mean it cannot gain market share it has lost in the intellectual marketplace. This will not be done only by forming political action committees and demanding the government conform to conservative Christian values. The church will make advances if it approaches the problem with truth and grace instead of with truth and anger. The way to tilt the balance back toward conservative Christian values is graciously serving the hurting and disenfranchised in our culture. "The world was Christianized even before Constantine proclaimed Christianity as the official religion because Christians were in the front lines of serving hurting people," Busbee said.

As a church serves its community, it earns a place in the intellectual marketplace, but it will only be effective if it does not approach the dialogue from a position of presumed dominance. "We need to shift our mind-set and understand we are not dominant. We need to enter the marketplace knowing we need to compete in an intellectual marketplace that has a lot of different competitive products," Busbee concluded.

On occasion this means standing up for truth and communicating clearly what we believe. When San Francisco Mayor Gavin Newsom authorized same-sex marriages on February 12, 2004, Busbee knew a public response was required. First, however, he approached the mayor privately and asked, "How do we tell our children to obey the law when the mayor of San Francisco won't?" After this personal appeal, Busbee went public with his opposition to the mayor's decision.

Pastor Busbee helped organize a march on Sunday, April 25, 2004, that included about seven thousand people demonstrating in defense of traditional marriage. "We wanted the mayor to know there is a group of people who are willing to go public about their belief in biblical marriage," Busbee said. "We don't want to be harmful or hurt anyone. But we want it to be clear that we uphold the sanctity of one man and one woman in marriage." He continued, "It would be easy [for Christians] to feel besieged and develop a fortress mentality, but we wanted to counteract that. We have a ministry to homosexuals in our church. We want to share the grace and truth of the Bible."[2]

Busbee's tone was gracious while his words were truthful. Later, when the California Supreme Court struck down the mayor's decision, the *San Francisco Chronicle* contacted Busbee for a reaction. He told them that limiting marriage to "one woman and one man" was "the law of the land established by the citizens of California and a moral standard that is in alignment with Scripture. The law comes from our spiritual heritage."

But Busbee didn't gloat while speaking the truth. His tone remained gracious as he lamented, "I feel a tremendous sense of regret and concern for those (same-sex married) couples. This will create a lot of emotional upheaval in their lives and their relationships."

## Will You Be My Neighbor?

Soon after he offered the parking lot for the grand opening celebration of the LGBT center, its director approached Busbee to let him know they would be sponsoring a block party for their constituents. It was going to be a huge gathering right in front of the church, requiring the city to shut down the common street they shared. The event was open to all who shared the center's values and would include things like female impersonators as part of the celebration. "Is there anything that's going to be significant about that day for you?" he asked Busbee. "Let me think about it, and get back to you," Busbee replied.

After praying about it, Busbee contacted with a simple request, "Please don't let anything happen on that day that would desecrate our property." He went on to explain the church's stance on homosexual behavior and emphasized he did not want any homosexual activity to take place on the church's property. Although disappointed in the pastor's beliefs, the director told him: "I'll have a group of people out there, and nothing will happen. We will not do anything that would dishonor your property. You've been respectful to us; we're going to be respectful to you."

Neither party had adopted the other's belief system, but both were being neighborly. The Scripture says, "A gentle answer turns away anger, but a harsh word stirs up wrath" (Prov. 15:1). Because Busbee led with grace and followed with truth, the man was gracious in return. Members of First Baptist attended the block party to pray and share Christ with those who came to celebrate their deviant lifestyles. Both sides managed the situation appropriately and demonstrated neighborliness.

That encounter became a model for Busbee when he had a similar exchange with a leader of Soul Force, a Christian gay-rights group. In that meeting Busbee opened the Bible and explained his position but then said, "I wanted you to know where I'm coming from, but I also want to make an agreement with you. I'm committing not to say anything to embarrass you in the public arena. I'm not here to wage war against your community. I'm not going to use the public arena to speak poorly of you or tear you down. And I ask you to make the same commitment to me." When they left the meeting, neither side had changed their perspective, but both had agreed not to battle each other in the public arena.

A few weeks later the Southern Baptist Convention passed a resolution about homosexuality, and it outraged many in the gay community. A representative from Queer Nation, a radical protest group headquartered two blocks from First Baptist, warned Busbee by e-mail that they were planning to show up at his church the next Sunday to disrupt his worship service in protest of the resolution. Busbee immediately picked up the phone and called his friend in the gay community, the LGBT director, and said: "We made an agreement. I know you're not with these people, but if there is any way you could get hold of them on our behalf and say that we are not their enemy and they don't need to disrupt our worship service, I'd really appreciate it." Two days later Busbee got an e-mail from Queer Nation apologizing for the threat along with an invitation for future dialogue.

None of those involved were agreeing to think like the others or behave like the others but just to be neighborly to one another. This process had begun with the church's initial offer of the parking lot. Later it would again be the church's turn to extend a hand of friendship to its neighborhood. There was a movement in the community to tear down the freeway that separated the Financial District and the Castro District in San Francisco. Workers had repaired the damage from the 1989 earthquake, but the highway was still a blight to many in the city.

The gay community took the position tearing down the freeway would be akin to tearing down a barrier for their movement to go mainstream. While First Baptist did not have a stake in the issue and certainly did not want to enter into the politics of it, they offered their facilities for community meetings. They were neutral facilitators of a discussion that was important to many in the community. The meetings generated a lot of midweek activity at the church, which was glad to offer hospitality to those who needed a restroom or to run a few copies. With tears in his eyes, one man told Busbee's wife, "This is the first time I've ever been inside of a church, and I was sure if I ever was in a church that I'd be hated." But he wasn't. He was loved.

The church never stopped standing for what they believed, but they led with grace. While planning for the celebration of the demolition of the highway, the LGBT center's director suggested the city ask the church to host the festivities. More than three thousand people, including the mayor, passed through the doors of the church. But the community did more than ask the church for use of their building. They also asked the church to provide the music for the event. That day the church proclaimed the gospel to all through the music chosen by their worship band.

When the church is neighborly and leads with grace, we affirm our neighbors do not have to be Christlike for the church to behave in a Christlike manner toward them.

## Contextual Ministry

Pastor Busbee usually did not do battle in the political or public arena. He chose, instead, to do it in the spiritual arena. At the block party he led church members to pray and share their faith. When the center was being constructed, he asked the contractor if the church could throw laminated Scripture into its foundation. "Hell yes," he said. "I don't care; we throw our cigarette butts and beer cans in there so I don't care what the hell you throw in there." Today, embedded in the foundation of the San Francisco LGBT Community Center, are laminated Scripture cards symbolizing the prayers and ministry of the church to its community.

The church also produced prayer guides for their members to use as they prayer-walked the block and even went on the inaugural tour of the facilities, praying for the people who would pass through its doors. On the tour someone asked, "What does First Baptist Church think about you guys being here?"

The guide responded, "I think they're glad we're in the neighborhood."

After hearing the reply and thinking about it, Busbee said, "Yeah, I'm glad they're here. I mean, I'd rather them be sitting across from my church than sitting across from Gold's Gym." He continued, "It's a sovereign placement. God put this church here a hundred years ago. He knew a long time ago what was going to be across the street from it." Busbee is not ministering in a vacuum. He works within a ministry context and chooses to minister to those who surround him. Churches cannot always choose the target demographic for their ministry. Sometimes God places them in the midst of a people group, and they must use whatever means necessary to reach them.

While ministering in rural Montana, David Hansen met a feisty ninety-four-year-old blind woman whose fierce independence buffeted his early attempts to minister to her. She chopped her own wood, cooked her own meals, and wouldn't accept help from anyone, much less a preacher. She would, however, allow him to drop by to serve her the Lord's Supper.

For the longest time he could not convince her that people loved her. "Love isn't in the Bible," she said. "The Bible calls it charity, not love." He continued to be faithful to minister to her on her terms.

With time she began to allow the church to bring meals by and even let the pastor chop some wood for her. Her cold exterior began to thaw. The church started helping her with her bills and assisted her niece in cleaning up around the woman's place. Pastor David began chopping wood for her on a regular basis. It was his way of showing Christ's love for one of His children.

Before her one-hundredth birthday, she went into a local nursing home where she received the care she needed. Though Pastor David did not chop wood for her anymore, he continued to minister to her. In his book *The Power of Loving Your Church*, he describes what happened after stopping by the nursing home to give her Communion one day.[3]

"Upon rising to leave, I stoop over and give her a hug. She reaches up and returns my embrace." Before leaving, he told her something powerful, "I have charity for you, Kathryn." And she responded, "Well, that's nice, a person needs a lot of that."

Jesus' love (excuse me, I meant charity!) can melt the hardest heart and heal the deepest hurts. Kathryn was right; a person needs a lot of it. Incarnational ministry for Pastor Hansen meant showing love to an elderly woman by chopping her wood while leaving her dignity in place while he did it.

Practical, get-your-hands-dirty ministry choices are meaningful demonstrations of love. Many Christians think only in terms of stories like this one when considering how to show love to others. But Phil Busbee did not live in a rural setting where love meant chopping wood. He lives in an immorality-embracing city that needs to hear the truth of the gospel in a gracious manner. If he lived in India, he would be trying to reach the Hindus. If he lived in Utah, he would be trying to reach the Mormons. Since he lives in San Francisco, he must try to reach homosexuals. Some church members were upset with Busbee's attitude and approach. They left the church, with one guy telling Busbee, "Homosexuals are not a people group that I want to reach."

Ignoring people in need is not a luxury Pastor Busbee had. He realized he was involved in a spiritual war, and—make no mistake about it—lives were at stake. By the grace of God, people were being transformed, people like Young.

For five years before coming to First Baptist, Young had been in a committed homosexual relationship. He was already HIV positive and was addicted to cocaine. One day he heard the music playing through the church's open doors and wandered inside with his partner. He continued to attend church services and activities. At times he got so caught up in the worship, he would fall to his knees before God with tears streaming down his cheeks.

One Sunday he got into a physical altercation with his partner during a worship service. Every time Young stood to worship, his partner would grab his hips and pull him back into the pew. Bobby, one of the deacons, sat down next to Young and said, "If there is anything I can do to help, I will." That day, on the front steps of the church, Young committed his life to Jesus Christ and left his gay lifestyle.

A few years later, Young went public with his whole story, giving glory to God during a testimony to the entire church on Easter Sunday. Young came to know the truth of the gospel because one church dared to share it with grace.

"I don't know how grace and truth live together," Busbee says. "I know what grace is. I know what truth is. All I know is that I'm going to try to live both of them right now."

## Postlude

Phil Busbee went to be with the Lord, after an extended illness through which he continued his pastoral leadership, on June 27, 2009. In his obituary the *San Francisco Gate* wrote, "Blessings, not condemnation, was the heart cry of Phil Busbee, Pastor at First Baptist Church of San Francisco," and quoted a Baptist Press article that said, "Afflicted with physical suffering that at times has been life threatening for him, there is a greater concern than his personal health. What weighs more in Phil Busbee's life is this: a burden and passion for people who inhabit San Francisco's 49 square miles, but do not know Christ."[*]

As far as the *San Francisco Gate* was concerned, Busbee accomplished his mission of sharing truth with grace. But their word is not the final word. God always has that. I believe my former classmate heard what we all long to hear at the final judgment, "Well done, my good and faithful servant" (Matt. 25:23 NLT).

Today, First Baptist Church continues its vibrant ministry while still sharing a common street with a newly remodeled and enlarged LGBT Community Center. People from the neighborhood continue to hear truth because of the gracious ministry the church provides. Built on Pastor Busbee's legacy, the church continues to reach out to the people—all the people—of San Francisco with the gospel.

## CHAPTER 15

# A MODEL SERMON ABOUT THE NEW MARRIAGE CULTURE

## *Jeff Iorg*

*This expanded outline, reshaped for use in a church setting, is based on the President's Convocation message delivered by Dr. Jeff Iorg, Golden Gate Baptist Theological Seminary, at Mill Valley, California, on August 29, 2013. While the biblical material included is appropriate in every context, pastors should customize this message with pertinent applications and illustrations for their context. Care should be exercised to consider the age range of persons in the congregation when determining appropriate applications and illustrations.*

Recent events in our culture mandate a message in response to the most significant change in American society since abortion on demand was legalized in 1973. Rulings by the United States Supreme Court have effectively legalized gay marriage in many states, with corresponding adjustments in policy throughout the federal government, including the military. The result: the legal battle over gay marriage is essentially over. This is the kind of societal change, even if reversed at some point in the future, which will have a multigenerational negative impact around the world for decades to come.

For those of us who consider the Bible a guide for life, legalizing gay marriage is an alarming affirmation of the final step of rejecting God's design for human sexuality and traditional marriage as the foundation of a stable society. In Romans 1, Paul addressed the church in the capital city—Rome—of an empire rampant with people promoting immoral behavior. He wrote of them, "Their thinking became nonsense, and their senseless minds were darkened. Claiming to be wise, they became fools" (Rom. 1:21–22). As a result, "God delivered them over in the cravings of their hearts to sexual impurity, so their bodies were degraded among themselves. They exchanged the truth of God for a lie, and worshiped and served something created instead of the Creator" (Rom. 1:24–25). Paul then became more specific, observing,

> Even their females exchanged natural sexual relations for unnatural ones. The males in the same way also left natural relations with females and were inflamed in their lust for one another. Males committed shameless acts with males and received in their own persons the appropriate penalty of their error. (Rom. 1:26–27)

While describing first-century Rome, the letter reads like a prophetic description of our country today. Paul's conclusion is sobering and also applicable to our situation. Sexual sins are not the final step on this cultural downward spiral. The last step of rejecting biblical morality is when people "applaud" or celebrate those who legitimize immoral practices (Rom. 1:32). We have reached that point in America.

This is why governmental affirmation and cultural celebrations of gay marriage are so troubling. Sexual immorality of all types has been part of the human experience throughout recorded history. The troubling issue today is not so much the rise of immorality; that cycle ebbs and flows with changing generations. The troubling issue is the applause (or approval) from kissing in the streets to White

House ceremonies celebrated through every media possible. Political, cultural, and educational leaders are effusively congratulating themselves on their so-called progress. The final act of an unraveling society is not immoral behavior; it's canonizing immoral behavior as a "new normal" and celebrating it as a "moral victory."

Our new normal now includes the legitimatization of homosexual behavior, including same-sex marriage. These changes will produce many new ministry dilemmas. For example, how will you respond when a boy brings his two fathers to family night at your Vacation Bible School? How will you counsel a business owner in your church who opposes providing employment benefits to same-sex couples? When a new Christian already in a gay marriage wants out of that relationship, will you advise him or her to get a divorce, even if it means losing custody and influence with his or her adopted children?

How will we respond to these and countless other situations we will now face as compassionate Christians committed to upholding biblical standards? Let's explore these questions more fully and begin answering them by considering this message, "Ministry in the New Marriage Culture," based on 1 Peter 4:1–11.

The first principle in this passage about ministry in the new marriage culture is *Christians must continue to affirm distinct moral standards.* In verse 3, Peter describes the behavior of unbelievers. The word *pagans* has pejorative implications for some modern hearers (1 Pet. 4:3). In context, it simply describes unbelievers, persons who have not yet committed themselves to Jesus as Lord and Savior. Their natural inclinations include "carrying on in unrestrained behavior, evil desires, drunkenness, orgies, carousing, and lawless idolatry" (1 Pet. 4:3).

Peter uses general words to describe common behavior in his day and ours. Peter characterizes behavior of unbelievers as marked by unrestrained use of drugs and alcohol, multiple sexual partners, and worshipping at the altar of "having a good time." His purpose, however, is not cataloging a comprehensive list of specific sins. His purpose is contrasting how believers formerly lived and how they are expected to live now. Peter reminded his hearers: "There has already been enough time spent in doing what the pagans choose to do" (1 Pet. 4:3). The clear implication is believers once behaved like unbelievers, and the time for such behavior is now past.

The focus in this short list is on "behaviors," not orientations. This is an important distinction. The Bible condemns behaviors—not inclinations, propensities, proclivities, feelings, or temptations. Same-sex attraction is a powerful reality for some people. Condemning a person for this desire, or in modern terms "orientation," is counter-productive. Just because a person has a desire, even a strong desire, toward a particular sexual activity does not mean they must translate desire into action. This conclusion contradicts what might be called "the doctrine of sexual inevitability," upon which modern morality is based. Sexual inevitability means whatever a person feels, desires, or wants sexually must inevitably be expressed so go ahead and own it as your "orientation" and express it. This is why many lampoon the abstinence movement. They mistakenly reason, "Everybody knows teenagers will inevitably have sex so why not help them do it right rather than teach them to manage their desires?"

Even people who claim to believe in sexual inevitability do not implement their doctrine consistently. For example, if someone claims "polygamist" as their sexual orientation, desiring multiple partners to be fulfilled, their behavior is still illegal and morally condemned by almost everyone. Adultery is considered morally reprehensible to almost everyone. Similarly, no person can claim "pedophilia" as their sexual orientation and express it without prosecution. All three of these sexual "orientations" are condemned in our culture. People who claim these "orientations" are expected to manage their temptations and control their behavior. When they do not, they face repercussions ranging from societal condemnation to lengthy imprisonment.

Christians must make a careful distinction at this point. We must oppose immoral behavior more than condemn people for immoral impulses. Most of us, if not all of us, have sexual interests, tendencies, desires, lusts, or temptations challenging our Christian convictions. We restrain those impulses not because it's easy but because we are trying to live up to moral standards that lead to a happier life, healthier families, stronger communities, and more stable societies. All of us, if we are honest, think immoral thoughts. We recognize those thoughts, left unchecked, can lead to immoral actions. We know we must "demolish arguments and every high-minded thing that is raised up against the knowledge of God, taking every thought captive to obey Christ" (2 Cor. 10:4–5).

Even with our spiritual resources, this is difficult for believers. It's much more difficult for unbelievers. Many of them have strong desires toward immoral behavior, unchecked by spiritual strength or societal mores. Their feelings are real and compelling. While recognizing this realty, we must not label those feelings, no matter how powerful, an "orientation" equated with sexual inevitability. We must help people find strength, through the gospel and Christian community, to make right choices about their sexual behavior.

As Christians, we make different behavioral choices reflecting a commitment to new moral standards. As a Christian, you have different moral standards than those in the culture around you. Some of you who are leaders in our church are expected to model even higher standards. While this seems obvious to many of us, it's getting harder to maintain distinctively Christian morality. Let me highlight two reasons for this today.

First, some Christians confuse acculturating the gospel with compromising moral behavior. A church planter tells his story of starting a church near Portland, Oregon, that illustrates this dilemma:

> We worked hard at creating a 'culture current' church that connected with people from the Pacific Northwest. We accommodated cultural distinctives from dress codes to worship style to program choices and scheduling. When we built our campus, it resembled a ski lodge in a forest setting—lots of exposed wood with blues and greens dominant in the color scheme. Because we were not like the other Baptist churches in our region, we endured some criticism from other Christian leaders. We were called compromisers and liberals.

It was painful, but we knew being culture current was a missional necessity.

While we accommodated culture in many ways, we were unwilling to compromise biblical doctrine or clear biblical teachings. Early in our church's development, we removed a man from our membership for brazen immorality. It was difficult, but it had to be done. Some traditionalists, who had previously criticized us, were surprised to learn our commitment to a culture current model did not equate with compromising biblical moral standards.

All of us should advocate for innovation, change, and creativity in church ministry. We should do all we can to connect with people in our unique cultural setting and communicate the gospel in terms they understand. International missionaries do this all the time. We have an increasing need to do so in our culture. But we must not make this mistake: advocacy for accommodation on nonessential issues does not include endorsing behavior clearly out of step with Christian moral standards described in the Bible. What is biblically wrong can never be politically correct, legally right, or a strategic part of healthy church life.

The second reason it is difficult to maintain Christian moral standards is some Christian leaders are at the forefront of the movement to undermine biblical morality. Clergy from some Christian denominations are now prominent endorsers of behaviors contrary to every orthodox expression of Christianity prior to the twenty-first century. These leaders are redefining what it means to be "Christian" in ways disconnected from historic Christianity. It's hard to uphold distinctive Christian morality when so many mixed messages are being disseminated by other Christian leaders. As a leader today, and in the future, I may find myself marginalized, but I will not compromise clear teachings about biblical morality. If you stand with me, you may be in the minority. We may be in the minority, even opposed by some prominent Christians; but we must bear up under this cultural pressure and stand strong together.

This leads us to the second major idea in our text about ministry in the new marriage culture: *Christian moral standards will be aggressively opposed.* Peter described unbelievers as being "surprised that you don't plunge with them into the same flood of wild living—and they slander you" (1 Pet. 4:4). The opposition to our standards comes in two phases.

First, unbelievers are surprised when Christians claim different moral standards and refuse to celebrate their choices. When a Christian voices a different moral code, relational tension often results. One adulterer was shocked when he told a chaplain about his fabulous mistress. The chaplain responded by warning him, with tears, of the destruction his behavior would bring to his wife and children. He accused the chaplain of being judgmental and unloving, which illustrates the second phase of opposition described in the text.

As a result of your unwillingness to affirm their choices, unbelievers will "slander you" (1 Pet. 4:4). Slander is verbal assault, uttering false charges or misrepresentations that demean or damage a person's reputation. In a media-saturated and social-media world, this is easier and more widespread than ever.

As a result of this message, I may be accused of hate speech, of denying homosexuals their civil rights, and of attacking people rather than showing them God's love. I will be called an uncaring, judgmental, narrow-minded, out-of-touch fundamentalist. I will be lumped in with racists, terrorists, and anarchists as an enemy of progress. I will be labeled a cultist and have the legitimacy of my Christian faith questioned. And, no doubt, the worst profanity used in modern America will be hurled my way. I will be called "intolerant."

You will be slandered in similar ways if you advocate Christian morality today. My prediction: today's slander is a precursor to more serious social, legal, and physical opposition coming in the next few years. We will discover how "tolerant" the tolerance advocates will be as they consolidate their political power.

In the face of aggressive opposition, how should we respond? Our text outlines our response, both a motivating reality and several specific actions. Let's discover them as we consider the final principle in the text related to ministry in the new marriage culture.

*Opposition to our moral standards requires a Christian response.* Before Peter outlined action steps, he first underscored a motivating reality. He wrote, unbelievers "will give an account to the One who stands ready to judge the living and the dead" (1 Pet. 4:5). Unbelievers who reject biblical morality are at risk of judgment. Don't read this passage as celebratory or vengeful. In its context it's a reminder to believers that unbelievers are in a perilous position. They are facing judgment, both the consequences of rebellious living in this life and eternal separation from God in the next. As believers, we cringe at the thought of people we know experiencing judgment. We want them delivered, not doomed. Coming judgment motivates us to do all we can to help as many people as possible avoid judgment. Only the most callous, embittered person would read these verses and think, *Finally, they'll get what they deserve!* The opposite must be true of us. Coming judgment motivates us to tell people about deliverance available through Jesus Christ.

Peter next outlines three action steps for us to counter opposition to our moral standards. The first step is share the gospel! This may surprise you. You might be expecting a call to civil disobedience or prophetic confrontation instead. Not so. Your first response to people who oppose Christian moral standards is sharing the gospel. Peter wrote, "For this reason the gospel was also preached to those who are now dead, so that, although they might be judged by men in the fleshly realm, they might live by God in the spiritual realm" (1 Pet. 4:6). This verse cannot mean preaching to people who have died. That's impossible. It means, in its context, the gospel was preached to people who have since died, prior to their deaths. The gospel was their means to deliverance in this life and their hope after death in the next life. The same is still true of all people today.

Your most significant message to people in a culture marked by moral decay and immoral living is the gospel. We must not become preoccupied with opposing immoral behavior, no matter its form. Moral choices emerge from a person's spiritual condition. Unbelievers act like unbelievers. While we uphold our moral convictions, expecting unbelievers to model Christian behavior is a misplaced hope. Your first and best response to immorality in your community is to preach, teach, share, witness, and live the gospel. The greatest need of every person in the world—lesbian, gay, bisexual, transgender, adulterer, fornicator, or straight-laced puritan—is still the gospel.

While certain parts of this message will anger secularists, this next section may draw fire from some Christians. Sharing the gospel with the LGBT community, including those who are in same-sex marriages, means we should welcome them to our worship services, invite them to our homes, and befriend them at work and in social settings. While holding to your moral convictions without any compromise, you must keep your focus on the greatest need of every person—no matter his or her behavior—which is hearing and responding to the gospel.

This is a personal challenge for many of you who find homosexual behavior repugnant. But remember, you too were once without hope, without Jesus. Think of what your life would be like if you did not have His grace to motivate you to live up to His standards! Some of you have friends, children, grandchildren, nieces, nephews, and cousins caught up in immoral lifestyles. Be heartbroken for them, not judgmental of them. Determine to pray for them, show them the love of Jesus, and share the gospel with them.

Our current cultural challenges test our belief in the power of the gospel. Is the gospel really "God's power for salvation" (Rom. 1:16)? Is it really true that "if anyone is in Christ, he is a new creation; old things have passed away, and look, new things have come" (2 Cor. 5:17)? Is the gospel inherently powerful, needing to be declared more than defended? My answer is yes to all three questions. Our current cultural challenges will also test our prioritization of gospel ministry. While political action is important, saving America by reforming social structures or creating new political coalitions around our values must not be our ultimate priority. We need a radical recommitment to communicating the gospel as our foundational ministry message.

Communicating the gospel seems to be a diminishing priority among Christians. In my denomination of Southern Baptists, we have thousands more churches and millions more members than fifty years ago; yet our capacity to tell people the good news about Jesus and see evidence of conversion through baptism is at an all-time low. We are better than ever at debating the gospel but not so effective at declaring it. Most churches no longer train people for personal evangelism. Preaching has degenerated to showing PowerPoint slides about how to have a better life. Giving an invitation to actually repent and believe the gospel is less and less common in worship services.

We have a decision to make, which must be made urgently. Will we return to gospel-centered ministry focused on growing our church, or continue our downward spiral toward irrelevance in sharing the gospel? Individually you have a decision to make. Will you recommit to gospel-centered personal ministry? Let's stop deceiving ourselves that we are sharing the gospel effectively and make the necessary changes to become better gospel tellers.

A second strategy in the face of opposition to Christian moral standards is being "serious and disciplined for prayer" (1 Pet. 4:7). These are sober times. We need serious and disciplined prayer to sustain us. Trying to get our church together for prayer is challenging because of work responsibilities, ministry commitments, and family obligations. Somehow—in our worship services, Bible studies, women's ministries, men's ministries, and youth group—we must reprioritize prayer. In our families, at mealtimes or family devotions, we must make more time for prayer.

Peter also advocates a third response when faced with opposition to our moral standards. He wrote, "Above all, maintain an intense love for each other, since love covers a multitude of sins" (1 Pet. 4:8). Peter then amplifies what it means to love each other by calling us to hospitality and using our gifts to serve one another (1 Pet. 4:9–11). These might be considered as separate action steps, but today let's combine them as examples of what it means to love one another.

The focus in these verses is on believers showing love to one another. Why is this so important? When attacked, we need one another to withstand the pressure. We must not cannibalize one another, weakening ourselves and our ministry efforts by needlessly attacking one another. We must "maintain an intense love for each other" (1 Pet. 4:8), meaning we intentionally choose loving responses to fellow believers. And, when other believers sin against us, we must learn to overlook offenses because "love covers a multitude of sins" (1 Pet. 4:8).

As our culture becomes more and more hostile to Christian morality, we must become more and more unified with other believers. We cannot allow debates over worship styles, missionary methods, and even lesser doctrinal issues to divide us. Yes, core doctrines that define the Christian faith must be defended. The Bible is clear about this in many passages. But we must become more discerning about what really matters and avoid attacking one another over lesser issues. We need one another and will need one another more and more as opposition to our values becomes more entrenched in governmental and societal systems.

While the focus on this passage is on loving other believers, there's also ample biblical mandates to love unbelievers, even those who attack us. Jesus said, "You have heard that it was said, Love your neighbor and hate your enemy. But I tell you, love your enemies" (Matt. 5:43–44). What does loving people who oppose our values look like? Some say love means affirming people for who they are, celebrating their choices as good for them, and accepting all moral standards as equally valid. That is not love. Love tells the truth, advocates healthy choices, and helps people achieve a higher quality of life. Love also protects people and values them as creations in the image of God. For this reason Christians must avoid verbal attacks, hateful actions, bullying, and violence directed toward individuals in the LGBT community or same-sex married couples. Love demands we tell the truth about immoral behavior while treating people with respect. Real love is much harder to demonstrate than the hollow, self-serving substitute some people demand instead.

We conclude then with this summary and these commitments. We affirm distinct moral standards described in the Bible and affirmed for centuries by orthodox Christians. We expect opposition to those standards and will respond appropriately. How will we respond? We will communicate the gospel to all people by every available means. We will pray, invoking God's power and presence in our lives. We will love one another, standing stronger when we stand together. We will love unbelievers, loving them enough to tell them the truth about God, the gospel, and a more fulfilling life resulting from healthier moral choices.

Toward that end, let's commit ourselves today to fulfilling the biblical instructions we have heard today.

# MEET THE WRITERS

**Gregory C. Cochran**

Dr. Gregory Cochran is associate professor in the School of Christian Ministries at California Baptist University, where he is the director of the Applied Theology program. He earned his PhD in Christian Ethics from The Southern Baptist Theological Seminary in Louisville, Kentucky. Dr. Cochran joined the faculty at CBU after serving for fifteen years in pastoral ministry. He blogs at www.GregoryCCochran.com. He has been married for more than twenty-five years and has seven children.

**Brad Dacus**

Mr. Brad Dacus is founder and president of Pacific Justice Institute and can be heard daily on *The Dacus Report* on radio stations across the country. He received his Juris Doctor from the School of Law at the University of Texas. If your church is dealing with any circumstances surrounding same-sex marriage issues or would like free legal counsel or representation with regards to your church polices, please contact Pacific Justice Institute for pro bono assistance at www.pacificjustice.org. He has been married for more than fifteen years and has two children.

**Rodrick (Rick) Durst**

Dr. Rodrick (Rick) Durst is professor of historical theology at Golden Gate Baptist Theological Seminary and is director of its Bay Area Campus in Fremont, California. During his tenure at Golden Gate, he has served as the Southern California campus director, Online Education program director and vice president of Academic Affairs. He is a two-time graduate of Golden Gate Seminary. Prior to his academic career, he served twelve years in pastoral ministry. He has published a variety of articles and journals, and has more than fifty theological videos available online. His latest book, soon to be released, is *The Trinity in the New Testament and the Church*. He has been married for more than thirty-seven years and has three children.

## Leroy Gainey

Dr. Leroy Gainey holds the J. M. Frost Chair of Educational Leadership at Golden Gate Baptist Theological Seminary. He was the first African-American elected as a faculty member by a Southern Baptist Seminary. Prior to joining the faculty in 1987, he was senior pastor at Central Baptist Church, Syracuse, New York, and a church planter in New Jersey. He earned his PhD from Syracuse University. Dr. Gainey is a popular conference speaker and lecturer. He has contributed to the Holman Family Bible and is the author of several articles and one book, *Why Have Plain When You Can Have a Rainbow*, and is contributing author to two books, *Sunday Schools That Really Excel* and *A Mighty Long Journey*. He has been married for more than forty-two years and has four children.

## Adam Groza

Dr. Adam Groza is associate professor of philosophy of religion and vice president for Enrollment and Student Services at Golden Gate Baptist Theological Seminary. Dr. Groza is a graduate of The Master's Seminary and earned his PhD in Philosophy of Religion from Southwestern Baptist Theological Seminary. He has been married for more than fifteen years and has four children.

## Ann Iorg

Mrs. Ann Iorg is a national leader in preschool ministry training. She has degrees from Hardin Simmons University and Golden Gate Baptist Theological Seminary. She regularly teaches and consults on preschool and children's ministry programs and teaches in the Partners in Ministry program at Golden Gate Seminary. Her publications include contributions to *The Christian Homemaker's Handbook* and the *One-Year Women's Devotional Guide*. She currently serves as the Sunday preschool director at her church. She has been married for more than thirty-five years and has three adult children.

### Jeff Iorg

Dr. Jeff Iorg is the president of Golden Gate Baptist Theological Seminary. He is a graduate of Hardin Simmons University, Midwestern Baptist Theological Seminary, and Southwestern Baptist Theological Seminary. Dr. Iorg is a popular conference speaker who also teaches leadership, preaching, and church ministry courses at Golden Gate Seminary. Prior to his service at the seminary, he was the executive director of the Northwest Baptist Convention. His publications include *The Painful Side of Leadership*, *The Character of Leadership*, *Is God Calling Me?*, *The Case for Antioch*, *Live like a Missionary*, *Seasons of a Leader's Life*, and *Unscripted*—along with dozens of articles and curriculum materials. He maintains a leadership resources website at www.JeffIorg.com. He has been married for more than thirty-five years and has three adult children.

### Paul Kelly

Dr. Paul Kelly is associate professor of educational leadership at Golden Gate Baptist Theological Seminary, joining the faculty in 2009. Kelly has a PhD in Christian education from New Orleans Baptist Theological Seminary. Prior positions include vice president of Ministry Resources at Student Life Publishing, editor in chief of Discipleship Resources in Student Ministry Publishing at LifeWay Christian Resources, and several years in youth ministry. Dr. Kelly is the founding president of an online ministry called SmallYouthGroup.com.

### Heath Lambert

Dr. Heath Lambert is assistant professor of counseling at The Southern Baptist Theological Seminary and Boyce College and

Associate Dean of Applied Studies at Boyce College. He earned his PhD at The Southern Baptist Theological Seminary. He has taught courses in biblical counseling since 2006, joining the faculty after serving several years in pastoral ministry. Dr. Lambert currently serves as the executive director of the Association of Certified Biblical Counselors. He is the author of *The Biblical Counseling Movement after Adams, Finally Free: Fighting for Purity with the Power of Grace,* and a coeditor of *Counseling the Hard Cases: True Stories Illustrating the Sufficiency of God's Resources in Scripture.* He has been married for more than eleven years and has three children.

### Richard R. Melick Jr.

Dr. Richard (Rick) Melick is distinguished professor of New Testament at Golden Gate Baptist Theological Seminary and director of the Academic Graduate Program. He currently teaches courses in New Testament, hermeneutics, and creative expository preaching. Dr. Melick earned his PhD at Southwestern Baptist Theological Seminary and has been an academic leader for more than forty years. In addition to his service at Golden Gate Seminary, he serves as professor and PhD dissertation supervisor at Evangelische Theologische Faculteit in Leuvin, Belgium. He is the author of numerous books; among the latest is *Called to Be Holy* and *Teaching that Transforms: Facilitating Life Change through Adult Bible Teaching,* coauthored with his wife, Dr. Shera Melick. His writings also include multiple articles, curricula, editing, and contributions. He has been married for more than forty-six years, has three children, and eight grandchildren.

### Tony Merida

Dr. Tony Merida is the founding pastor of Imago Dei Church in Raleigh, North Carolina. He also serves as associate professor of preaching at Southeastern Baptist Theological Seminary in Wake Forest, North Carolina. Dr. Merida is a graduate of New Orleans Baptist Theological Seminary with a PhD in preaching. His books include *Faithful Preaching, Orphanology, Ordinary: How to Turn the World Upside Down,* and *Proclaiming Jesus.* He also serves as a general editor of the new Christ-Centered Exposition Commentary series published by Holman Reference. He has been married for more than eleven years and has five adopted children.

## Christopher W. Morgan

Dr. Christopher (Chris) Morgan serves as dean and professor of theology in the School of Christian Ministries at California Baptist University in Riverside. He is also an affiliated professor of systematic theology for the PhD program at Golden Gate Baptist Theological Seminary. He earned his PhD from Mid-America Baptist Theological Seminary. He has written or edited sixteen books, including *Jonathan Edwards and Hell*, *A Theology of James*, *Hell under Fire*, *The Glory of God*, *Fallen*, *Why We Belong*, and *The Community of Jesus*. He has been married for more than twenty-three years and has one daughter.

## Debbie Steele

Dr. Debbie Steele is associate professor of Christian counseling at Golden Gate Baptist Theological Seminary. She taught previously at California State University, Fresno, and as adjunct faculty at Fresno Pacific University, Fresno City College, Tulane University, Southeastern Louisiana University, and Elizabethton College. Since 2004, she has operated a private practice as a licensed marriage and family therapist, providing Bible-based counseling to the local community. Her website, www.paradoxministries.com, provides additional resources for counseling ministries. She has written numerous publications and presented at international, national, and local professional conferences. Dr. Steele is coeditor of *Psychiatric Nursing* textbook and is a contributor to *Advanced Psychiatric—Mental Nursing*. She has been married for more than thirty-three years and has two children.

## Paul Wegner

Dr. Paul Wegner is professor of Old Testament at Golden Gate Baptist Theological Seminary. He earned degrees from Moody Bible Institute and Trinity Evangelical Divinity School, and holds a PhD from the University of London. He has taught at Moody Bible Institute, Phoenix Seminary, and now serves at Golden Gate Seminary. Dr. Wegner has written numerous articles and books including *The Journey from Texts to Translations: The Origin and Development of the Bible, A Student's Guide to Textual Criticism: It's History, Methods and Results,* and *Using Old Testament Hebrew in Preaching: A Guide for Students and Pastors.* He has been married for more than thirty-two years and has two children.

### Jim L. Wilson

Dr. Jim L. Wilson is professor of leadership skills formation at Golden Gate Baptist Theological Seminary and is director of the Doctor of Ministry Program. He holds degrees from Golden Gate Seminary and Wayland University. He is an award-winning writer with hundreds of articles featured in more than sixty publications. Dr. Wilson has written or contributed to more than a dozen books; among his latest are *Future Church* and *Soul Shaping.* He is a premium contributor for sermons.logos.com and operates his own website at FreshMinistry.org. He has been married for more than thirty-three years and has two children.

# NOTES

## Chapter 2

1. Charles Pope, "The First Blow to Marriage: No-Fault Divorce," September 2, 2014, http://blog.adw.org/2009/09/the-first-blow-to-marriage-no-fault-divorce.

2. Rich Miller, "Is Everybody Single? More Than Half of the U.S. Now, Up From 37% in '76," September 16, 2014, http://www.bloomberg.com /news/2014-09-09/single-americans-now-comprise-more-than-half-the-u-s -population.html. See also: D'Vera Cohn, Jeffrey S. Passel, Wendy Wang, and Gretchen Livingston, "Barely Half of U.S. Adults Are Married—a Record Low," September 2, 2014, http://www.pewsocialtrends.org/2011/12/14 /barely-half-of-u-s-adults-are-married-a-record-low.

3. Gretchen Livingston and Kim Parker, "A Tale of Two Fathers: More Are Active, but More Are Absent," September 5, 2014, http://www.pewsocialtrends .org/2011/06/15/a-tale-of-two-fathers.

4. W. Bradford Wilcox, "The Evolution of Divorce," August 17, 2014, http:// www.nationalaffairs.com/publications/detail/the-evolution-of-divorce.

5. Ibid. In 1960 there were 9.2 divorces per one thousand married people. This increased to 22.6 divorces per one thousand married people by 1980.

6. Nicholas H. Wolfinger, *Understanding the Divorce Cycle: The Children of Divorce in Their Own Marriage*s (Cambridge: University of Cambridge Press, 2005), 8.

7. "The Decline of Marriage and Rise of New Families," September 3, 2014, http://www.pewsocialtrends.org/2010/11/18/the-decline-of-marriage -and-rise-of-new-families.

8. Andrew J. Cherlin, "In the Season of Marriage, a Question. Why Bother?" September 3, 2014, http://www.nytimes.com/2013/04/28/opinion/sunday/why -do-people-still-bother-to-marry.html?pagewanted=all&_r=0.

9. Barbara Ray, "Adulthood: What's the Rush?" September 3, 2014, http://www.psychologytoday.com/blog/adulthood-whats-the-rush/201303 /baby-marriage-is-fast-becoming-the-norm-0.

10. Gary J. Gates, "How Many People Are Lesbian, Gay, Bisexual, and Transgender?" August 25, 2014, http://williamsinstitute.law.ucla.edu/research

/census-lgbt-demographics-studies/how-many-people-are-lesbian-gay-bisexual
-and-transgender.

## Chapter 3

1. David E. Garland, *1 Corinthians, Baker Exegetical Commentary on the New Testament* (Grand Rapids, MI: Baker Academic, 2003), 3.

2. Anthony C. Thiselton. *The First Epistle to the Corinthians: a Commentary on the Greek Text. The New International Greek Testament Commentary*, ed. I. Howard Marshall and Donald A. Hagner (Grand Rapids, MI: Eerdmans, 2000), 16–17, italics added by author.

3. Paul's epistles are variously dated, but most scholars accept the date of the midfifties for these epistles. It should be noted that Paul wrote Romans from Corinth, perhaps adding to the concerns of Roman cities addressed in it.

4. Nero had a public ceremony with the young teenager, whom he castrated and dressed as the bride. Sporus traveled with Nero dressed as a woman. Nero called him "Mistress" and "Empress," and he consulted with him instead of his wife before his death. Nero also raped a vestal virgin and had regular incest with his mother. Other sexual irregularities are well known and were repudiated by Roman historians.

5. Romans 1:24, 26, 28 (NIV).

6. The progression is best supported by the fact that the first, Romans 1:24, identifies lust as the driving force; Romans 1:26 describes the motivation as "dishonorable passions"—the same "passion of lust" that Paul references as habitual in 1 Thessalonians 4:5.

7. Often the practice is associated with the training or mentoring of boys in the ways of society, particularly pederasty.

8. The word is plural, better translated as "people who practice *porneia*," and it occurs twice.

9. Judging, of course, does not relieve one of thinking biblically about conduct. Some activities are absolutely wrong, and the church must stand against them. Paul's point seems to be that we should not be preoccupied with judgment. Our business is grace.

10. The biblical worldview is a critical distinction rather than "Christian worldview." In our age "Christian" has often been watered down to refer to attitudes of acceptance and action far different from those affirmed in Scripture. For clarity, "biblical" provides focus.

11. Obviously the Old Testament was written in Hebrew, but the early church used the Greek translation, the Septuagint (LXX), since the world spoke Greek. The Greek words there reflect the Hebrew.

12. Paul's word is *phusis* (nature), which can be used in differing ways. Here it refers to the natural order of things, as it often does.

13. See, for example, the inscriptions (graffiti) at Pompeii noted in Garland, *1 Corinthians*, 240. "We keep mistresses for pleasure, concubines for daily concubinage, but wives in order to produce children legitimately"—Apollodorus.

14. For that matter, in discussion of marriage in the New Testament, there is almost no mention of procreation. Marriage is always symbolic of God's relationship with His people or related to proper spousal relationships.

## Chapter 4

1. Voice of the Martyrs, *Extreme Devotion* (Nashville: W Publishing Group, 2001), 269. See http://www.persecutionblog.com/2009/10/zahids-release.html.

2. Andreas J. Köstenberger, "The Gospel for All Nations," *Faith Comes by Hearing: A Response to Inclusivism*, ed. Christopher W. Morgan and Robert A. Peterson (Downers Grove, IL: IVP Academic, 2008), 209.

3. Anthony C. Thiselton, *The First Epistle to the Corinthians: A Commentary on the Greek Text*, NIGTC (Grand Rapids, MI: Eerdmans, 2000), 1,190.

4. Ibid., 1,191.

5. Oliver O'Donovan, *Resurrection and the Moral Order: An Outline for Evangelical Ethics*, 2nd ed. (Leicester, England: Apollos, 1994), 56.

6. Graeme Goldsworthy, "Gospel," in *New Dictionary of Biblical Theology*, ed. T. Desmond Alexander and Brian S. Rosner (Downers Grove, IL: IVP Academic, 2000), 524. Thanks to Matthew Emerson for pointing to this.

7. Matthew Y. Emerson, "Victory, Atonement, Restoration, and Response: The Shape of the New Testament Canon and the Holistic Gospel Message," *Southeastern Theological Review* 3/2 (2012): 193–94. Emerson here quotes John Webster, "Gospel," in *Dictionary for Theological Interpretation of the Bible*, ed., Kevin J. Vanhoozer (Grand Rapids, MI: Baker Academic, 2005), 263–64.

8. Clint E. Arnold, "Power," in *Dictionary of Paul and His Letters*, ed. Gerald Hawthorne, Ralph Martin, Daniel Reid (Downers Grove, IL: InterVarsity Press, 1993), 724.

9. Gordon D. Fee, *The First Epistle to the Corinthians*, NICNT (Grand Rapids, MI: Eerdmans, 1987), 95.

10. Ibid.

11. Ibid.

12. Ibid. Paul makes a similar point in 1 Corinthians 4. First, Paul reminded the Corinthians that he had become their father in the faith through the gospel (4:15). Next, he admonished them to follow him, meaning his teaching and his actions. Yet there was division. Others were opposing Paul's teaching and offering other interpretations of the gospel life. Paul then made a sharp distinction between the words spoken by his opposition and the words which he himself would bring. The difference would not be eloquence but power (4:20).

13. See Christopher W. Morgan, "The Church and God's Glory," in *The Community of Jesus: A Theology of the Church*, ed. Kendell H. Easley and Christopher W. Morgan (Nashville: B&H, 2013), 213–35. For more on how God displays His purpose of unity and Himself as one through the church, see Christopher W. Morgan, "Toward a Theology of the Unity of the Church," in *Why We Belong: Evangelical Unity and Denominational Diversity*, ed. Anthony L. Chute, Christopher W. Morgan, and Robert A. Peterson (Wheaton, IL: Crossway, 2013), 19–36.

14. Stephen J. Wellum, "Beyond Mere Ecclesiology: The Church as God's New Covenant Community," in *The Community of Jesus: A Theology of the Church*, 207.

15. For more detail on 1 Corinthians 6:9–11, see the helpful essay by Richard Melick Jr. in this volume. See also David E. Malick, "The Condemnation of Homosexuality in 1 Corinthians 6:9," in *Bibliotheca Sacra* 150 (October–December, 1993), 479–92.

16. Anthony Thiselton, *1 Corinthians: A Shorter Exegetical and Pastoral Commentary* (Grand Rapids, MI: Eerdmans, 2006), 91.

17. Our understanding and comments in this section have been shaped by the following works on 1 Corinthians 13: Jonathan Edwards, *Charity and Its Fruits* (reprint, Orlando: Soli Deo Gloria, 2005); D. A. Carson, *Showing the Spirit: A Theological Exposition of 1 Corinthians 12-14* (Grand Rapids, MI: Baker, 1987); Ajith Fernando, *Reclaiming Love: Radical Relationships in a Complex World* (Grand Rapids, MI: Zondervan, 2012); David E. Garland, *1 Corinthians*, BENTC (Grand Rapids, MI: Baker, 2003); Michael Green, *To Corinth with Love* (Dallas, TX: Word, 1988).

18. Carson, *Showing the Spirit*, 66.

19. Edwards, *Charity and Its Fruits*, 237–40.

20. Note the title of Mark Dever's recent book, *The Church: The Gospel Made Visible* (Nashville: B&H, 2012); for more on the church as God's display people, see Morgan, "The Church and God's Glory," in *The Community of Jesus*, 213–35.

21. Francis A. Schaeffer, *The Mark of the Christian* (Downers Grove, IL: InterVarsity Press, 1970), 29; http://www.ccel.us.shaeffer.html; see also Timothy George and John Woodbridge, *The Mark of Jesus: Loving in a Way the World Can See* (Chicago, IL: Moody, 2005), 19–21.

22. Rosaria Champagne Butterfield, "My Train Wreck Conversion," *Christianity Today*, February 7, 2013, 112. See http://www.christianitytoday.com /ct/2013/january-february/my-train-wreck-conversion.html?paging=off.

## Chapter 5

1. For more about transformation see Eric Swanson and Sam Williams, *To Transform Your City: Whole Church, Whole Gospel, Whole City* (Grand Rapids, MI: Zondervan, 2010), 127–30.

2. Paul G. and Frances F. Hiebert, *Case Studies in Missions* (Grand Rapids, MI: Baker Book House, 1987).

3. See E. Glenn Hinson, *The Early Church: Origins to the Dawn of the Middle Ages* (Nashville: Abingdon Press, 2010), 64–65.

4. The name has been changed to protect confidentiality.

5. Probably believer's baptism should better be understood as disciple's baptism since the command of Christ in Matthew 28:18–19 is to make and baptize disciples and not merely believers.

6. Linda Bergquist and Allan Karr, *Church Turned Inside Out: A Guide for Designers, Refiners and Re-Aligners* (San Francisco: Jossey-Bass, 2010), 120, where the conversation uses the metaphor of bounded sets.

7. E. Y. Mullins, *Axioms of the Christian Religion* (Atlanta: Mercer University Press, 2010, originally published 1908), 80, where the chapter subtitle asserts, "The Holy and Loving God Has a Right to Be Sovereign."

8. *The Baptist Faith and Message* 2000 can be found online at http://www.sbc .net/bfm2000/bfm2000.asp. Accessed August 23, 2014.

9. Note the full title of John Howard Yoder's classic practical ecclesiology, *Body Politics: Five Practices of the Church before the Watching World* (Nashville: Discipleship Resources, 1992); cf. Charles Lawless, *Membership Matters: Insights from Effective Churches on New Member Classes and Assimilation Findings* (Grand Rapids, MI: Zondervan, 2005).

10. L. Jones Stanton and Mark A. Yarhouse, *Ex-Gays?: A Longitudinal Study of Religiously Mediated Change in Sexual Orientation* (Downers Grove, IL: IVP Academic, 2007); Kim Schaffer, L. Nottebaum, P. Smith, K. Dech, and J. Krawczyk, "Religiously-Motivated Sexual Orientation Change: A Follow-up Study," *Journal of Psychology and Theology*, 2007, vol. 27: 329–37.

11. See http://videos.huffingtonpost.com/entertainment/michael-bussee-and-his-fight-against-exodus-international-517829621, June 21, 2013, self-described ex-ex-gay left Exodus when he and the cofounder Gary Cooper confessed their relationship.

12. See http://videos.huffingtonpost.com/entertainment/exodus-head-alan-chambers-full-apology-to-the-lgbt-community-517829623, June 14, 2013; here Alan Chambers, then current head of Exodus International, apologizes not for the biblical standard to which Exodus is committed but for the pain caused by Exodus and its affiliate leaders causing "shame, sexual misconduct, and also false hope" to many who sought their help. He renounced reparative therapy which seemed to promise change in sexual orientation. Biblical convictions about faith meant that Exodus would cease to be an ex-gay organization and become a "Christian organization teaching people how to be faithful to God in the midst of their sexual reality."

13. Charlene E. Hios, "Leaving My Lesbian Past: The Church That Walked with Me Away from Homosexuality," *Leadership Journal.net*, Fall 2013, 26–29; "The Pastor's Side of the Story," 29.

14. Gregory Wills, *Democratic Religion: Freedom, Authority, and Church Discipline in the Baptist South 1785–1900* (New York: Oxford University Press, 1997), 35.

15. Timothy and Denise George, eds., *Baptist Confessions, Covenants and Catechisms* (Nashville: B&H, 1996).

16. John W. Drakeford, *People to People Therapy: Self Help Groups: Roots, Principles and Processes* (San Francisco: Harper and Row, 1978), 10–22.

17. See http://videos.huffingtonpost.com/entertainment/web-exclusive-interviews-an-ex-gay-womans-decision-to-be-celibate-517829618, "Singleness as a possibility for my whole life," June 21, 2013; Our Eulogy for Exodus International, http://www.christianitytoday.com/ct/2013/june-web-only/ eulogy-for-exodus-international.html, Dorothy and Christopher Greco, June 24, 2013, accessed August 31, 2014, "In our experience, Exodus has been filled with

vulnerable, well-meaning men and women who took up an impossible task without adequate support and were then shamed by their own kin for failing. Despised and rejected by both the church and the gay community, it's no wonder Exodus succumbed to this auto-immune attack."

## Chapter 6

1. Graham Bell, *The Masterpiece of Nature: The Evolution and Genetics of Sexuality* (Berkeley, CA: University of California Press, 1982), 19.

2. Mark Ridley, *The Cooperative Gene* (New York, NY: Free Press, 2011), 108, 1,011. Quoted in Bert Thompson and Brad Harrub, "Evolutionary Theories on Gender and Sexuality" in *The Journal of Creation*, vol. 2, issue 1 (2004), 97–104.

3. Macklemore and Ryan Lewis, "Same Love" on *The Heist* (Macklemore LLC, 2012).

4. Bono, "Man and a Woman" on *How to Dismantle an Atomic Bomb* (Island/Interscope, 2004).

5. Saint Augustine, *Confessions*, ed. Michael Foley (Indianapolis, IN: Hackett Publishing, 2006), 3.

6. G. K. Beale, *We Become What We Worship: A Biblical Theology of Idolatry* (Downers Grove, IL: InterVarsity, 2008).

7. Aristotle, *Nicomachean Ethics* (New York, NY: Barnes & Noble Books, 2004), 25–41.

8. Will Durant, *The Story of Philosophy: The Lives and Opinions of the World's Greatest Philosophers* (New York, NY: Pockets Books, 1991), 87.

## Chapter 7

1. John R. W. Stott, *Between Two Worlds* (Grand Rapids, MI: Eerdmans, 1982), 136.

2. Ibid., 137.

3. Ibid.

4. Tim Keller, *Center Church* (Grand Rapids, MI: Zondervan, 2012), 101.

5. Tim Keller, *The Meaning of Marriage* (New York, NY: Riverhead Books, 2013), 195.

6. Keller, *Center Church*, 79.

7. I'm indebted to our friends at Redeemer City to City for walking our elders through this particular exercise.

8. I'm indebted to Keller for helping me think through this process and to Steve Timmis for the language of "contact" and "conflict."

## Chapter 9

1. Joe Dallas and Nancy Heche, *The Complete Christian Guide to Understanding Homosexuality: A Biblical and Compassionate Response to Same-Sex Attraction* (Eugene, OR: Harvest House, 2010), 13–15.

2. Mark Yarhouse, *Homosexuality and the Christian: A Guide for Parents, Pastors, and Friends* (Minneapolis, MN: Bethany House, 2010), 120.

3. Asa Sphar and Argile Smith, *Helping Hurting People: A Handbook on Reconciliation-Focused Counseling and Preaching* (Lanham, MD: University Press of America, 2002), 17.

4. Paul Metzger, *Connecting Christ: How to Discuss Jesus in a World of Diverse Paths* (Nashville, TN: Thomas Nelson, 2012).

5. Yarhouse, *Homosexuality and the Christian*, 124.

6. Charlene Hios, "Leaving My Lesbian Past," *Leadership Journal* (Fall 2013), 27–29.

7. Alan Brash, *Facing Our Differences: The Churches and Their Gay and Lesbian Members* (Geneva: World Council of Churches, 1995).

## Chapter 10

1. See for example Simon R. Crouch, et. al., "Parent-Reported Measures of Child Health and Wellbeing in Same-Sex Parent Families: A Cross-Sectional Survey," *BioMed Central Public Health* (June 2014), 635; Daniel Potter, "Same-Sex Parent Families and Children's Academic Achievement," *Journal of Marriage and Family* 74 (June 2012), 556; and Timothy J. Biblarz and Judith Stacey, "How Does the Gender of Parents Matter?," *Journal of Marriage and Family* 72 (February 2010), 3.

2. See William Meezan and Jonathan Rauch, "Gay Marriage, Same-Sex Parenting, and America's Children," *The Future of Children* 15:2 (Fall 2005), 97.

3. Erik H. Erikson, *Identity: Youth and Crisis* (New York, NY: W. W. Norton, 1968), 128–35.

4. Ibid., 26–29.

5. Laura E. Berk, *Exploring Lifespan Development, 2nd ed.* (Boston, MA: Allyn and Bacon, 2011), 293.

6. Ibid.

7. Ibid.

8. Walt Mueller, *Youth Culture 101* (Grand Rapids, MI: Zondervan, 2007), 167.

9. Berk, *Exploring Lifespan Development*, 294.

10. Jeffrey Jensen Arnett, *Adolescence and Emerging Adulthood: A Cultural Approach* (Boston, MA: Pearson, 2013), 253.

11. Ibid., 263.

12. Ibid.

13. Jose Bauermeister, et. al., "Relationship Trajectories and Psychological Well-Being among Sexual Minority Youth," *Journal of Youth and Adolescence* (2010) 39:1,148.

14. Arnett, *Adolescence and Emerging Adulthood*, 263.

15. Mark A. Yarhouse, *Understanding Sexual Identity: A Resource for Youth Ministry* (Grand Rapids, MI: Zondervan/Youth Specialties, 2013), 45–65.

16. Arnett, *Adolescence and Emerging Adulthood*, 385.

17. Berk, *Exploring Lifespan Development*, 295.

18. Mueller, *Youth Culture 101*, 340.

19. Kara E. Powell, Brad M. Griffin, and Cheryl A. Crawford, *Sticky Faith: Youth Worker Edition* (Grand Rapids, MI: Zondervan, 2011), 86.

20. Christian Smith with Melinda Lundquist Denton, *Soul Searching: The Religious and Spiritual Lives of American Teenagers* (New York, NY: Oxford University Press, 2005), 261.

21. Jim Burns and Mike DeVries, *Partnering with Parents in Youth Ministry* (Ventura, CA: Gospel Light, 2003), 20–30.

## Chapter 12

1. R. L. Barnes, "The History of Interracial Marriage: Colonial America to Loving v. Virginia (1967)," *US History Scene*, accessed November 1, 2014, http://www.ushistoryscene.com/uncategorized/the-history-of-interracial-marriage-colonial-america-to-loving-v-virginia-1967.

2. Maggie Maclean, "History of American Women," October 16, 2007, accessed November 1, 2014, http://www.womenhistoryblog.com/2007/10/puritan-women.html.

3. "Anti-miscegenation laws in the United States," Wikipedia, the free encyclopedia, accessed November 1, 2014, http://en.wikipedia.org/wiki/Anti-miscegenation_laws_in_the_United_States.

4. "Three-Fifths Clause," from The Heritage Guide to the Constitution, accessed November 1, 2014, http://www.heritage.org/constitution#!/articles/1/essays/6/three-fifths-clause.

5. "Anti-Miscegenation Laws in the United States," Wikipedia, accessed November 1, 2014, http://en.wikipedia.org/wiki/Anti-miscegenation_laws_in_the_United_States.

6. "The Emancipation Proclamation," U.S. National Archives & Administration, accessed November 1, 2014, http://www.archives.gov/exhibits/featured_documents/emancipation_proclamation.

7. "The Rise and Fall of Jim Crow", PBS, accessed November 1, 2014, http://www.pbs.org/wnet/jimcrow/segregation.html.

8. Barnes, "The History of Interracial Marriage: Colonial America to Loving v. Virginia."

9. "Jim Crow Laws," American Public Media, accessed November 1, 2014, http://americanradioworks.publicradio.org/features/remembering/laws.html.

10. "Civil Rights Movement: History, Causes, and Purpose," accessed November 1, 2014, http://www.english-online.at/history/civil-rights-movement/civil-rights-movement-history-and-causes.htm.

11. "Time Line of Same-Sex Marriage," Wikipedia, accessed November 1, 2014, http://en.wikipedia.org/wiki/Timeline_of_same-sex_marriage.

12. "Slogans," Wikipedia, accessed November 1, 2014, http://en.wikipedia.org/wiki/LGBT_slogans.

13. "Impact of the Civil Right Laws," U.S. Department of Education, accessed November 1, 2014, http://www2.ed.gov/about/offices/list/ocr/docs/impact.html.

14. "History and Timeline of the Freedom to Marry in the United States," Freedom to Marry, accessed November 1, 2014, http://www.freedomtomarry. org/pages/history-and-timeline-of-marriage.

15. Matt Slick, "What Does the Bible Say about Homosexuality?," Christian Apologetics and Research Ministry, accessed November 1, 2014, http://carm.org/ bible-homosexuality.

16. "List of Christian Denominational Positions on Homosexuality," Wikipedia, accessed November 1, 2014, http://en.wikipedia.org/wiki/ List_of_Christian_denominational_positions_on_homosexuality.

17. Raymond Johnson, "Gay Population Statistics," About Relationships, accessed November 1, 2014, http://gaylife.about.com/od/comingout/a/popula-tion.htm.

18. "Gay as the New Black," Huffing Post Interviews, accessed November 1, 2014, http://live.huffingtonpost.com/r/segment/comparing-civil-rights-gay-rig hts/510a8c422b8c2a138f000395.

19. "Racial Classifications," Wikipedia, accessed November 1, 2014, http:// en.wikipedia.org/wiki/Race_(human_classification).

20. Stephen Zunes and Jesse Laird, "The US Civil Rights Movement (1942– 1968)," Nonviolent Conflict, accessed November 1, 2014, http://www.nonviolent -conflict.org/index.php/movements-and-campaigns/movements-and-campaigns -summaries?sobi2Task=sobi2Details&catid=17&sobi2Id=22.

21. Kelly M. Vaillancourt, "Antibullying Initiatives: An Update on Federal Legislation," NASP Publications, accessed November 1, 2014, http://www.nasp online.org/publications/cq/40/8/advocacy-in-action.aspx.

22. Jason Whitely, "How Same Sex Marriage Decided State by State," USA Today, accessed November 1, 2014, http://www.usatoday.com/story/ news/politics/2014/10/26/jimmy-carter-same-sex-marriage/17963533/?utm_ source=feedblitz&utm_medium=FeedBlitzRss&utm_campaign=usatoday-new-stopstories.

23. "History of Marriage in California," Wikipedia, accessed November 1, 2014, http://en.wikipedia.org/wiki/History_of_marriage_in_California.

24. Jeffrey Toobin, "The Obama Brief: President Obama's Judicial Legacy," The New Yorker, accessed November 1, 2014, http://www.newyorker.com/ magazine/2014/10/27/obama-brief.

25. "America's Civil Rights Timeline," International Civil Rights Center & Museum, accessed November 1, 2014, https://www.sitinmovement.org/history/ america-civil-rights-timeline.asp.

26. "Time Line of Same Sex Marriage," Wikipedia, accessed November 1, 2014, http://en.wikipedia.org/wiki/Timeline_of_same_sex_marriage.

27. George Chauncey, "The Long Road to Marriage Equality," The New York Times, June 26, 2013, accessed November 1, 2014, http://www.nytimes. com/2013/06/27/opinion/the-long-road-to-marriage-equality.html?_r=1&.

28. "History and Timeline of the Freedom to Marry in the United States" Freedom to Marry, November 1, 2014, http://www.freedomtomarry.org/pages/ history-and-timeline-of-marriage.

29. Jason Whitely, "How Same Sex Marriage Decided State by State."

30. "Treatment for Homosexuality," American Psychological Association, accessed November 1, 2014, http://www.apa.org/pi/lgbt/resources/guidelines.aspx.

31. For a counter argument to Vines and a scholarly treatment of the biblical texts consistent with the church's historically high view of Scripture, see R. Albert Mohler Jr., ed. *God and the Gay Christian?: A Response to Matthew Vines* (Louisville, KY: SBTS Press, 2014).

32. "Position Statements," Southern Baptist Convention, accessed November 1, 2014, http://www.sbc.net/aboutus/positionstatements.asp.

33. David Badash, "Anderson Cooper Asks Baptist Leader about Gay Marriage," Huffington Post, accessed November 1, 2014, http://www.thenew-civilrightsmovement.com/anderson-cooper-asks-baptist-leader-about-his-gay-marriage-linked-to-n-korea-nuclear-war-claim/politics/2013/04/04/64378 and http://www.huffingtonpost.com/news/rev-fred-luter.

## Chapter 13

1. Public accommodation laws require businesses to conduct their business without discriminating against identified classes of people (race, religion, gender, sexual orientation, etc.).

## Chapter 14

1. "Same-Sex Marriage: What Can I Say?" *Leadership Journal*, Summer 2004, http://www.christianitytoday.com/le/2004/summer/3.54.html.

2. Kelli Cottrell, "San Francisco Churches Rally to Defend Traditional Marriage," Baptist Press, May 21, 2004, http://www.bpnews.net/bpnews.asp?Id=18326.

3. David Hansen, *The Power of Loving Your Church: Leading through Acceptance and Grace* (Grand Rapids, MI: Bethany House, 1998), 169–70.

4. "Phillip D. Busbee," obituary, July 5, 2009, http://www.legacy.com/obituaries/sfgate/obituary.aspx?page=lifestory&pid=129204906#sthash.ep7c62wX.dpuf.